Overcoming

How Faith, Family & Friends Helped One Black Man Beat the Odds

PRAISE FOR OVERCOMING

Overcoming is thought-provoking and so relevant to those of us who face health and personal challenges as part of our daily life journey. Willie Dean provides sound advice and a life example about overcoming the most difficult situations and challenges. With faith, family, friends, and perseverance, Dean shows us we can overcome.

During our life journey, all of us face crises, challenges, and disappointment. Dean's thought-provoking book provides real-life examples of overcoming tragic and deeply challenging situations. Facing health crises, racism, the death of his spouse, and job disappointments, he still managed to overcome and provide a lifetime of distinguished service to others.

Overcoming is an inspiring and thought-provoking book. Dean traces the history and development of his family and the struggles of his parents, who overcame poverty and racism to provide their children with a better life. His family gave him a strong foundation in Christian faith, self-confidence, and determination—strengths that guided him through life's tragedies. Yet, Dean made it through and remained steadfast as an outstanding servant leader, who lives a life of significance, helping others as his highest priority.

—HAROLD MEZILE, Former President/CEO,
YMCA of the Greater Twin Cities, Minneapolis, Minnesota

One of the things that I believe is critical for our personal and spiritual growth is the sharing of stories along our life journey—both the good (joyful) and the bad (painful). When we can be transparent about our struggles and speak to the faithfulness of God in spite of adversities that we face, then we do ourselves and others (family and friends) a tremendous service because our journey can encourage someone who's going through challenges to stay the course and remain faithful. I also firmly believe that God is perfectly okay with us NOT always liking the path we are on or the struggles we face, but what pleases God is our willingness to stay on the path, with the faith and belief that things will not only get better but trusting that God is with us during times of challenge, loss, and uncertainty.

In *Overcoming*, Willie Dean shows both his human vulnerability and spiritual faith (that without question grew deeper and stronger from every adversity and challenge he faced, endured, and overcame). I applaud Willie for being candid about the struggles and setbacks he's faced professionally and personally and his openness about God's faithfulness during these times.

In my blessed time of knowing Willie, it was quickly clear how much he cherishes his faith, family, and friends. He is a man of deep integrity, humility, and compassion. It is my sincere prayer that readers of this memoir are both encouraged and blessed and that this book will be a tool for all (especially men) to share and uplift one another.

—REV. CARLA M. MITCHELL,
Former Pastor, St. Peter's AME Church, Minneapolis, Minnesota

African American men and boys, it is well-known and documented, face and experience many unique challenges in America. In fact, many of the obstacles and hurdles that Black men and boys encounter as a result of the social circumstances in which they are often born, including intergenerational poverty, racism, microaggressions, etc., contribute to the fact that many Black boys and men psychologically have little self-esteem or self-worth and often never believe in themselves to where they do not develop aspirational dreams because of how society has historically viewed Black men and Black boys.

Black men and boys need inspiration, guidance, mentorship, and a toolkit to which they can find resources that will assist them in realizing that they too can set aspirational goals which they can work toward achieving. Because I, myself, have authored a success tips book, entitled, *It Isn't Difficult To Do It IF You Know How To Do It*, which is a book designed to provide a roadmap for success for Black men and boys and others, I am particularly proud to endorse and recommend Dr. Willie Dean's book, *Overcoming: How Faith, Family & Friends Helped One Black Man Beat The Odds,* as a valuable resource to assist and enlighten readers as to how they can overcome obstacles in their own lives.

To this end, Dr. Dean has written a superb summary, replete with detailed accounts, of the numerous spiritual blessings he has received. This memoir also shows how reliance on his faith, family, and friends and listening to the voices of his ancestors have accounted for the many successes he has achieved. These techniques have helped him overcome significant challenges such as racists, bullies, serious health challenges, divorce, and the death of loved ones and go on to accomplish much in his lifetime in both his personal and professional life.

—DR. CHARLES S. MODLIN, Urologist,
Medical Director of Equity, Inclusion & Diversity,
Kidney Transplant Surgeon and Author,
MetroHealth Medical Center, Cleveland, Ohio

A must-read, *Overcoming* is not only a classic example of how a Black man navigated a path to success in a world so obstinately opposed to him, but it also is a moving illustration of the power of love...love of God, family, and mankind. Insightful, timely, sensitive, and transformative.

—GLORIA SPIGHT,
Former Teacher, Memphis City Schools

Overcoming
How Faith, Family & Friends Helped One Black Man Beat the Odds

Willie Dean, Ph.D.

Foreword by
Rev. Dr. Byron C. Moore

Austin Brothers
— PUBLISHING —
www.abpbooks.com

Overcoming

How Faith, Family & Friends Helped One Black Man Beat the Odds

Willie Dean, PH.D.

Published by Austin Brothers Publishing, Fort Worth, Texas

www.abpbooks.com

Copyright 2022 by Willie Dean

Cover Photo Copyright 2022 by J. Mone' Photography

The copyright supports and encourages the right to free expression. The purpose is to encourage writers and artists to continue producing work that enriches our culture.

Scanning, uploading, and distribution of this book without permission by the publisher is theft of the author's intellectual property. To obtain permission to use material from the book (other than for review purposes) contact terry@abpbooks.com.

ISBN: 979-8-9867751-1-1

Printed in the United States of America
2022 -- First Edition

Dedication

*In loving memory of my parents,
Eddie and Mattie Dean,
my first role models.*

Contents

Foreword	1
Prologue	5

Part One
Childhood And Adolescence – The Formative Years

Faith – Hope in the Face of Doubt	33
Family – Ties That Bind	37
Friends: Essential to the Soul	61
Elementary School: The Wonder Years	63
Junior High: Age of Discovery	69
The Tumultuous Sixties	81
Trauma, Violence, and Bullying	85
Senior High: Caring for Others, Discovering Self	87

Part Two
Young Adulthood: Making My Way In The World

Boy to Man – My Transition to Manhood	103
Grad School – Age of Enlightenment	111

Part Three
Middle Age – God's Purpose For My Life

The Great Commission and My Role in Discipleship	121
Giving Back – Service Beyond Self	125
A Rewarding Career – Self-Actualization	127
Health Challenges – The Patience of Job	165
Being Black in America	183
First Pitch – A Lesson on Humility	221

Caring for Aging Parents	227
Achieving Balance in My Life	237

Part Four
The Golden Years – Fruits Of My Labor

Finding My Soulmate	249
The Lord is My Shepherd – He Guides Me the Right Way	257
Love and Unity – What the World Needs Now	261
Epilogue	269
Acknowledgements	303
About The Author	307

FOREWORD

IT WAS THE AUTHOR William Cowper who penned the Christian hymn "God Moves in a Mysterious Way" in 1773. Those words could not be more appropriate in describing my relationship with Dr. Willie Dean. We both were servants of the African Methodist Episcopal Church in the early 2000s. While Dr. Dean was serving in the office of Steward at Saint Peter's AME Church in Minneapolis, I was serving as the Pastor of Saint James AME Church in Saint Paul, Minnesota. Our respective journeys have led us to reconnect at the Saint Andrew AME Church in Memphis, Tennessee. This reconnection has been such a tremendous joy that it could only be described as a divine déjà vu. I have watched Dr. Dean as a devoted Christian, a loving husband, a conscientious scholar, and a man of ethical convictions.

I am blessed with the unique experience of serving as Dr. Dean's pastor, an honor and privilege that I do not take lightly nor for granted. As a pastor, my life often intersects with the lives of persons from various vocations and stations. It is in this context of pastor and parishioner that I share in relationship with Dr. Dean. While my educational pursuits have certainly prepared me for the vocation of the clergy, Dr. Dean's academic pursuit has been nothing short of stellar, trailblazing, and inspiring. My circumstances related to achievement, both academically and professionally, pale in comparison to the conditions under which Dr. Dean has pursued the sharpening of his intellect and the development of his character. It is the duress of racism, health challenges, and an unaccepting society that has prepared him to render tremendous contributions to the academic, business, and faith-based venues in which he engages.

The undertaking of a memoir, while being offered for public consumption, is a peek into the private life and legacy of an individual. Dr. Dean has taken up the much-needed task of exposing the complexities and difficulties of the

African American male within the context of venues that are very rarely found to be acknowledging and reluctantly accepting of persons of color. The narrative of African American men has too often been rendered to a statistical or negative stereotypical descriptive rendition that fails to acknowledge the emotional pain, spiritual pull, intellectual prowess, and ethical promise that African American males manifest in our society daily. Moreover, Dr. Dean addresses these narratives from the perspective of the historical and contemporary contexts, inclusive of family values, keen societal observations, and a strong spiritual foundation rooted deep within him from his upbringing.

This memoir will take the reader on a journey filled with the overt and covert obstacles that too often present themselves amid rare and precious opportunities. The ethical depth and intestinal fortitude needed to rise above the cantankerous criticisms, racial ridicule, and human degradation are on full display in this treatise. Our media and cinematic portrayals of African American life, while sometimes being very skillfully and artistically depicting, fall severely short of the authentic experience of the unique process of maturing from a Black boy to a Black man. This is especially true when your manhood is often challenged, confronted, and questioned by a world that feels more comfortable with you in a perpetual state of arrested development than to promote the blossoming of your humanity into the purpose-filled individual that lies within all of us.

If there was ever a person perfectly suited and qualified to chronicle a narrative of overcoming the odds and challenging the status quo while remaining true to a sincere foundation of faith, family, and focus, it is certainly Dr. Willie Dean. As an African American male who is quite familiar with the myriad of trials of attempting to strive and succeed against the long-standing barriers to brilliance, I both embrace and recommend this masterpiece of literary insight. Dr. Dean is the epitome of what is known in the faith community as a living testimony. Great works of art of any nature are not necessarily created but simply expressed through the lens of the experience of the artist.

While this work centers on the experiences of a man who refused to let external forces extinguish his internal fire, anyone who has ever had to keep going despite the circumstances that could have derailed their destiny can relate to this narrative. If you have ever had to face situational stagnation, been confronted with a reasonable rationale to quit, or if you've been in the grip of grief, Dr. Dean offers us a testimonial of triumph. If you are in need of a living witness who goes beyond the theoretical assumptions of what racism, despair, and profound pain look and feel like, you must read this memoir. It is a tremendous work presented to us by an authority on the often-excruciating experiences of life not only as an African American male but as a man on a mission to make a difference. May we all be so blessed with the faith, the family, and friends to live a life that exemplifies what it truly means to overcome.

—REV. DR. BYRON C. MOORE
Senior Pastor
Saint Andrew AME Church
Memphis, Tennessee

PROLOGUE:

DISCOVERING GOD'S PLAN FOR MY LIFE

He has showed you, O man, what is good; and what does the Lord require of you but to do justice, and to love kindness, and to walk humbly with your God? Micah 6:8 (Revised Standard Version)

Like many Christians, at a point in my faith journey, I began to ask myself, "What is God's plan for my life?" "What does He require of me?" Many of the answers to these questions can be surmised from scriptures like Micah 6:8 (...to do justice, and to love kindness, and to walk humbly with your God...). However, I wanted to look at my life through a comprehensive spiritual lens to see whether my actions meet God's expectations. I embarked on writing this book to document and share my life story and lay bare to the world how I have used God's gifts. My story is one of how—with the support of my faith, family, and friends—I was able to beat the odds stacked against Black men, like me, in America and overcome the many obstacles that I faced in my life. This book is intended to illustrate how the intersection of race and religion played prominent roles throughout my life and how by the grace of God, I not only survived...I thrived! This book is also intended to serve as inspiration for my sons and other Black men, women, boys, and girls, who may find it useful as a guide to help them beat the odds that are stacked against people of color in this country!

I was born on March 15, 1951, in Potts Camp, Mississippi, but my journey began more than 2,000 years ago on Calvary when Jesus Christ laid down His life so that I might "have life and have it more abundantly." My birth, assisted by a midwife, in an iron bed in my maternal grandparents' modest home, was the beginning of a life filled with love, hope, and many challenges that I had to overcome. I learned how to survive and thrive in a culture wrought with systemic racism that is stilted against persons like me. I thank the Lord for His grace and mercy, for without Him, I don't know where I would be. It is because of Him that I was able to achieve success in many areas of my life and use wisely the gifts that He has given me.

This book is my story, one that I hope will be a testament to the trials and tribulations I have overcome as well as a lasting legacy of the contributions that I made—by the grace of God—to American society. This is a success story that I hope will inspire my sons and other Black men, women, boys, and girls who must cope with racism in this country, in addition to the everyday challenges of life. I also hope that my White peers will read these words and stop to ask themselves what it's like to be a person of color in our culture. More importantly, I pray that as God continues to reveal His plan for my life that I will be attentive and obedient to His will.

My story highlights how I beat the odds and overcame—or at least managed as best I could—numerous adversities in my life. My school and church involvement during the 1960s caused me to realize that I am endowed with certain gifts from God. My placement in advanced classes in grade school and my success on my junior high basketball team are testaments to my academic and athletic achievement. I was blessed to graduate from high school, for the data (1970 U.S. Census) shows that nearly one out of three (29.4 percent) of Black male students dropped out of high school nationwide in 1970, the year after I obtained my diploma. I was "blessed" to graduate from high school and go on to attend college and earn bachelor's, master's, and doctoral degrees.

The intersection of my faith, family, and friends helped me overcome obstacles such as racism and other atrocities frequently faced by Black Americans. These problems—often manifested as disparities in housing, education, healthcare, wealth, voting access, poverty and employment opportunity, etc.—act to place people of color at a distinct disadvantage in our country.

My story tells how my reliance on my faith, family, and friends helped me overcome racists, bullies, serious health challenges, divorce, the death of loved ones, and go on to accomplish much in my lifetime. By the grace of God, I was able to provide leadership to churches throughout the nation, become a loving husband and father, care for my ailing parents, ascend to the highest ranks in the YMCA, obtain a Ph.D. in Education and earn a black belt in Tae Kwon Do. God is good…all the time!

VOICES OF MY ANCESTORS

The voices of my ancestors are constantly with me, reminding me that they laid the foundation for my life and blazed the path for my family's future. Their lives, like mine, were guided by their faith in God and the love of family and friends. Many of my ancestors were likely enslaved people who came to this country—against their will—from West Africa around the early 1600s. Against all odds, they found ways to overcome tremendous obstacles and survive; however, more than 400 years after the first enslaved Africans were brought to these shores and nearly 160 years after the abolishment of slavery, many of my people are still "not free," and are treated as second-class citizens in our beloved country.

I am indebted to my son, Cedric, for his work tracing our family's genealogy. Using *23andMe*, he discovered that my DNA make-up includes: Sub-Saharan African, 82.2 percent; European, 14.8 percent; East Asian and Indigenous American, 2.4 percent; trace ancestry, 0.1 percent; and unassigned, 0.5 percent. My ancestors are linked to early North Carolina, early South Carolina, and early Virginia African Americans. According to *23andMe*:

> The majority of Black Americans who can trace their roots back to North Carolina in the 1700s have ancestors from coastal West African countries along the Gulf of Guinea, including the Congo, Cameroon, Nigeria, Benin, Togo, Ghana, and the Ivory Coast. Although many Black Americans during this period were enslaved, some had gained or purchased their freedom before the 1700s, when indentured labor and slavery weren't always lifelong sentences. Others escaped and lived in a free, independent community in the Great Dismal Swamp on the Albemarle Sound near Edenton, North Carolina.
>
> Most African Americans in the early Virginia African American community can trace their ancestry back to West Africa in the present-day Republic of Cameroon, the Republic of the Congo, Nigeria, Ivory Coast, Ghana, Benin, and Togo. Over a two-hundred-year period, many were enslaved and brought to Virginia to work on tobacco farms. While early Virginia plantations were concentrated on the coastal plains, slave-owning planters gradually moved westward in search of new opportunities, shifting populations of enslaved people inland. Life for both free and enslaved Black Virginians grew more difficult as race-based laws restricted their social, political, and economic rights. Black Virginians responded with rebellions and cultural innovations. Spirituality, and the church, in particular, became critical for Black people as they found unique ways to communicate with one another.

Willie Dean

Due to slavery, many members of my family probably migrated—or more accurately, were forced—westward from early North Carolina, early South Carolina, and early Virginia to Kentucky, Tennessee, Georgia, Alabama, and Mississippi. According to *23andMe*:

> Most African Americans in this community [early North Carolina, early South Carolina and early Virginia] can trace their ancestry back to West Africa in present-day Republic of Cameroon, the Republic of the Congo, Nigeria, Ivory Coast, Ghana, Benin, and Togo. From the ironworks of South Carolina and Tennessee, the forests of northern Alabama, and the cotton fields of Mississippi, these African Americans formed deep bonds to family and land. Oppressed by law and custom, many moved to Chicago at the beginning of the 20th century, looking for better lives for themselves and their children. They turned their experiences into soulful treasures such as blues, jazz, and gospel, a rich culinary culture, and religious traditions that helped make the South and Chicago what they are today.

My family has roots in Marshall County and Lafayette County, Mississippi. Many Black families, like some of my relatives, fled oppression and poverty in the South and moved to other sections of the country. Some members of my family relocated to Memphis, Tennessee, for good-paying jobs and better life opportunities. Others moved to St. Louis, Missouri, Gary, Indiana, Buffalo, New York, and other "progressive" cities.

Many of my relatives left the South in the 1950s and 1960s and found better jobs and opportunities for themselves and their families in the industrial Midwest and the culturally diverse North. A number of uncles and cousins found jobs in the steel industry in Gary, Indiana, and in the automobile industry in Buffalo, New York. Often, when relatives relocated and found employment, they helped other relatives from the South get jobs and often helped them with housing for their families until they could get on their feet. I had two uncles who married two sisters. They both got jobs in the automobile industry in Buffalo, New York, and together bought a duplex where they lived, one family upstairs and the other downstairs. Many of my ancestors opened the door to other relatives from the South to obtain jobs in the northern cities where they worked, relocating and lifting whole families out of poverty.

Cedric traced the "Pye" branch of our family tree due to many matches sharing this rare surname, from which he made connections to White enslavers who are our progenitors. Sadly, like numerous enslaved Black women of the period, some of my Black female ancestors were likely raped or otherwise forced into unholy and unwanted unions by their White enslavers, causing unimaginable pain and humiliation for the women and girls, anger, and emasculation for their fathers, husbands, brothers, and friends, and shame and degradation for their families and their mixed-race children.

Through all that they faced, many of my ancestors found ways to overcome Jim Crow laws and other practices that were designed to disenfranchise Black people through bias in the workplace, police brutality, and unfair practices in voting, housing, education, health care, and public accommodations. Through it all, my ancestors were God-fearing people. Their strength of character also meant that despite these atrocities, remarkably, they did not hold hate in their hearts. Many of them found ways to not only survive but to thrive in a culture that did not provide equal opportunity for all.

My maternal grandfather, McKinley Brown, married my maternal grandmother, Malrea Dukes. "Daddy Brown" and "Mama Rea," as we affectionately called them, lived in Potts Camp, Mississippi, and were believed to be some of the earliest Black landowners in the community. Daddy Brown was an independent Black farmer who owned farmland that was fronted on a major highway in Potts Camp.

My paternal grandfather, Anderson Savon Dean (nicknamed "Poppa," a.k.a. "Sammie"), like my father, was a sharecropper. He lived with us for much of his declining years after his wife, my paternal grandmother, Annie May Pye Dean (nicknamed "Mama May"), passed away. Poppa loved to weave cane chairs and whittle wooden objects as well. He rotated, staying a week at a time at each of his children's homes. There was tremendous love and respect for him, the patriarch of our family. Poppa chewed tobacco, dipped snuff, and smoked a pipe. This was not the best role model for my developing mind. However, I never wanted to do any of these things. I did, however, put "talcum powder" in one of his old pipes to emulate his smoking. The upside was that "smoking" my pipe with talcum powder helped stop my dyspepsia, a spitting compulsion. Poppa's dark, wrinkled skin was weather-worn and a constant reminder of the countless days he must have spent toiling long hours under the hot Mississippi sun in the cotton fields of White landowners.

My father told me about a night when Poppa's life was spared by a group of White men who were members of the Ku Klux Klan (KKK). Dad said the clansmen—who were threatening to lynch Poppa—let him go when they learned he was a Mason. Whites treated Blacks with disdain; however, there was an odd kinship between members of White and Black Masonic lodges. White Masons didn't fellowship with Black Masons, but there was a strange relationship between them and deference given to their Black "brothers." I can't help but think that if my grandfather had been lynched that night, what would have happened to his family and mine? I would never have been born!

Unfortunately, this fate did befall many Blacks who were lynched at night, under cover of darkness, or publicly during the day for all to see. Their bodies were often left hanging in trees as a constant reminder to others who might dare to be insolent or to stand up for their rights. According to *Wikipedia*, "The Tuskegee Institute has recorded the lynching of 3,446 Blacks and the lynching of 1,297 Whites, all of which occurred between 1882 and 1968, with the peak occurring in the 1890s, at a time of economic stress in the South and increasing political suppression of Blacks." Most Whites were lynched for crimes like cattle rustling or theft, etc. In addition, a number of Whites who were sympathetic with Blacks and fought against racism were also lynched.

When I think about the plight of my ancestors—many of whom likely came to this country in chains—I am inspired by their resilience. I remember how difficult it was for me as an adolescent to pick cotton during only one week of "vacation" with my mother on my maternal grandparents' Mississippi farm. The sun was brutally hot, bugs were everywhere, and no matter how hard I tried, I couldn't pick much cotton. I can only imagine how much more difficult it was for my forefathers to toil—sunrise to sunset, day in and day out—under the oppression of slavery.

Yanked from their families, culture, and familiar environs in Africa, my ancestors, like countless others, were chained together and piled like cargo into the dank, pest-infested hulls of slave ships. Many died during the months-long Middle Passage to America. Not recognized as whole human beings, they were forced into involuntary servitude, with fears of torture, rape, degradation, family separation, and little hope for a brighter future. Those that dared to escape were hunted down like animals by slave hunters, forerunners of modern-day police.

I think about how many lynchings and other atrocities have been inflicted on Black Americans—at night, in the woods, or in other desolate locations—often by so-called "upstanding" White men from the community, wearing hoods to cloak their identities. I don't know if I could have survived what my forefathers had to endure. I ask myself, "Would I have been strong enough to withstand the pain and degradation of slavery, Jim Crow, or the KKK?" "Would I have been tortured and killed by angry Whites for being 'uppity' or 'out of my place,' as was Emmett Till?" (Till, a 14-year-old Black boy from Chicago, was tortured and killed by angry White men for allegedly making remarks to a White woman and whistling at her in Money, Mississippi, in 1955.)

History aside, it is even more frightening to realize that the chances of my sons, or me, dying at the hands of law enforcement—"living while Black"—is a real possibility in this country even today.

My ancestors, like many other Blacks, were not allowed to look Whites in their eyes when addressing them and were always expected to be subservient. I never saw my father resort to shuffling his feet; however, I could sense a shift in his demeanor when addressing White people. White and Black children growing up in the South were often friends and were on a first-name basis. Black children called their White friends by their first names, "Charles" or "Sally," etc. However, somewhere about the age of puberty, the relationships changed, as did the power dynamics, and Blacks were expected to refer to Whites as "Mr. Charles" or "Miss Sally." I can only imagine the humiliation I would have felt as a Black man if I had to refer to a White child as "Mr." or "Miss."

Many of the issues with systemic racism in this country are rooted in slavery, often referred to as "America's original sin." White supremacy, which has led to feelings of superiority of the White race over other races, has made it difficult and nearly impossible for Blacks and other people of color to live and thrive in America. "White privilege"—a phenomenon that is often not recognized or realized by Whites—provides advantages to the majority group (Caucasians in this country) and serves to disadvantage other groups. Ironically, many historians, anthropologists, and sociologists describe race as a social construct that is used to categorize groups of people. In effect, there is but one race, the human race.

Like the trauma of slavery, the genocide of Native Americans, the only indigenous people who inhabited America before Christopher Columbus "discovered" it, is a scourge upon our nation's history. Native people were systematically removed from the land where their ancestors had hunted, fished, and lived for generations until European-Americans bought, stole, or cajoled it from them. I have an affinity for Native Americans, for their ancestors were mistreated by "upstanding" citizens of this country just like mine.

The maltreatment of enslaved Blacks negatively affected my ancestors and, consequently, many of their descendants for more than 400 years. I believe that police brutality, generational poverty, housing discrimination, educational inequities, healthcare disparities, and voter suppression can be traced to early discriminatory practices dating back to the founding of this nation. The Declaration of Independence of the Thirteen Colonies from Britain—"We hold these truths to be self-evident, that all men are created equal, that they are endowed by their Creator with certain unalienable Rights, that among these are Life, Liberty and the pursuit of Happiness"—has not yet been realized for people of color and women in this country.

I pray that my research studying barriers to upward mobility and advocating for diversity, equity, and inclusion will reveal inequities in American society and play a meaningful role in helping to overcome barriers and rid our nation of the evils of racism.

APPRECIATING DIVERSITY AND INCLUSION

My education and employment afforded me many opportunities to appreciate diverse cultures, domestically and internationally. I've lived and worked in several regions of the United States and have experienced the differences in cultures, and racial attitudes, in multiple cities in the South (Potts Camp, Mississippi; West Memphis, Arkansas; Memphis, Tennessee); the Southwest (Arlington, Texas; Fort Worth, Texas; Mansfield, Texas); the Midwest (St. Louis, Missouri; Omaha, Nebraska; Bloomington, Minnesota; Minneapolis, Minnesota), and the East (Cleveland, Ohio). I have also been privileged to travel and experience the cultures of multiple foreign countries, including Canada, Mexico, Jamaica, Colombia, the Netherlands, Germany, and Sweden. My life experiences have given me a greater appreciation for diversity, equity, and inclusion than I would otherwise not have had.

My career allowed me to meet many interesting people, including *YMCA* members and participants, community residents, mayors, and governors. I also met celebrities, including pop singer Usher, former St. Louis Cardinals Major League Baseball pitcher and member of the Baseball Hall of Fame Bob Gibson, former Texas Rangers Major League Baseball pitcher and member of the Baseball Hall of Fame Nolan Ryan, former TV personality and 1970 Miss USA semifinalist Jayne Kennedy, and members of the Dallas Cowboys Cheerleaders. I also had the honor of throwing out the first pitch at a Texas Rangers Major League Baseball game. And I am proud to have met Capt. Charles L. White, one of the original Tuskegee Airmen.

I am blessed that my exposure to persons of diverse cultures and backgrounds has broadened my national perspective and helped me appreciate others who are different from me. I am proud that my cosmopolitan experiences have made me a better global citizen, and to value worldviews that are different from mine.

Life in the Dean Household

Home-cooked meals, holiday celebrations, and church were emblematic of life growing up in the Dean household. We used to make homemade ice cream in an old-fashioned wooden churn. My sister, brothers, and I would take turns spinning the manual crank. We would stop churning before the custard was ready, eat some of the ice cream, and restart the process to fluff it up again, albeit in a thinner form. We also had an old family recipe for a seltzer to treat stomach aches that was made of vinegar, baking soda, sugar, and water. The concoction, remarkably like Alka Seltzer, usually did the trick. However, we liked to drink it just for fun.

I loved holidays and special occasions. Easter Sunday with service at our church, followed by an egg hunt on the church grounds (or at a family member's home), was a highlight for us kids. I was never very good at finding eggs and would often step over ones that were in plain sight. Frequently my parents would take my hand and point out eggs that were right under my foot. Christmas—the celebration of the birth of Jesus, gifts from family and friends, and a visit from Santa Claus—was the most highly anticipated day. It seemed the year passed by ever so slowly as I waited for that special day. I remember going to bed early to avoid Santa "putting ashes in my eyes" if I was awake when he arrived. I never really reconciled why there was no "Black Santas" in the stores or on television. I remember Children's Day at our church, a day when each child was given a speech to recite. As nerve-racking as it was trying to memorize and give a speech in front of the congregation, I recognize now that it was good training for developing my oratorical skills and confidence with public speaking.

Compartmentalization
An Effective Coping Skill?

I learned to compartmentalize challenging and uncomfortable situations in order to overcome, or at least manage, difficult events in my life. Two marriages that ended in divorce, the deaths of my second wife, mother, and father; systemic racism; serious health challenges; and the loss of a citywide junior high basketball championship all forged me into the man that I am today. I learned to compartmentalize my emotions as a coping mechanism to process disappointment, grief, and fear. However, this technique has not always helped me build good interpersonal skills and relationships.

Some have interpreted my steady demeanor as indifference. I've been told by loved ones, employees, and others that my lack of affect, my "poker face," makes it hard to know what I'm feeling. The Arlington (Texas) *YMCA* Board of Directors required me to take the Dale Carnegie course—"How to Win Friends and Influence People." I went kicking and screaming to the class; however, I was voted the top student by my classmates. Maybe you "can teach an old dog new tricks." However, I still need to work on my interpersonal skills. I need to let people know that I care about them and their problems. There is a lot of truth in the adage, "People don't care how much you know until they know how much you care."

I thought having a calm, even disposition was an asset. In hindsight, I recognize the need to share my emotions with others, especially those close to me, and that doing so is not a sign of weakness. Had I to do it over again, I would be more demonstrative of my feelings. I recognize now that it is important to let others know where you stand on issues, to let them know whether you are pleased, displeased, happy, sad, grief-stricken, fearful, confident, anxious, euphoric, or angry. Real men do share their emotions! I have learned it is critical that we deal with situations on a conscious level and let those around us know how we feel.

Looking back, I ask myself, "Should I have spoken up and been more demonstrative with my feelings when I was confronted with racism, and other matters, in my community, on my job, and in my sons' lives?"

NEW BEGINNINGS
STARTING A FAMILY AND A CAREER

I got married in 1973, and Cedric, my eldest son, was born later that year. I was 22 years old. My wife, Cedric, and I lived briefly with my parents and then moved to an apartment my cousin was vacating in Castalia, a neighborhood just a few miles away. The apartment was affordable, at only $68.00 per month; however, it was infested with roaches and located in a high-crime area. Growing up in my parents' household, I was not accustomed to either of these problems. I also was not used to being the head of the household and putting food on the table, paying for pediatric doctor appointments, and more.

I soon realized the need for more income. Although I was working 40 hours per week at a community center and part-time on weekends at my father's job, I was part of the working poor. We were living paycheck-to-paycheck. Fortunately, I got a job with the *YMCA* of Memphis and Shelby County in January

1974, which helped to ease the budget crunch I felt. I was hired as program director for the Glenview Branch *YMCA*, a position I held until March 1975.

My family and I moved to Fort Worth, Texas, in April 1975, following my acceptance of the position of Executive Director of the McDonald Branch *YMCA*, a branch of the *YMCA* of Metropolitan Fort Worth. At age 23, I was one of the youngest *YMCA* branch executives in the nation. Like my branch in Memphis, however, this was a Y that served the Black community. A pattern in my hiring was beginning to develop. I didn't know it then, but I was beginning to be typecast as only being qualified to lead and serve in Black communities.

Cedric's mother and I divorced in 1977. I obtained custody of Cedric, and at the age of 26, I found myself a single parent. I was blessed to have had access to convenient and affordable childcare through the Y's before- and after-school childcare program. I was also blessed to have grown up in a loving two-parent family and to have had parents that I could look to as role models for good parenting. I also had a mother that I could call long-distance and get cooking advice and a father and brother who would drive 500 miles to be by my side following surgery.

As a young executive director, I worked long hours, which left little time to develop friendships or female relationships. Cedric and I were inseparable. I spent most of my free time with him, attending school functions, helping him with his homework, or going to the park, a movie, or a monster truck show. I took joy in drawing a cartoon on Cedric's lunch bag each morning. It seemed to ease his apprehension about going off to school. One Halloween, I dressed up as Count Dracula and surprised Cedric's grade school class.

Cedric spent many summers with my mother and father when I was a single parent. We drove the nearly 500 miles from Fort Worth to Memphis to drop him off at the beginning of each summer. I have fond memories of that special bonding time together. We talked, laughed, and sang all along the way. We often played a game where we each tried to be the first to identify the brand names of 18-wheel trucks that we passed on the interstate. *Mack*, *Peterbilt*, and *Ford* were most prevalent. Cedric loved to gesture to truck drivers as we passed them by, pretending to blow an imaginary air horn; most truckers obliged him by blowing their horn in response.

We often used our Citizen's Band (CB) radio to communicate with other drivers along our journey. We frequently used channel 19 to find the location of speed traps by saying: "Break 1-9 for a Smokey report." We referred to cops as "Smokey," a nod to "Smokey the Bear," a cartoon character popularized in the 1940s and 1950s by the United States Forest Service. Another term that we used was "There's a bear in the air" to let other drivers know that a police helicopter or airplane was being used to clock the speed of vehicular traffic. First widely used by long-haul truckers, the CB radio provided a means to call out for help to other drivers and police during emergencies and a sense of community for its users that was akin to social media communities today. CB radios fell from prominence with the proliferation of cell phones in the 1990s. Many younger generations have no idea what fun CB radios brought to their users. I consider myself lucky to have experienced this cultural phenomenon.

Cedric and I relocated to St. Louis, Missouri, in 1981, upon my acceptance of the position as Executive Director of the Monsanto Branch *YMCA* and District Director of the City North District, a branch of the *YMCA* of Greater St. Louis. I was a single parent in a new city, and I relied on my family for support. I am indebted to my late cousin, the Reverend Quinton Ross, and his family with whom I stayed that first summer. Quinton graciously allowed me to stay in the guest room of their home in Black Jack, Missouri, a northern suburb of St. Louis. (This area is near Ferguson, Missouri, which would be the hotbed of racial unrest after the killing of a Black man, Michael Brown, Jr., by a White Ferguson, Missouri police officer in 2014. Even when I moved to Missouri in 1981, the northern suburbs were becoming increasingly Black and low-income.)

Cedric spent the first few summers with my mother and father in Memphis, giving me a break and allowing me to settle into my job. I packed Cedric a sack lunch, placed him on a *Greyhound* bus in the seat behind the driver, and sent him to live with his grandparents after his school was dismissed for the summer. Initially, we both had inhibitions about the nearly 300-mile, seven-hour bus trip for an eight-year-old traveling alone. However, neither of us let on to the other that we were nervous. (Not sharing emotions and compartmentalizing feelings would become a trend in my life.) By the grace of God and attentive drivers who made sure Cedric remained on the bus during stops and ate his lunch at the prescribed time, he always arrived safely and well-fed, to be picked up by his grandfather. This is another example of God watching over us and my family stepping up to help in our time of need.

Cedric went to the farm daily with his granddad over the course of the summers he stayed with my parents. He helped where he could and played by himself or with another boy who joined them on the farm from time to time. Cedric loved his grandparents, and he especially bonded with his granddad. I don't know what I would have done if my parents had not wanted—or had not been able—to care for Cedric during the summer months when he was out of school. Being a single parent was difficult; however, it would have been much harder without their love and support. I thank God for having loving parents and their ability to help raise my son.

I also relied on my extended family. In addition to living with my cousin, Quinton, and his family, during my first summer in St. Louis, my cousin, Ella Oatts, aided me by babysitting Cedric when I went out on occasional dates. Cedric grew close to Ella's fraternal twins, Charles and Charlene. The support of my family allowed me to have a social life, which was a rare commodity for me as a single parent in a new city, where I knew few people.

With the modest salary increase I received when I moved from Fort Worth to St. Louis, I was able to buy a three-bedroom home in Olivette, a suburb of St. Louis. This was the first home that I purchased. It was a charming ranch-style house with a single-car garage (actually a closed-in carport) and a finished basement on a lot with mature trees. Our neighborhood had a circular street pattern with one way in and out, which reduced traffic dramatically. A downside to our neighborhood was there were few kids of similar age to Cedric. His only friends were ones he met at school, who lived near the school that was about a mile away.

We lived in the Ladue School District, which included residents of the cities of Ladue and Olivette. Ladue was one of the most affluent communities in the St. Louis area. When the Chief Financial Officer of the Y asked where I was going to live and the school district Cedric would attend, he seemed surprised that I could afford such an expensive area. In retrospect, he probably didn't realize that the city of Olivette, where I lived, was much more modest than the city of Ladue. While Cedric benefitted by attending school in an affluent district with adequate resources, it had its shortcomings. By the time Cedric got to high school, we noticed that a number of his classmates had their own cars, and many drove their parents' luxury vehicles to school. Although Cedric never said anything, I suspect that he and his middle-class friends sometimes felt uncomfortable juxtaposed with their wealthy classmates.

I also wonder about the motivation and biases that the primarily White faculty had working with Black students. Studies have shown that White teachers often have lower expectations for school success for Black students—especially Black male students—than do Black teachers. I graduated from a high school with only Black students and mostly Black teachers. In contrast, I ask myself, "Did I do my Black son a disservice by enrolling him in an affluent, resource-rich, mostly White school district with mostly White teachers?"

Cedric took music and, for some reason, chose, or was assigned, to play the string bass. At nearly six feet tall, the instrument was taller and nearly as heavy as Cedric. We couldn't afford to rent a second instrument that he could keep at home for practice, which meant we had to transport the huge bass to school on days that he had music class. It must have looked funny to neighbors and other commuters to see Cedric and me driving to school with his string bass sticking out of the moonroof of my little Toyota Supra. The things we do for our children.

I learned much later that when Cedric accompanied me to the Y for evening meetings or after day camp in the summer, he often got into fights with neighborhood children. (Cedric would also tell me years later that he had to fight almost daily at school when we moved to Omaha upon my acceptance of the position of President/CEO of the Omaha/Council Bluffs Metropolitan YMCA.) Like me when I was his age, Cedric didn't tell anyone about the violence that confronted him. I wonder now if I had somehow signaled to Cedric that men are supposed to handle problems without crying when we hurt and not tell when someone bullies us. Nobody likes a tattletale, or so many children may think. Cedric later met and married his wife, Melissa.

Cedric joined the United States Navy after graduating from Millard South High School in Omaha, Nebraska, in 1992. This decision helped him mature and gave him valuable career skills. Already skilled with technology—he built his own computer while in high school—Cedric worked in avionics in the navy. He traveled around the world as a crewmember of the U.S.S. Carl Vinson, a U.S. Navy carrier. Cedric learned new skills and was introduced to new cultures as he related to the 5,000-member crew and the people living in the many countries he visited. He often tells stories about his naval experiences. He saved his money while in the navy and was able to buy a car, clothing, and apartment furnishings. I am very proud of his service to our nation and the mature, responsible adult he has become!

Cedric uprooted his life and moved from Memphis, Tennessee, to Bloomington, Minnesota, in 1999, after my wife, Pam, suffered oxygen deprivation following surgery and lapsed into a chronic vegetative state. Without Cedric and my dad, I don't know what I would have done during what was one of the most challenging periods of my life.

Pam, my second wife, and I met in the summer of 1985 at the Monsanto YMCA in St. Louis, Missouri, where I was the branch executive director. I was concerned about fictitious persons being added to our payroll, so I often went over paychecks with my administrative assistant on payday. Our paychecks only listed employees' first and middle initials and last names. A couple of times during my reviews, I inquired, "Who is P.P. Williamson?" I was told that

P.P. Williamson was a school teacher who had been hired as our Summer Day Camp Director. One day I looked out of my office door and saw the back of a woman's head. She had a shag haircut that flowed down her back. Out of curiosity, I asked my assistant who the lady was, and she replied, "That's P.P. Williamson."

Soon, I mustered up the courage to speak with Pam after she came to my office under the guise of looking for a pair of scissors. I first met Jarrod, my second son, when he, a precocious three-year-old, accompanied his mother, Pam, to my office. Jarrod was inquisitive and "as busy as a bee," picking up everything on my desk that was not nailed down.

Eventually, I asked Pam out on a date to see the movie *Beverly Hills Cop*. I wanted to be discreet. While she didn't report directly to me, I didn't want to create an appearance of favoritism. For that reason, we kept our relationship low-key until after the summer, when she no longer worked for the Y.

Pam and I fell in love and got married in October 1985. Our son, Matthew, was born the next year. Pam, Matthew, Jarrod, Cedric, and I lived together in our Olivette, Missouri home until we relocated to Nebraska in 1989. Tragically, Pam suffered oxygen deprivation following surgery in 1998, when we lived in Bloomington, Minnesota. She lapsed into a chronic vegetative state and passed away in 2001.

Pam was a loving wife and mother who loved her family and a dedicated educator who loved teaching and her students. Our children and her students adored her. She would give you the shirt off of her back. We lost an angel when she passed away. Because of our faith, we know she is resting peacefully now with the Lord in Heaven and that she continues to watch over us.

Jarrod and I grew to love each other as any father and son would, with the occasional differences of opinion about who was in charge. He would tell me years later that he remembers me fondly playing music on Sunday mornings that included LPs of my favorite musicians, like Bootsy Collins, Sly and the Family Stone, George Duke, The Commodores, The Isley Brothers, George Clinton, and Prince! Looking back, I didn't realize the impression I was making on Jarrod with something as simple as my love of music. Imagine the routine and often unconscious decisions we make every day that impact the impressionable minds of young people in our orbits, especially our own children.

Jarrod is a talkative soul and makes friends easily. He is smart and loves reading, which helped him to excel in school. In high school, he developed a love for writing and a penchant for drawing, the former he would take up as his career aim.

Willie Dean

Driving Jarrod to Florida to attend Florida International University (FIU) is one of my fondest memories of our time together. We drove 26 hours from Minneapolis to Miami, stopping only for gas, food, and restroom breaks. It was a special time for us to bond as father and son. Once during our trip, I awakened when Jarrod was driving, saw palm trees, and asked if we were in Florida. Jarrod answered, "Yes." Several hours later, we passed a sign that said, "Welcome to Florida." I looked at Jarrod, he looked at me, and we both laughed out loud because we thought we were already in Florida.

After resting the Sunday night after reaching Miami, Jarrod and I attended several FIU orientation sessions for new students and parents the next day. When the orientation was over, and it was time for me to fly back to Minnesota, Jarrod asked me at the airport, "What do I do now?" I could sense the trepidation in his voice, and I knew he needed reassurance. I said to him as I gave him a hug, "You'll figure it out." He didn't realize that I was as nervous for him as he was, but I didn't let it show. (Once again, I didn't show my emotions and perhaps falsely signaled to Jarrod that nothing could rock me.) Jarrod went on to have a successful experience and made many new friends at FIU. He received his Bachelor of Science degree in Print Journalism and Mass Communication, becoming the first person in the second generation of our family to graduate from college!

Jarrod is an extrovert and a people person who seeks new adventures and looks forward to new challenges. He likes to explore new cities and neighborhoods and take photos of street art. His independent spirit is evidenced by his ease at living in new environments and making new friends.

Jarrod has lived in multiple cities and regions of the United States. He lived in Miami, Florida, when he attended FIU. After college, he worked for a New York magazine and lived in East Harlem, New York, and West New York, New Jersey, when he worked in the digital video archives at MTV. Jarrod later lived with his aunt and her family in St. Louis, Missouri, when he interned for *FleishmanHillard*, a global marketing and public relations agency, and as a retail salesman for *Enterprise Rent-A-Car*. Jarrod also lived in Los Angeles, California, when he worked as a public relations assistant at the *California Science Center*. He also served as a freelance writer and wrote some articles for several music magazines. Jarrod returned to Florida and lived with friends in mid-town Miami. He then spent some time in the hospitality industry, where he was a concierge at a hotel and also worked at the *Four Seasons Hotel*.

Jarrod couldn't afford a car when he moved back to Miami, so he resorted to riding around the city on a motorized scooter. This was a cost-effective way to travel and get to his part-time job. This mode of transportation worked well until one day; a dog charged at Jarrod while he was passing by and caused him to wipe out on the pavement. In addition to some minor scrapes and bruises, Jarrod suffered a separated shoulder and broke his foot.

Without health insurance to have his shoulder rehabilitated, Jarrod did research on *YouTube* and set out to do it on his own. After weeks and months of working out in the gym, Jarrod transformed himself from the proverbial "97-pound weakling" to a muscle-bound young man. He has enjoyed bodybuilding and has maintained his new 190-pound physique. Jarrod discovered his ability to motivate others and got into personal training to teach people that they are stronger than they think.

After rehabbing himself, Jarrod lived with his brother, Matt, Kristine (Matt's wife), and me in Richfield, Minnesota. During this period, he worked for *Lifetime Fitness* as a personal trainer. He also worked as a barback and a bartender at *Seven*, a posh Minneapolis restaurant and bar. After working at Seven, Jarrod worked as a senior bar assistant at *Parlour* in Minneapolis, considered one of the top bars in the Twin Cities.

Jarrod's next adventure involved a return to California to the city of San Diego, where he worked as a bartender at the *Downtown Westin Hotel*; however, his goal was to become a copywriter. Jarrod later worked as the Social Media Community Manager at a social media advertising agency. There he oversaw the company's social media communities, among other tasks. His interview turned out to be a group interview fashioned like a game show on Facebook Live.

Later, Jarrod learned the ins and outs of copywriting from his friend, Ryan Warnberg, who he's been friends with since the eighth grade. Jarrod worked with Ryan, writing and managing the social media channels for Ryan's photo app. They also worked on several freelance projects together. During this time, Jarrod was also writing freelance for a nonprofit's blog and anyone interested in his services.

Jarrod's first search engine optimization (SEO) internship was at an agency called *Pacific*. It was originally only supposed to be for three months. But, based on his work ethic and contributions to the SEO Department, they extended the internship to six months and then to nine months. This was also a way for them to get around hiring Jarrod full-time and providing him benefits. They said they didn't want to hire him because of his lack of experience. After that period, Jarrod worked as an intern at the agency part-time and at *Club Monaco*.

Jarrod was struggling to make it, so after nine months, he left the agency for his first full-time SEO role, which lasted five months. Jarrod now lives in Los Angeles, where he is working as an SEO analyst. He is still pursuing his dream to be a writer for a music magazine.

I remember fondly driving with Jarrod from Minneapolis to San Diego in 2016 to start his life anew in California. After breakfast, hugs, and a "near-emotional" sendoff from Matt and Kristine, we piled into Jarrod's little 2012 *Toyota Scion* and headed south through Minnesota to Iowa and then west to Nebraska and the beautiful mountains of Colorado. (Driving in Colorado brought back wonderful memories of my undergraduate days backpacking in the "Rocky Mountain State." More on that later.).

We had been driving a long while in Utah when a clerk at a gas station warned us to be careful after we passed the snow fences ahead. She said we should be on the lookout for deer and antelope that run across the highway, especially at night. Jarrod had driven several hours when I awakened and, in the darkness of night, saw what I thought were deer or antelope on a collision course with our vehicle. I yelled, "Lookout Jarrod!" As we got closer, Jarrod said calmly, "It's okay, Dad, they're just tumbleweeds!" We had a good laugh…as we passed the marauding tumbleweeds!

I mention Jarrod's odyssey and quest to find himself, in such great detail, in order to say to young Black men, "Don't give up on your dreams." Discover your passion, seek a good education, training, and experience, obtain a mentor, and settle for nothing less than a rewarding career that allows you to support yourself, your family, and your community.

Jarrod, the loquacious three-year-old that I met in my office at the Y more than three decades ago, has grown to be a focused man that I am proud of and adore today.

Matthew, my youngest son, was born on August 25, 1986, at *Baptist Hospital* in St. Louis, Missouri. His mother, Pam, had a history of false labor pains, causing us to make several disappointing trips to the hospital. When her labor started for real, I discovered I had left my car low on fuel and had to stop at a gas station en route to the hospital. I never quite lived this down. After we arrived at the hospital, Pam was in labor for quite a long time, so long that I got hungry and left the delivery room to get a bite to eat. When I got back, Matt was on the way, and the nurse said I almost missed his birth. I was so excited that I forgot all the duties I had learned during our Lamaze classes. When Matt entered the world, he had a full head of black hair and was as cute as a button!

Pam and I brought Matt home from the hospital and showered him with love and affection. His name, "Matthew," which means "gift from God," was almost prophetic. Our children grew and developed typical sibling rivalries as they each jockeyed for attention. Matt liked riding on my shoulders nearly everywhere we went.

Matt enjoyed playing on my dad's farm. He especially liked buying firecrackers, placing them in piles of fresh cow manure, and running for cover as poop exploded into the air. Matt also liked going to the farm and riding the tractor with his grandddad. (This scene would be repeated numerous times with my grandchildren and their great-grandfather.) The farm became a favorite place for family members to visit whenever we were in Memphis.

Matt experienced several febrile seizures at a young age. The first happened when I was on a *YMCA* business trip to Chicago. Pam phoned me at my hotel late one night and told me what had happened; Matt had suffered a seizure and had been transported by ambulance to a nearby hospital in Sarpy County, Nebraska. We were told that febrile seizures sometimes occur in young children with high temperatures and that they often grow out of this abnormality.

After a while, Matt seemed to be free from the disorder. Then one evening, when I was home, I heard Pam's terrifying scream. I knew something was terribly wrong. Not knowing what was happening, I ran up the stairs, almost injuring my ankle, to find Pam holding Matt, who was having a seizure. Matt's eyes had rolled back in his head, and he was unresponsive. He was clenching his teeth, and I feared he might bite off his tongue, but I knew not to insert anything into his mouth. We called 911 and went with him to the ER at Sarpy County Hospital. The ER doctor on duty treated Matt and later became his pediatrician. Matt eventually grew out of having febrile seizures; however, that was not the end of his medical challenges.

Sometime later, Matt began having difficulty swallowing. It was a frightening time for him and our whole family. After numerous trips to his pediatrician, we were referred to a specialist at a hospital in Saint Paul, Minnesota. It seemed his inability to swallow was both physiological and psychological. Fortunately, in time he grew out of this condition.

A few years later, when Matt was age 16, he suffered a seizure and was transported by ambulance to the ER at *Southdale Hospital* in nearby Edina, Minnesota. I was home that afternoon working on homework for my doctoral studies. From my upstairs office window, I noticed Matt's car pull into our driveway. Shortly, the doorbell rang. I thought this was odd, "Why was Matt ringing the doorbell?" I thought perhaps he had lost his key or had left it at home that morning. When I got to the door, I recognized two of Matt's friends from his high school and immediately knew something was wrong. They said that Matt had suffered a seizure and was taken to the hospital by ambulance. The police had asked them to drive Matt's car home. I was annoyed that the police had allowed Matt's friends to drive his car, but my first concern was getting to Matt's side.

I drove immediately to the hospital, where I was told Matt had suffered a seizure. If that was not scary enough, the doctor said they needed to place him into a medically-induced coma to protect his vital organs. This was eerily similar to his mother's coma following a hysterectomy just a few years before, from which she lapsed into a chronic vegetative state and never recovered. My days were a blur, traveling to the hospital to care for Matt, ensuring Jarrod got off to school and dealing with my own fears and anxieties about what the future held.

I constantly prayed for Matt to recover fully. By the grace of God, Matt's condition improved. Eventually, he was brought out of the coma, and he was on the road to recovery. However, Matt wanted to go home immediately. He remembered what had happened to his mother, and he was deftly afraid of hospitals. His fears resulted in him becoming combative with his doctor, who he threatened with physical harm. Fortunately, the doctor understood Matt's fears and did not report the threats, for which Matt could have been criminally charged. The Lord was looking after us. Soon Matt was released from the hospital and has not had any additional episodes. We never exactly knew what caused Matt's seizures.

Once when our family traveled from Omaha, Nebraska, to Kansas City, Missouri, to visit a waterpark, Matt experienced a near-drowning. He and I were in the wave pool with hundreds of other park visitors. At the time, Matt didn't know how to swim, and he clutched me and the pool wall as we walked toward the growing waves. Suddenly, Matt lost his grip on the wall, and he was being sucked into the deep water. Instinctively I reached out, grabbed him by the hand, and held onto him. I knew he might drown. Matt climbed up my arm and clutched my neck in a near-death grip. After we left the pool, we decided to go to a nearby urgent care facility to have Matt examined. He was determined to be okay. Years later, after overcoming his fear of water (and numerous swimming lessons), Matt learned to swim at the Southdale *YMCA* in Edina, Minnesota. He is now a good swimmer and is confident around water. God is good!

Matt has always been a good athlete. (I like to think that he gets his athleticism from me.) After we moved to Bloomington, Minnesota, Matt and Jarrod participated in Bloomington Athletic Association baseball, football, and lacrosse. They also enjoyed skating, skateboarding, snowboarding, and bike riding. Sports were a great outlet for their energies and helped to keep them positively engaged at times when negative influences might have been competing for their attention.

Matt has always loved animals, especially dogs. However, I was uneasy about having a dog live inside our household, and the cold Minnesota climate did not allow for a dog to live outdoors. I did, however, permit Matt to have a plethora of other pets, including a teddy bear hamster, a regular hamster, goldfish, a rabbit, and a snake. One day Matt noticed that the male hamster that we had bought was actually a female upon the birth of her babies.

Matt's snake managed to push aside the screen top on its aquarium, which was weighed down with a brick, and escaped into the house on two occasions. The second time it was missing for more than two months. It was an eerie feeling knowing that a snake, albeit not poisonous, was loose in some unknown place in our house. I pondered, "Was I going to have to disclose to potential buyers that a snake was on the loose in the house when I got ready to sell the property?" Or, "Would I be awakened some night with a snake in my bed?" Fortunately, we found Matt's snake on both occasions.

One night after retiring to our bedroom, Pam and I heard what sounded like someone prowling around the outside of our house. I got a flashlight and retrieved my .357 magnum, and began searching the house. I found nothing on the inside that was amiss and was just about to phone the police when I noticed Matt's teddy bear hamster, "Teddy," pushing against my walk-in closet door. I quickly surmised that this was the source of the sounds that we had heard. Imagine our relief that no one was trying to break into our home and that we hadn't phoned the police. Can you imagine the laughter they would have had back at the station discussing a call for help from a big burly guy like myself, involving a harmless hamster?

Matt met his future wife, Kristine, in high school, and they have been a couple ever since. They got married in Jamaica. Their destination wedding included all the thrills and frills of a Caribbean resort get-a-way. I traveled from Minneapolis, as did Jarrod and a host of relatives and friends. Others traveled from around the country to witness and share in the wedding gala.

Matt graduated from Jefferson High School in Bloomington, Minnesota, and earned his Associate of Arts degree from the Minnesota School of

Willie Dean

Business. Matt and Kristine live in Bloomington, Minnesota, near friends from high school, and enjoy trips to the lake and international travel. They are a loving couple who enjoy their time together and taking care of their fur baby, Layla, an affable five-year-old Pit Bull. I am very proud of Matt and Kristine and love them both dearly.

My sons, as many teens do, veered away from their religious upbringing as they got older, opting for other activities and discovering their own personalities. They engaged in sports and other extracurricular activities while in school. Cedric embraced football, fell in love with computers, and played in the band while in high school. Jarrod and Matt enjoyed skateboarding, listening to music, and participating in sports like skating, skateboarding, football, baseball, lacrosse, and snowboarding. I drove Jarrod and Matt around town to practice their skateboarding skills. I even built a skateboard ramp in our driveway where they practiced risky jumps and other tricks; fortunately, they sustained no serious injuries.

My children have been a blessing to me. They have inspired me to be a positive role model and a good father—someone that they can always count on—as my father was for me. I thank God for having a loving family.

Overcoming

Dad, a sharecropper for much of his life, could never make enough profit to fully pay his debts to White landowners, leaving our family trapped in poverty.

Mom was a homemaker, however, she never had to work outside of our home or take in laundry, or cook for others.

Joe, the eldest child in our family, was the first to graduate high school.

Willie Dean

I became the second in our family to graduate high school, following in Joe's footsteps.

My little sister, Chris, also graduated high school, becoming the third child in our family to do so.

My little brother, Eddie Jr. (Bug), the only child born in Memphis, left school before graduating. He spent most of his life working odd jobs and caring for our parents.

Cedric, my firstborn, grew up in Memphis, Tennessee, Fort Worth, Texas, Saint Louis, Missouri, and Omaha, Nebraska.

Jarrod, my middle son, was a precocious three-year-old when I met him and his mother, Pam.

Pam and I got married in 1985 and our son Matthew, "a gift from God," was born a year later.

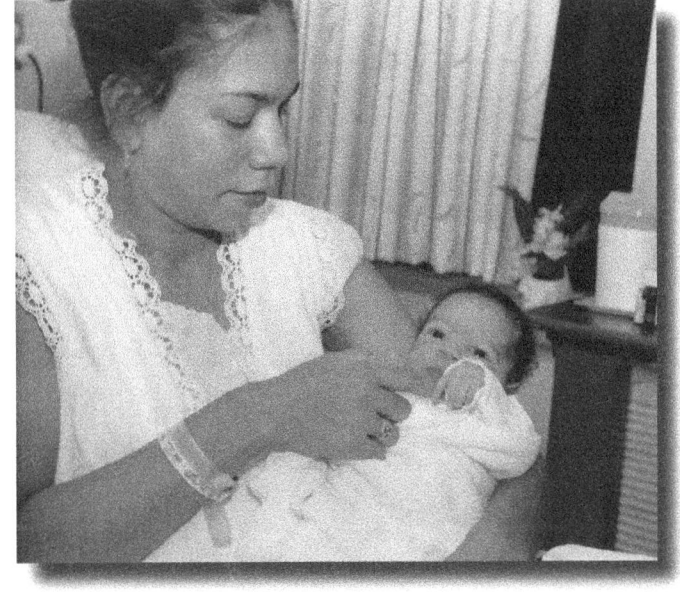

PART ONE

CHILDHOOD AND ADOLESCENCE - THE FORMATIVE YEARS

Faith – Hope in the Face of Doubt

"Now faith is the substance of things hoped for, the evidence of things not seen."
Hebrews 11:1 (King James Version)

My family has been religious since before I was born. I remember seeing my mother, grandmother, and aunt singing hymns and Negro spirituals while sitting on the Mother's Board or ushering on Sunday mornings when we journeyed to our country church in Mississippi. I remember my father sitting on the Deacon Board, offering prayers and collecting offerings. Church and religion were part and parcel of life growing up in the Dean household. I am convinced that our faith gave us the values and principles to live by that helped us overcome numerous challenges that faced Black Americans in the second half of the 20th century. Without faith, I could not have beat the odds that were stacked against me. Without faith, I don't know where I would be.

I confessed my faith in Christ along with my brother, Joe, at our family's longtime place of worship, Baptist Hill Missionary Baptist Church in Potts Camp, Mississippi. I remember attending "Revival," a special week set aside for prayer and preaching aimed at renewing the spirit of congregants and welcoming new believers into the fold. As a young boy, about nine or ten years of age, I sat on the "mourner's bench"—a pew or seat at the front of a church set aside for repentant sinners seeking salvation—with Joe and other youth from the community. Night-after-night ministers preached, choirs sang, and people shouted, showing their love for God. Mud daubers, flying insects that resemble wasps (however, they do not have stingers), flew unimpeded throughout the sanctuary. And, without fans or air conditioning, the sweltering August heat was almost unbearable. Sweat drenched our clothes and rolled off our brows as mothers fanned their children and themselves, trying to keep cool.

Near the end of the weeklong Revival, I believed I felt the Holy Spirit and confessed my acceptance of Jesus Christ as my Lord and Savior. That Sunday, I was baptized along with my brother and the other young converts in a muddy pond on a neighbor's farm. Knowing I did not know how to swim, I was fearful of what was about to happen. However, after being dunked under the water by a deacon, I triumphantly arose, symbolic of Christ's death, resurrection, and eternal life.

The church was the center of activity for families in the Black community in both the rural and growing urban areas of the South. With no air conditioning, our church's sanctuary became a virtual sauna during the hot days of summer. After service on some Sundays, the women of our little country church opened the trunks of their families' cars to serve "dinner on the ground." Youth and adults went from car-to-car fellowshipping and sampling food and desserts from some of the best cooks in the community. Without refrigeration, I don't know how the food was kept cool and did not spoil in the Mississippi heat. Since there was no indoor plumbing at our church, we had to use one of two outhouses that were kept stocked with discarded Sears and Roebuck or J.C. Penney catalogs, which were used instead of toilet paper.

Mealtime for our family, as with most Black families, was a time for family and friends to gather and share good and bad times. We always ate "family style" with meats and entrees served from platters that were placed in the center of the table. My father always sat at the head of the table and offered the same devotion at every meal, "Lord, we thank you for the food that we are about to receive, for the nourishment of our bodies, for Christ's sake. Amen." I still offer this devotion and find solace in repeating the words that I heard my father say for seven decades.

My father's job during my early years required him to work weekends, and my mother didn't drive, which prevented our family from attending Sunday church services regularly. The fact that I didn't attend regular church services was a source of embarrassment when my classroom teacher discussed on Monday mornings what had transpired at church the previous day. For the first time in my life, I felt singled out; the irony is that it was for something for which I had no control.

As Joe and I got older, we were allowed to walk to our Aunt Mary Edna's church in Castalia, a community that was a couple of miles from our home. Sometimes we took a shortcut along the railroad tracks. I was always afraid we might encounter a "hobo" or a frightening animal along the desolate tracks. As I look back, there was not much danger on the tracks compared to the violence on many of our streets today.

Later on, we attended Cane Creek Missionary Baptist Church, which was only a 10-minute walk from our home. Although the church was located nearby, it was on the other side of U.S. Highway 51 (known then as Bellevue, now Elvis Presley Blvd.). The busy highway did not have a stoplight or a crosswalk near our church, which made it dangerous for pedestrians, especially children, to cross. This is the same highway where I caught a glimpse of U.S. President Lyndon B. Johnson as he traveled from the airport to downtown Memphis in the 1960s. I remember thinking that his head viewed through the window of his presidential limousine looked to me like he was larger than life. Looking back, perhaps his contributions to American life were.

Joe and I drove the family car to church after we got our driver's licenses. I attended Sunday school and later, at age 13, taught an adult class. Then at age 16, I was named Assistant Sunday School Superintendent and was issued keys so that I could open up the church on Sunday mornings. When I look back, I realize how mature I was and how blessed I was to be given such responsibilities at such a young age. These experiences in the church helped prepare me for leadership later in my family, my school, and my career.

Getting our driver's licenses gave our mother, Joe, and me mobility that we never had before. Unfortunately, Joe and I didn't appreciate this privilege and asked our mother for money for gas to take her places. When our father learned of this, he was livid. He sat us down and said in no uncertain terms, "If you can't take your mama where she needs to go without charging her, you can just park the car!" That heated lecture set us straight, and to this day, I don't charge anyone when they need a ride. This was perhaps the beginning of my charitable and giving spirit.

As I grew, so did my faith. I don't know how I would have coped with the challenges in my life if I had not had a strong religious foundation. My belief in God and His unconditional love have carried me through many difficulties, ranging from loss of employment, health crises, divorces, and the deaths of family members. My faith has been the bedrock of my existence, providing a firm foundation upon which I have built a humble, God-fearing life.

Family – Ties That Bind

"Honour thy father and thy mother, that it may be well with thee, and that thou mayest live long on the good land, which the Lord thy God gives to thee."
Exodus 20:12 (King James Version)

My parents, Eddie Dean, Sr., and Mattie Delilah Brown were married on August 25, 1947. The second of four children, I enjoyed family life with my parents and my siblings: older brother, Jonenathan (Joe), younger sister, Christine (Chris), and younger brother, Eddie Jr. (Bug). My parents were caring and nurturing. They provided us with everything we needed: food, clothing, shelter, and most importantly, love. We were more fortunate than I realized at the time to have grown up in a stable family environment.

My father, affectionately known as "Eddie B.," was born in Potts Camp, Mississippi. He was the son of Anderson Savon "Sammie" Dean and Annie May Pye Dean and brother of Warrean, Essie, and Lester Dean. Dad was married to my mom for 49 years until her death in 1997.

My mother was also born in Potts Camp, Mississippi. She was the daughter of McKinley Brown and Malrea Dukes Brown and the sister of William, Willie Calvin, Eddie, M.C., and Mayetta.

My mother had only a fifth-grade education, and my father went to school through only the eighth grade. Because of their limited education and lack of time, my parents didn't check our homework often after we got beyond the fifth grade. Nor did they attend parent-teacher conferences or sporting events and other activities that we participated in at school. Even though they had limited education, my parents were among the smartest people I have ever known. They produced offspring who earned three bachelor's, three master's, and two doctoral degrees.

Reared during the Great Depression, my parents knew the difficulties of raising a family in austere times. I didn't realize until much later in life that growing up in a two-parent household was not the norm for many children in the Black community where I was reared. We never went hungry, lacked clean clothes to wear, or were left alone out of the necessity for our parents to work multiple jobs. I was blessed to grow up in a family with both a mother and a father present.

My parents' roles were typical for fathers and mothers in nuclear families in mid-20th century America. My father, a truck driver for most of his working life, was the breadwinner for our family, while my mother, whose role was every bit as important, was a stay-at-home mother who took care of us kids and our household. My father was the disciplinarian in our family. I remember when my mother got exasperated with my behavior, she would bellow those dreaded words, "Wait until your father gets home!" My parents were of the ilk that, "If you spare the rod, you spoil the child." When we misbehaved, we had to often get a belt or a switch from a tree for the administration of our punishment. I didn't enjoy corporal punishment; however, it did curtail our negative behavior. At least I never heard my parents utter the proverbial phrase, "This will hurt me more than it will hurt you!"

MISSISSIPPI TO MEMPHIS – A GAME CHANGER

My father shared with me that it was increasingly difficult for a young Black family to make ends meet in mid-20th century Mississippi. Scarce jobs and an unfair sharecropper system under which he and other Black farmers labored all but ensured continued poverty for many Black families. Getting what seemed like a serendipitous opportunity to get a good job and lift his family from poverty would prove to be a game-changer for my father and our family.

My father's plight was reminiscent of the dilemma faced by the character, John Q. Archibald, played by Denzel Washington, in the 2002 movie *John Q.* In the movie, Archibald's son was in a hospital badly in need of a transplant, but his health insurance wouldn't cover the procedure, and alternative government aid was not available. Archibald's wife implores him to "do something!" In desperation, Washington's character takes hostages in the hospital emergency room and demands medical care for his child.

My dad must have felt he "had to do something," as he was "at the end of his rope" and had no other alternative than to contemplate stealing milk for his hungry children. I imagine that my dad felt similar desperation like the character, John Q. because, knowing him as I did, it would have been uncharacteristic for him to engage in illegal activity. Poverty, however, has a way of making even good people make bad choices.

On a whim on a Saturday afternoon in 1951, my father got onto the back of a pickup truck and rode with friends 68 miles from Potts Camp, Mississippi, to Memphis, Tennessee, where he was offered a truck-driving job with Frisco Transportation. Having been a poor sharecropper most of his life and a worker in a sawmill for a brief period, this was Dad's first "good-paying job." I came across one of his old W-2s recently that showed he earned $4,270 from his truck-driving job in 1956 (equivalent in purchasing power to about $43,768 today, well above the $27,750 poverty guideline in 2022 dollars for a family of four). Just think, "Our family's income in 1956, as a result of Dad's good-paying job, was well above the U.S. poverty guideline!" I marvel that a chance encounter—that I believe was actually providence—resulted in his being hired for a good-paying job that lifted my family from poverty and changed our trajectory forever.

My father commuted to Memphis weekly, returning home to Potts Camp on weekends. During the week, he stayed in Memphis with an uncle, who lived in a rooming house on E.H. Crump Blvd. near the bridge spanning the Mississippi River from Tennessee to Arkansas. His uncle worked for *Frisco Railroad* and was instrumental in helping my father get hired by the company's trucking division. (Another example of a family member helping a relative find employment and temporary housing.)

My father periodically visited and cared for his uncle, who was an alcoholic, throughout the years. He sometimes took me with him on these visits; however, I never got out of the car and didn't see the conditions inside the rooming house where his uncle lived. Judging from the appearance of the neighborhood and the outside of the building, his living conditions probably left much to be desired.

As a child, I didn't understand the devastating effects of alcoholism; however, I understood the love and care that my father displayed toward his uncle. No one in my immediate family drank, although a number of my uncles and cousins did, some of them to excess. One of my uncles had numerous drunk-driving encounters with the police and even was charged with striking a pedestrian while driving drunk. I thank God that I didn't have such negative role models in my mother or father. Looking back, I realize how alcohol and other drugs have plagued many American families. I know that alcohol addiction is a disease, and it should be treated as such. We shouldn't denigrate individuals who have addictions. Rather, we should seek to get them the medical treatment and other help they may need.

Our family moved from Potts Camp, Mississippi, to West Memphis, Arkansas, when I was about a year old. My mother chopped cotton only two days after we moved to West Memphis. She was a dutiful wife, mother, and homemaker who cared for my father, brother, and me and was integral to our family's cohesiveness and stability, despite our limited financial resources.

My father and my maternal grandfather, McKinley Brown (Daddy Brown), built our house in West Memphis with their own hands. They framed it up over the course of two weekends and worked together to finish the original two rooms. We lived at the end of the street, next to a mosquito-infested bayou. My brother, Joe, and I were often chased by an aggressive bantam rooster when we went to the outhouse. Later my father added two more rooms, a bathroom, and indoor plumbing to our house. We lived down the street from Uncle M.C. (Buck) and Aunt Alvinia (Auntie) Brown.

The Black Arkansas soil was rich with nutrients but would crack open during the hot, dry summer months. My mother said that baby chicks would sometimes fall into the crevices and couldn't get out! Mosquitoes that attacked us daily were exacerbated by our proximity to the bayou at the end of our dead-end street. Fortunately, we had a screened-in porch that provided a means for us to sit outside comfortably at night. This, too, was built by my father, who was handy and could build or fix almost anything.

I remember driving to my maternal grandmother's house, in Potts Camp, on many Sundays. We would attend church in the morning and gather at Mama Rea's for family dinner. I relished the delicious meal that often-included homemade dishes like turnip greens, cabbage, chow chow, fried chicken, chitterlings, baked ham, mashed potatoes and gravy, cornbread, cakes, and pies. I played with my brother and cousins and often tore the knees of my pants and the flesh of my knees, climbing through barbed wire fences that separated the yard from the adjacent pasture and hog pen. The trip to Potts Camp always seemed long, although the distance was only about 68 miles. However, the return drive seemed shorter, probably because my siblings and I were exhausted from the activities of the day, and we would fall asleep as soon as we laid down in the backseat of our family's car. Having a car, I realized later, was an anomaly for Black families in the 1950s. I was blessed and didn't even know it.

I never had or desired to have a pet; however, I was tasked with feeding my father's hunting dogs. I remember Jim, a redbone, and Kingfish, a coon hound that I fed daily. My father loved to go hunting with family and friends. This was one of his few forms of recreation. I helped my father dress the small game that he brought home, including quails, rabbits, squirrels, raccoons, and opossums. I realized later that, in addition to recreation, hunting was one of my father's ways of supplementing our family's food supply. I had the opportunity to accompany my father on a squirrel-hunting trip. Although I was a good shot, much to my disappointment, I didn't bag a squirrel on our outing.

Joe and I watched drive-in movies from our bedroom window. Late at night, we could even hear the sound coming from the tiny speakers a half-block away. Once, we witnessed the vandalism of our mailbox by individuals driving by late at night; however, we didn't report the destruction to our parents. Looking back, I don't know why we failed to share this information. It may have been we didn't understand the gravity of the situation, or we were reluctant to be witnesses for fear of retaliation from the perpetrators.

I often witnessed rendezvous between men and women on the desolate land near the drive-in movie that was across the street from our house. The couples would meet, leave in one car and later return. Now, I surmise that they may have been cheating on their spouses. This was something that my young mind didn't understand. As I got older, I saw this scene, albeit in different forms, repeated over and over again by individuals who were untrue to their wedding vows. Fortunately, based on the role model established by my parents and the teachings from the church, I believed in monogamy. This belief would serve me well in dating and later in marriage.

Our relocation to Memphis was a game-changer that altered the trajectory of our family. It allowed us to move from an unfair sharecropper system and poor agrarian economy to the middle class. It didn't, however, allow us to escape the cruelties and unfair practices of racist Jim Crow laws that limited our pursuit of happiness and access to quality education, gainful employment, and other facets of the American dream. My father credits the fact that a Jewish developer was willing to sell our family property—for one of three new tract homes built in the community—as the reason he and my mother were able to get a loan and build our home.

My family's relocation from Potts Camp, Mississippi, to West Memphis, Arkansas, and later to Memphis, Tennessee, was a godsend! Like the 1970s television situation comedy, *The Jeffersons*, we were "moving on up" into the middle class. And, like the sitcom's characters, George and Louise Jefferson, who moved from a meager, working-class lifestyle in Queens to "a deluxe apartment in the sky" in Manhattan due to the success of their dry-cleaning business—Mom and Dad moved from a sharecropper's debt-ridden fate on the farm and poverty, to the middle class and a better life for our family in the city!

My Father – My Role Model

Dad was a God-fearing man who served many years as chairman of the Deacon Board of Baptist Hill Missionary Baptist Church in Potts Camp, Mississippi, and as a member of the Deacon Board at New Fellowship Christian Church in Olive Branch, Mississippi.

Dad learned early on about the inequities of life as a Black man in the South in 20th century America. He grew up in rural Marshall County, Mississippi, at the height of Jim Crow, a period in American history when southern Whites—through the enactment of unjust and discriminatory laws and policies—sought to carry on the vestiges of slavery by denying Black citizens access to quality education, healthcare, housing, employment, and the right to vote, among other things.

Dad, like his father before him, was a sharecropper. For much of his adult life, he farmed land owned by Whites. Like many Black families in the South of that era, our family lived "rent-free" on the land, grew crops for our own consumption, and "shared" part of the harvest each year with a White landowner. Our family, like thousands of other Black families, was indebted to a White landowner for housing, use of their farmland, equipment, seed, fertilizer, etc.

In his later years, my father told me that when he was sharecropping, he could never produce enough crops to clear a profit and get out of debt. The cycle of poverty created by this system of indentured labor—that perpetuated poverty and decimated families—was little better than slavery. Because most Black sharecroppers had little education, they had no knowledge or ability as to how to break this cycle. My father said that at the end of the harvest, the landowner would share the results for the year and would invariably say, "Eddie, you almost made enough this year to cover your debts." Year after year, my father found himself unable to get out of debt and unable to seek a better life for our family.

My father told me about a time when he secretly helped one of his sisters and her husband "escape" from a farm where the White landowner refused to let her leave because of interminable debt amassed from year after year of sharecropping without a profit. My father helped my aunt and uncle load their vehicle and escape under cover of the night. This sounded like something from a novel or a movie, but sadly it actually happened.

Dad also recounted how when he was a child growing up in rural Mississippi, he and other Black kids had to walk to school while White kids rode a bus to a different school that was modern and better equipped. As the bus passed the Black kids on the narrow rural roads, the White kids often taunted them, called them "nigger," and threw debris at them from the bus windows. What a demoralizing experience. I can only imagine the pain and degradation this must have caused countless Black youth and their families.

Through all of the pain and humiliation, my father and countless other Blacks learned to play the game by being outwardly friendly, respectful, and subservient to their White counterparts, even when it was demoralizing. This they did out of a strength of character and out of necessity, for what else could they do when the system was corrupt. Who do you tell when those in charge—employers, law enforcement, the courts—are all aligned against you simply based on the color of your skin? How do you redress wrongs when the system is biased against you? America, "home of the free, home of the brave," had become a caste system where Blacks and other people of color were literally and figuratively at the bottom of society.

Dad had tremendous courage to move our family from Mississippi to West Memphis, Arkansas, in the early 1950s and later to Memphis, Tennessee, where his career as a truck driver lasted more than 35 years. A proud Teamster, he could drive anything on wheels, from mule-drawn wagons to farm tractors and 18-wheelers. Years later, I learned that labor unions, like the Teamsters, did not always welcome Blacks into their membership.

A lover of the outdoors, Dad was an avid hunter and farmer. He was a man of many talents. He could build cabinets, sew leather for homemade ankle weights, slaughter hogs, pick cotton, change brake shoes, and repair most anything.

A member of Keystone Lodge 39, Dad—like his father, Anderson, and my brother, Eddie Jr.—was a proud Mason.

Dad loved our family and treasured the occasions when we spent time together. He especially enjoyed his pilgrimage to South Africa with Joe, Tana (Joe's partner), Chris, and Skip (Chris' husband) to celebrate his 80th birthday. Dad would spend hours showing his pictures of folk he met on his journey and the sites and scenes of the African continent. He was especially touched by the site of the brutal Robben Island Prison, where Nelson Mandela spent the first 18 years of his 27 years of imprisonment under the unfair apartheid system.

Dad also enjoyed gathering family and church members on his farm for cookouts. I remember when he invited a busload of church members from a church in Chicago, Illinois, to the farm for a barbecue when they were in town for a joint service with Baptist Hill M.B. Church in Potts Camp. Dad and his church members also enjoyed going to Chicago on a reciprocal visit.

Dad worked hard and made it so that Mom never had to work outside the home, take in laundry, or clean houses for White folks. Always the dutiful husband, Dad spent hours on end caring for his dear Mattie during her long illness. Mom and Dad were a team, and while they didn't always agree, they put forward a united front when determining how we kids were to be raised. Dad was the biblical head of our household, and Mom was his helpmate. He treated Mom with dignity and respect. Her role as homemaker and primary caregiver for us kids was as consequential to our family as Dad's role as the breadwinner and disciplinarian.

Dad loved and nurtured his children and was an excellent role model for our developing personalities—each in our own way. He was gentle but firm in his demeanor. Dad was more of a doer than a teacher. He would let me assist or watch him in his woodshop, but he didn't give step-by-step instructions on how to do things. What I learned from Dad was by observation.

Growing up on a farm, Dad likely didn't have much time or opportunity to play sports. He did, however, like watching Major League Baseball on television later in life. He also enjoyed traveling with Joe to watch Joe's son, Nathan, during spring training in Florida, when Nathan played baseball for Haverford College. This was an important time when Dad, Joe, and Nathan bonded and enjoyed their time immensely together.

While Dad never attended my basketball games when I played in junior high or high school, he developed a love of college and professional basketball in his later years. We especially liked watching the Memphis Grizzlies of the NBA on television.

Dad had a generous spirit. He often shared vegetables from his farm with family, friends, and church members. I remember going with him to take vegetables to women in our community to help feed their families. I also remember him taking produce to his church for distribution to members of the congregation and their families.

My father could fix practically anything and would often help others in need. I remember Dad spending hours on end taking apart, repairing, and reassembling the carburetor on my car. He changed the oil, resurfaced the brakes, repaired flat tires, and did general maintenance on all of our vehicles. With limited resources, he relied on his own skills to repair or build things.

My father was fearless with animals. In addition to owning hunting dogs, at various times he kept a raccoon and a squirrel in a cage in our garage. He sometimes let the squirrel loose in the house. I remember it scampering up the curtains to perch atop the cornices in our living room as we kids ran for cover! It's a wonder we never were bitten or contracted rabies or other maladies.

I helped my father build cabinets in our garage and often helped him install them in customers' homes. As I said earlier, Dad was a doer and not a teacher. If you watched him work, you could learn from him; however, I don't remember him ever giving me specific instructions on how to do something. Rather, he provided a positive role model to his children: he cared for our financial needs, put a roof over our heads, and was always there for us. My father was symbolic of an often-heard mantra in the Black community, "You have to see a man to be a man."

Dad spent much of his "free" time on his 7.4-acre farm in Olive Branch, Mississippi, that he bought in 1986 from another Black farmer. He tilled the soil to grow vegetables, including corn, green beans, turnip greens, tomatoes, sweet potatoes, and Irish potatoes and also raised cows and an occasional goat. For several years he even raised hogs on our cousin's farm just up the road. (The property where he had his pigpen is now the site of a housing development. If the new homeowners only knew!)

My father worked full-time on his truck-driving job during the day and went to the farm to work until after the sun went down. Being industrious, he collected wood, tin, and other building materials to construct a small farmhouse, barn, and toolsheds on the property. He added electricity, a septic tank, and running water to provide creature comforts, including a television, window air conditioners, kitchen, bathroom sinks, and a toilet. He also acquired a couple of farm tractors and an assortment of farm implements that he used to work the soil.

Each fall, Dad would gather the crops that he had grown. He would give much of his harvest to church members or sell it to customers in the community that he had established over the years. When winter came, we often would slaughter hogs. This was a communal activity that involved my father and other men (family members and friends). The hog that had been pent up and grain-fed to clean out its system was led through a chute to an area separate from the other hogs. Invariably, the hog that was to be slaughtered was excessively agitated. Did it somehow know it was about to become sausage and bacon?

When the men were positioned, and a 55-gallon drum of water had been brought to a boil on a nearby fire, my father would aim his .22-caliber rifle between the hog's eyes. With just one shot, the hog would fall to its knees. One of the men would take a butcher knife and slit the hog's throat and reach down to stab its heart. This was done to release blood to ensure it would drain from the carcass when it was hung to be dressed. As gory as it may sound, slaughtering a hog in this manner was humane as the hog died almost instantly.

A slit was cut behind the hoof of each hind leg, exposing a tendon that would be used to hang the carcass on a two-by-four attached to a fence. The two-by-four was used as a lever to raise the hog and place it into the boiling water to remove its body hair. When that was completed, two hefty men would hoist the carcass and hang it from a sturdy tree limb.

One of the men would then take a very sharp knife and cut open the carcass from its rectum to its throat, taking care to remove its internal organs. Almost all of the hog was kept to be consumed. The organs were set aside for cooking. The tenderloin, chops, ribs, feet, and ears were separated, and the carcass was quartered into shoulders and hind sections (or hams). The shoulders and hams were placed on a wooden table and rubbed with salt and sugar cure to help draw blood from the meat while it hung in the smokehouse over the winter. Salt was used to cure the meat as there wasn't enough room in the freezers to hold all of it.

The use of salt to cure, or prevent the meat from spoiling, hearkens back to the days when there was little or no refrigeration available—especially to poor and Black people—to freeze food. Many foods were cured and seasoned with salt. (I believe that this practice was likely a contributing factor to the prevalence of elevated blood pressure in the Black community. I also believe that my hypertension was caused, in part, by heredity and the high-sodium diet I consumed when I was young.)

Slaughtering hogs was done on a cold day to minimize the risk of meat spoiling. The days were so cold that my fingers felt like they would fall off; however, my father and the other men didn't seem to be bothered. I don't remember any of the men wearing gloves. I guess that was the difference between a green city boy like me and the weather-worn men who grew up on farms in the rural South who helped with this annual ritual.

My father would set aside some of the lean meat to make sausage. He would mix up salt, pepper, and sage to season the meat and then grind the sausage in his meat grinder. (Occasionally, he would take a whole side of pork to our neighborhood butcher to be ground into sausage.) My mother would fry sausages, bacon, and eggs for breakfast the next morning. We would have delicious liver, tenderloin, ham, shoulder, and pork chops with rice, onion, eggs, or gravy throughout the year.

To defray the cost of running the farm and feeding the animals, my father made an arrangement to pick up discarded table scraps, lettuce, and vegetables from several area restaurants. We drove by the restaurants in the evenings near closing and picked up their discarded food. Often as not, the table scraps included plates, cups, and cutlery that inattentive workers had thrown out with the trash. It's a wonder the restaurants stayed in business after losing such enormous amounts of dishes and cutlery.

My father's farm was a godsend for him. It allowed him to work the soil and maintain his connection with the earth. The farm was particularly important in my father's life after the company he worked for, *ET&WNC Transportation*, went out of business in 1986, and he lost his job. The farm was cathartic and provided my father a respite from the pressures of urban life and helped him put food on the table for our family. Some of the happiest moments I observed with my father were when he was plowing in the garden, feeding the cows, or enjoying the fresh air with his children, grandchildren, and great-grandchildren.

My father was my role model and my hero!

MY MOTHER – HOMEMAKER-IN-CHIEF

My mother was an excellent cook, which provided her tremendous satisfaction and a sense of self-worth. Her contributions to the family were invaluable. Mom never used a recipe. She made the best fried chicken, baked ham, and smothered tenderloin, which she often served with rice, corn, potatoes, macaroni and cheese, fried green tomatoes, purple hull peas, and green beans. One of my favorite dishes was my mother's chicken and dressing, made with real cornbread, not store-bought stuffing. She made delicious desserts, including chocolate, pineapple, coconut, caramel, and white cakes. She also made great pies, including sweet potato, egg custard, pecan, peach cobbler, and apple cobbler. I remember her fondly letting me lick the filling from the mixing bowls when she made her delicious desserts.

My mom likely learned her culinary skills from her mother. Growing up on her family's farm in rural Mississippi, she had ample opportunities to learn how to become a good cook. I remember going to Mama Rea's for Sunday dinner and seeing my Aunt Mayetta catch a chicken in the yard, wring its neck, pluck it, and fry it the same day for dinner. There was something special about eating fresh vegetables and knowing the chicken you were eating was as fresh as it could be.

I didn't know it then, but chickens on farms like my grandparents' were what are now referred to as "free-range." They had the run of the farm and were put up in a henhouse only in the evenings to prevent them from being eaten by foxes or coyotes. I remember going into the creaky old henhouse to collect eggs that were laid that day. How mother hens know which eggs have been fertilized and contain embryos is beyond me.

My mother canned fruits and vegetables from our family's farm to provide food for our table and to stretch our household budget. She and I often sat for hours shelling purple hull peas, snapping green beans, or husking corn while watching TV. She sterilized Mason jars, and after cooking the fruits or vegetables in a pressure cooker, she carefully filled and sealed the jars. We stored the canned goods beneath our beds, in closets, or in the kitchen cabinets as we didn't have a traditional cupboard. The canning process kept the food from spoiling and as fresh as when we first put it away.

My mother was more than a housewife; she was the glue that held our family together. She prepared our breakfast, ushered us off to school with our neatly packed brown lunch bags, and welcomed us home to a home-cooked dinner with the entire family. She was there to guide and direct us, and we never came home to an empty house. We were not "latchkey" children, but we didn't fully appreciate the value of Mom being at home to supervise our before- and after-school activities.

Although my mother did all the cooking and washed our clothes, she taught me how to hang laundry on the clothesline, iron clothes, and clean the house, skills that have been invaluable to me as an adult and as a single parent. I wish I had taken home economics in school to learn more about cooking, sewing, home budgeting, etc.

My mother became ill when I was in grade school, and my father taught me how to make cornbread. It was my job to bake the bread daily before he got home from work. This was a tangible way for me to help out at home. I felt jealous when Joe got a job mowing our neighbor's yard. I wanted to earn money just like him. I had an early yearning to work and pull my own weight. Working hard was a value instilled in us by our parents.

Our meals were served family-style, which in retrospect, led to my overeating. I believe that if we had had to get up from the table to serve ourselves at the buffet, we would not have eaten as much at each meal. Dad took pride in the fact that I would eat anything, and I was always a member of the "Clean Plate Club." I loved pig feet and pig tails; however, at one meal, I ate too many and became very ill. I have not eaten either dish since. We each had our favorite piece of chicken. Much of my family's life revolved around food and eating together in our dining room.

My mother never learned to drive and spent considerable time watching television soap operas. She and my Aunt Mayetta watched these weekday programs religiously. For good or bad, TV became my mother's window to the world. She learned new things, and in some cases, television reinforced negative stereotypes about people and situations. Given Mom's limited education, I rarely saw her reading the paper. Neither Mom nor Dad read books to us; however, they bought an expensive set of *World Book Encyclopedias* (one volume was shipped each month), so that we could do research for our homework. Mom and Dad were committed to providing us with a good education and ensuring we had opportunities they had not had.

My mother got a Social Security card in order to run a home daycare for neighbors' children, the only job she ever held. She provided a valuable service for young mothers with children who lived nearby. Through the years, many young adults who she cared for as children came back to express their appreciation for all my mother had done for them.

Mom was a special lady who loved and cared for her family! I loved her dearly!

My Big Brother

My older brother, Joenathan, nicknamed "Joe," born March 26, 1948, has been one of my role models from an early age. I followed in his footsteps in elementary and high school. And I emulated him in numerous ways, including playing basketball for our high school, drawing pictures, enjoying photography, and obtaining a doctorate.

After graduating from Hamilton High School, Joe was accepted by the University of Tennessee, Knoxville (UT), to study architecture. He matriculated in the fall of 1966 in a school that had desegregated only five years earlier. The university and the city seemed a lifetime away. I remember driving with my father or uncle to take Joe to the campus in the fall and pick him and his belongings up from his dorm room at the end of each school year. I can still see the mountain of luggage, books, and papers that he stored in our garage when he spent a summer abroad. He came back from Europe with hundreds of color slides that documented his overseas adventure. His beautiful pictures piqued my interest in photography.

Joe and another young Black man from Memphis were just two of a few Blacks among thousands of White students on campus. In addition to the college and its students, faculty, and staff, even city sanitation workers in Knoxville were White. This must have been a culture shock for Joe and his friend, coming from our South Memphis community where almost everyone was Black.

Years later, when discussing his college experience at UT, Joe lamented that he was at a disadvantage, having graduated from an inner-city school that didn't have resources like the schools located in Memphis' suburban communities. This was perhaps even more acute when he attended graduate school at Princeton University, where he earned a Master of Architecture and Urban Planning degree and a Doctor of Philosophy degree in Architecture and Urban Planning. After college Joe became an architect. I admired his ability to draw plans for buildings and communities. As an urban planner, Joe has the skills to merge form with function to enhance residential, commercial, and public interests in designing aesthetic and functional urban communities.

I am indebted to Joe for the many trails he blazed for me and our younger siblings.

My Little Sister

I was four years old when my sister, Christine, was born on November 14, 1955, in West Memphis, Arkansas. We called her "Sis" when she was young. Now, as an adult, we refer to her as "Chris." I take pride I taught my sister how to walk by dragging a biscuit around a coffee table in our living room, coaxing her to stand, let go, and take her first steps! I've been one of her big brothers ever since.

As a toddler, Chris was nearly bald; however, my mother daily brushed and plaited what little hair she had. Eventually, Chris' hair grew long and flowed down to her shoulders.

Chris followed Joe and me to Dunn Avenue Elementary School. After finishing elementary, she was assigned to Hamilton Jr. High School, the school that I had wanted to attend upon my graduation from sixth grade. She graduated in 1972 from Hamilton High School, Joe's, and my alma mater also.

Chris was talkative and made friends easily. One of her best friends was a petite girl named Deborah. I drove Chris and Deborah all over the community to attend church teas and fashion shows. They were inseparable. They continued their friendship when they moved to the East coast. Deborah passed away in 2020, leaving a huge hole in Chris' heart.

After high school, Chris attended Boston College in Boston, Massachusetts, where she earned a Bachelor of Arts degree in Sociology. She later attended American University in Washington, D.C., where she earned a Master's degree in the Administration of Justice.

I love my sister and feel we have a special bond, perhaps because of her biscuit training and learning how to walk!

My Little Brother

My younger brother, Eddie Jr., was born on April 10, 1959. "Bug," as he was nicknamed, was born at McLemore Clinic, one of the few healthcare facilities that were open to Blacks in our community at that time. It happened that when Bug was born, I was in the same clinic overnight. When I heard what I thought was a baby crying late one night, I left my room searching for my baby brother. My love and dedication to my brother continued after he came home.

We had just moved from West Memphis, Arkansas, to a new tract home on Menager Rd. in Memphis, Tennessee, about the time of Bug's birth. Our house, one of three new homes in the neighborhood, was on a corner lot with a view overlooking a drive-in movie theater. I learned later that my parents were able to buy our home only threw a Jewish developer. It was rare for Black families to be able to buy a new home in the 1950s in Memphis because of redlining—government-sanctioned discrimination against Black home ownership in certain neighborhoods.

Bug had curly Black hair and chubby cheeks that I loved to pinch. One day while holding Bug on my lap he began to slide towards the floor. I heard my mother scream as she scooped him from my arms and to safety.

Bug grew up in the same loving household and attended Dunn Avenue Elementary like his three siblings before him. He loved dogs and took over the task of caring for my father's hunting dogs when he got old enough. He recounts the times fondly when he accompanied my father on hunting trips.

Bug was invaluable as a companion for my dad after my mom passed and in helping to care for him when he became ill. They often took long drives around the county and frequently ended up on Mud Island to watch the tugboats on the Mississippi River and the people nearby. Bug and I drove dad to doctors' appointments, family gatherings, and the grocery store. When my father became terminally ill and was placed in home hospice, Bug and I worked as a team along with his hospice caregivers to provide a comforting and loving experience for my father in his final days.

Bug serves on the security team at his church, New Fellowship Christian Church in Olive Branch, Mississippi, where he has a close relationship with his pastor, the Reverend Dwight Saulsberry, and First Lady Phyllis Saulsberry.

Life for Bug was traumatizing after Dad's passing. His dog, Tiger, who he had raised from a puppy, died the same year. Bug is learning to live independently and loves the support he receives from his church, family, and friends.

Bug and I, too, have a special bond. We love and look out for one another.

COMING OF AGE IN THE 1960S

My family took summer vacations by car. Looking back, I'm uncertain whether this mode of transportation was for pleasure, economic reasons, or because of discrimination against Blacks—difficulties finding public transportation, using restrooms, and eating at "Whites Only" restaurants along the way. We always kept an empty soda bottle in the car for use by us boys if we were not near a restroom that we could use. I don't know what girls did in those situations.

When Joe and I got old enough, we stayed with our Aunt Warrean and Uncle Drew Norris in Como, Mississippi, during the week our mother, father, Chris, and Bug were away on vacation. It didn't occur to me at the time that riding my bike down the dusty gravel road, shooting birds with my BB gun, and walking the length of a football field to get water from a faucet at the White landowner's horse trough, was not as much fun as going to visit family in Buffalo, New York or experiencing the wonder of Niagara Falls.

My mother chastised me for shooting birds that I wasn't going to eat. I stopped doing it, and I began to develop a deeper appreciation for the sanctity of life and the importance of the environment that would guide my life going forward.

I was always an active child. I often tore the knees out of pants—mine and Joe's—on the pavement or under barbed wire fences. And I frequently sustained lacerations to my knees and elbows. When I was younger, I received hand-me-down clothes that Joe had outgrown. In fifth grade, I was nearly his size. By junior high, I was his size and wore his clothes, much to his consternation.

In 1961, our family took a road trip to Oklahoma, where we visited Aunt Indiana "Indy" Dunn. Aunt Indy, who lived in Oklahoma City, was a boisterous and outspoken woman with a "gravelly" voice. While driving us back to her home—in my father's Buick—from a sightseeing trip, Aunt Indy hit the door of a man's car up the street from her house. She damaged the front fender of my father's car. Rather than stopping, she kept driving. After we got to her house, the man, who had suddenly opened his driver-side door into traffic, walked to her house and asked, "Do you know that you hit my car door?" Aunt Indy said without hesitation, "Yes. You shouldn't have opened it carelessly!" That incident and the dented fender on my father's car was a teachable moment for me, even though I was not yet of age to drive.

I remember seeing backyard oil wells and was fascinated by the golden exterior of a bank building. This was my first recollection of visiting another major city. I realized later in life, when trying to recruit kids to attend Y summer camp in Omaha, Nebraska, that many inner-city youths have never traveled outside of their communities. It also became apparent that many Black parents were leery of overnight camping, as they had heard stories about the lynching of Blacks—during slavery and the Jim Crow era—that often occurred in the woods.

When I turned age 16, I worked with the Neighborhood Youth Corp., a federal jobs program "created to give underprivileged youths the opportunity to work, particularly over the summer months, in order to prevent delinquency, show the value of hard work, engender self-respect, provide hope for the future, and to instill a sense of confidence in the government." I was assigned to work at Hamilton Elementary School during the summer of 1966 before starting high school. Mr. O.C. Duckett, head custodian, taught me how to mop, strip, and wax floors, operate a buffer, and clean the building. This was my first job where I received an actual paycheck. For a teenager, $1.25 per hour was a good wage for that era. Looking back, I wish someone had taught me about money management and saving. I spent everything I earned and lived paycheck-to-paycheck. This was a poor habit that I maintained, throughout much of my young adulthood, having to take out numerous high-interest bill consolidation loans. Unfortunately, I, like my parents, failed to teach my sons about money management when they entered the work world.

I learned to drive on the unfinished streets of Gaslight Square, a new subdivision across from our home that was developed from a defunct drive-in movie theater site. (This new development brought more middle-class families to our neighborhood.) As I practiced driving my father's old beat-up blue 1954 Ford F-150 pickup truck on the streets of the unfinished development, I had difficulty mastering the clutch to shift gears smoothly. My mother teased me and said that while I "bucked" in the pickup trying to shift gears going forward, I could back up just fine. For a while—when it seemed I would never get the hang of it—I mused about just driving around town in reverse! Eventually, with my father's patience and frequent practice, I learned how to slowly let the clutch out and shift gears smoothly. Like learning to ride a bicycle, shifting gears is a skill that remains with you for life. (Years later, I wished that *YMCA* hiring committees would remember this fact when considering me for CEO positions after I had been away from the organization for several years due to a family emergency. I could still "ride a bike." I could still be a CEO; however, no one would give me a chance.)

I loved driving, with or without passengers. I often picked up catalog orders for my mother at *J.C. Penney* and *Sears and Roebuck* and returned them when the items she ordered didn't fit or were not what she had expected. I willingly took my mother to the grocery store and other places. Once I ran out of gas—in front of the Mid-South Fairgrounds—while taking her on an errand. This was one of the busiest days of the fair, with tens of thousands of fairgoers and thousands of vehicles on the busy street. I left my mother in the hot car in the middle of traffic while I went to get gas. When I returned, the police had ticketed our car and, needless to say; my mother was fit to be tied. For more than 60 years hence I have not run out of gas again.

My first auto accident occurred while I was on a date to celebrate my girlfriend's 16th birthday. I had taken her to dinner and a movie. A newly licensed driver, I was making a left turn from Mississippi Blvd. onto McLemore St. in South Memphis. The driver of an oncoming car ran the stoplight and clipped the right rear fender of my father's 1959 Buick. Thankfully, neither my girlfriend nor I was injured; however, I slumped over the steering wheel in despair, wondering to myself how I would tell my parents what had happened. I was devastated. Fortunately, my high school math teacher was in the area and witnessed the accident. He gave the license plate number of the hit-and-run vehicle to the police.

After finishing the police report, I dropped my girlfriend off at her home and made the long drive—which was only about 15 minutes but seemed like an eternity—to my home. After I arrived home, I nervously awakened my mother and father and told them what had happened. They were relieved that no one had been injured, and to my surprise, my father didn't yell at me. And, I don't think he checked the damage to the car until the next morning. This was one of the longest nights of my life. I felt terrible that I had been involved in an accident and had damaged the family car, the car that was my father's pride and joy. It was the same car that transported us to church, to my grandmother's house for Sunday dinner and the same car that saved our lives on a lonely Oklahoma highway. (More on this later.) That car almost had human attributes, for it, along with our house, was an outward symbol of my family's status in the small but growing Black middle class.

Unfortunately, after the police tracked down the hit-and-run vehicle, the owner maintained that a relative had taken his car without his permission. Furthermore, the owner of the other car denied responsibility, and we were stuck with making repairs to our vehicle. We didn't have money to get our car professionally repaired, so my father hammered out the dents as best he could. Perhaps it was fitting the car had dents that became a constant reminder for me to not make assumptions about what other drivers will do. To this day, I drive defensively and don't turn left when a traffic signal changes from green to red, recognizing that the oncoming traffic may fail to stop and run the stoplight.

I started 10th grade at Hamilton High School in September 1966. Our principal, Harry T. Cash, an impeccably dressed man of small stature, was a strict disciplinarian. I remember hearing stories about how he would apply the "Board of Education" to the backsides of unruly students. (This was before the era banning corporal punishment in schools.) Joe had graduated from high school in May of the same year.

Joe became the first person in our family to attend college when in the fall of 1966, he went off to the University of Tennessee in Knoxville to study architecture. In September 1969, I matriculated at Memphis State University (MSU), becoming only the second person in our family to attend college. (Once again, I was following in Joe's footsteps.) This was just three years after MSU had been forced to admit its first Black students. My sister, Chris, would later enroll at Boston College, becoming the third person in our family to attend college.

I got married in 1973 and started a family. I soon learned that my meager income as a recreation assistant at a community center was not going to be sufficient to support a wife and child.

Willie Dean

School of Hard Knocks

I have been rambunctious from an early age and had to learn a number of life lessons the hard way. I wouldn't say that I was rebellious; however, I learned many lessons from the "school of hard knocks."

When I was a toddler, I fell from my crib while reaching for my father's shiny ink pen in the pocket of his shirt that was hanging on a doorknob nearby. When I fell, I struck a nail and split my head open. Living in rural Mississippi in the early 1950s meant there were no clinics or hospital emergency rooms nearby. And even if there were, a Black family would not have been welcomed.

I had long locks that my mother used to plait—leading some to assume I was a girl upon first meeting me—that the doctor had to shave so he could sew stitches in my scalp. To this day, I have a long scar on top of my head, a permanent reminder of my inquisitive nature. This scene would be repeated multiple times during my life with everything from scraped knees to broken bones.

I learned a valuable lesson about lying and stealing at a young age in the kitchen of my family's home. One day when I was about five years old, my mother cooked one of my favorite dishes for lunch—fried catfish. After lunch, she placed the leftovers in a dish and covered them with a napkin on the kitchen table for our dinner. Wanting more of my favorite dish, I went into the kitchen and—without asking permission—got some more catfish.

When I heard my mother coming into the kitchen, I dove under the table and tried to gobble down the fish. (I remember this incident like it was yesterday.) I guess I thought, "If I could get rid of the evidence, there would be no crime." Immediately fishbones got caught in my throat, and—crying in pain—I had no choice but to come from under the table. When my mother realized what I had done, she yelled, "I ought to whip you. I ought to whip you!" But like the good mother that she was, she gathered me up into her arms and tried to console me.

Frantically, my mother telephoned for a taxi—as she never learned to drive. She had Joe phone my Aunt Alvinia, who lived up the street, to let her know what was happening. Joe called Auntie and, in his excitement, told her, "Mama is taking Willie to the doctor; he swallowed a 'buffalo-catfish' bone!"

When we arrived at the doctor's office, the waiting room was packed with patients waiting to be seen. Upon seeing me in pain, with blood gushing from my throat, several of the patients said to my mother, "Go ahead and take your child in to see the doctor!" After the doctor removed the bones from my throat, he told me that I should never want to eat fish again.

Fish is still one of my favorite meals; however, I learned a valuable lesson about stealing and lying that day. You see, I "stole" the fish without asking for it, and I attempted to swallow it and hide beneath the table to cover up my misdeed, or in effect, I was "lying" about what I had done. God's admonishments in the Ten Commandments: "Thou shalt not steal" and "Thou shalt not bear false witness" have special meaning to me as a result of this painful lesson.

My next health scare happened when I was age six. I was watching television one Sunday evening while lying on the living room couch. When I tried to get up, I was unable to stand. My father and my Uncle Buck scooped me up and took me to the hospital. After what seemed like days of tests, I was diagnosed with measles, which had gone into my stomach. I had to endure dozens of shots in my backside. While my condition was serious, through the grace of God, I was eventually released with no ongoing concern.

One day while playing in the backyard, I accidentally broke the window of our garage door while throwing a toy tractor tire against the cinderblock wall. I reluctantly told my father what had happened. He was angry at me for being careless; however, he didn't punish me for my mistake. From this incident, I learned that honesty and taking responsibility for mistakes is the best policy.

On another day, while sliding on the ice in our backyard, I lost my balance and slammed my chest into the swing set. I thought I had broken my breastbone; however, I didn't tell anyone. Not telling others when I encountered hurt in my life had become a pattern. Maybe I sensed—erroneously—at an early age that "real men don't cry." This is a habit that I am still trying to break, for unknowingly, I modeled this poor behavior to my sons when they were growing up in my own family. Had I to do over, I would have been more emotive and discussed my feelings with others, especially my loved ones. I now know that "real men do cry."

One night in 1959, my father was working on the stove in our kitchen. When he disconnected the gas line without first turning off the gas at the meter, gas began to escape into the house. My father quickly covered the gas orifice with a rag and held it in place with his hands to try to keep the gas from escaping. Even though the gas had ignited from the lit pilot light and was burning his hand, my father calmly sent me outside to turn off the gas. He told me to take an adjustable wrench, go to the meter and turn the valve on top to the right until it wouldn't turn anymore. While I was only seven years old and had never shut off a gas line before, I realized that our home, with my father inside, could explode if I didn't do exactly as he instructed. Through the grace of God, I was able to figure out how to turn the gas off, and we were spared a major disaster.

The lesson that I learned about gas in 1959 saved my family's home in Minnesota more than 40 years later. (Although the emergency could have been averted had I not repeated my father's mistake.) When preparing to sell a gas clothes dryer before moving to Ohio in 2005, I disconnected a flexible aluminum gas line and tried to quickly cover the opening before capping it. Gas began to escape. I realized the danger that my family was in and summoned my son, Matt. I calmly instructed him to take a cordless phone outdoors and call 911. Firefighters arrived in minutes, turned off the gas, and aired out our house. The utility company came later and put a lock on the gas shutoff valve in the basement and required me to have a licensed plumber put in a rigid gas line with a shutoff valve within three feet of the gas appliance. The lesson learned from a similar incident four decades earlier allowed me to avoid a tragedy. I should have known better.

Most of these lessons, learned the hard way, would prevent me from making costly mistakes in the future. My mother used to say, "You would argue with a signpost." It wasn't that I was a "know-it-all"; rather, I felt confident in my ability to grasp situations, and I was young and very opinionated. I often had to experience things for myself. I guess you could say that I was an experiential learner. That may explain why later I enjoyed living in Missouri; the "Show Me State."

SINGLE-PARENTHOOD – TRAINING FOR THE FUTURE

I got married at age 22, and my son, Cedric, was born the following year. With no prior parenting training, my wife and I emulated how our parents raised us. Young and inexperienced, we had a number of obstacles. We lived with my parents for about a year in an effort to help make ends meet. We lived paycheck-to-paycheck and got into trouble using credit cards for everyday items and frills. We also developed the bad habit of taking out high-interest bill consolidation loans that kept us in debt. If only my parents, or someone, had taught me money management early in my life.

I was working full-time as a program director with the *YMCA* in Memphis and Shelby County, Tennessee, when I applied for a position as executive director of a branch Y in Fort Worth, Texas. Knowing no one in Texas, my family and I packed our belongings and headed on an adventure to an unfamiliar community. Due to a number of issues, my marriage ended in divorce after just four years.

Single parenthood at various times during my life—caused by divorce or the death of my spouse—forced me to be both mother and father for my children. I didn't fully understand the impact of single-parenthood on Cedric, Jarrod, and Matt as it was happening. In retrospect, I can see that I should have reached out more to family and friends to aid in my sons upbringing.

There was no manual for being a good parent. I relied on the examples that my parents provided me and emulated their parenting style. I tried to be a good role model, made sure my sons were well fed and clothed, provided a roof over their heads, ensured they got a good education, and most importantly, made sure they were baptized in the church. I tried to give my sons a foundation built on the Christian principles that I have held dear for over 60 years. I made sure we worshipped together as a family. I regret, however, that when I took a job in Minneapolis as National Field Executive for the *YMCA* of the USA, a position that required significant travel, our church attendance was sporadic.

Looking back, I see that the lessons that God taught me as a single parent following my divorce in my 20s prepared me for single-parenthood in my 50s when my wife unexpectedly lapsed into a chronic vegetative state following surgery and later passed away. The situation was unimaginable and another painful life lesson that made me a stronger person. "God is good!"

Friends Essential to the Soul

"Greater love hath no man than this, that a man lay down his life for his friends."
John 15:13 (King James Version)

THE MOTTO OF MY beloved Omega Psi Phi Fraternity, Inc.—"Friendship is essential to the soul"—speaks to the importance of friends in our lives. Friends can buttress our values in the face of negative influences that seek to defeat or destroy us. Whether friendships are forged in childhood or later in life, they can support us in good times and bad, keeping us grounded in who we are and who we aspire to be.

I didn't have many friends from my neighborhood or from school when I was growing up in Memphis. My mother, an introvert like me, didn't encourage individuals to visit inside our home. Even our father's friends usually visited with him on the driveway or in his garage workshop. My mother was most comfortable with close family members. We rarely hosted parties or large family gatherings. I only learned about playing cards and dancing when Joe and I stayed at the home of our Aunt Warrean and Uncle Drew Norris in Como, Mississippi.

I enjoyed playing under the bushes in our front yard, imagining I was in the great outdoors. This was perhaps a precursor to my love of camping and the friendships I would make with members of the Outdoor Recreation Club at Memphis State University during my undergraduate years.

While I didn't have many friends from my neighborhood when I was growing up, I bonded with teammates on my basketball teams and with classmates from school. My introverted tendencies and the lack of encouragement from

Willie Dean

my parents for me to get out and meet kids in my neighborhood contributed to me becoming a loner. We were often homebodies. I count among my few childhood friends my next-door neighbor and classmate, Rufus Pulley, and another classmate, William Henry Tate, Jr., who lived down the street from my cousin in Castalia. William and I grew close when we worked together during our senior year in high school as salesmen at a nearby department store.

The bulk of my friends today are people that I have worked with professionally through the *YMCA*, served with in service clubs, or worked with at churches in the cities where I have lived. I tend to compartmentalize my feelings and don't communicate with friends or family as often as I should. However, I take pride in sending text messages to family members and friends on holidays like Christmas, Easter, Mother's Day, and Father's Day. Now, in retirement, I look forward to forging deeper friendships with former colleagues, high school classmates, fraternity brothers, and church members. Support and encouragement from my friends have been important to me as I have faced numerous challenges in my life.

Elementary School
The Wonder Years

"Train up a child in the way he should go: and when he is old, he will not depart from it." Proverbs 22:6 (King James Version)

I STARTED FIRST GRADE in August 1956 at the all-Black Wonder Elementary School in West Memphis, Arkansas. This was two years after the landmark 1954 U.S. Supreme Court Brown v. Board of Education decision that ruled unconstitutional the practice of "separate but equal" facilities in public education. Despite this ruling, for the next 18 years, from elementary through high school, I would attend "Black schools." only when I was in high school did I have several White teachers; however, all of my classmates were Black. With school resources tied to property taxes, children who attended schools in poorer communities were disadvantaged. Unfortunately, this practice continues to this day with poor educational and socioeconomic outcomes for people and communities of color.

My first fight was with a girl at school; she beat my butt. When I got home, to add insult to injury, my father "tanned my hide," 1) for fighting and 2) for fighting a girl. Looking back, my father's dual message was not lost on me. I would have only one other fistfight in my life. It happened during a varsity basketball game when I retaliated against an opposing player who was holding my trunks to prevent me from rebounding. We both got ejected from the game. I learned critical lessons from these incidents: 1) fighting does not solve problems, and 2) one's ability to help their team is severely curtailed if they're not in the game. I also learned that not everyone plays by the rules. Some break the rules while others use their power and influence to flout them.

Willie Dean

When I was in the first grade at Dunn Elementary School in Memphis, Tennessee, I was confronted by our school's secretary—a petite older lady with what I perceived as a mean disposition. She chastised me for being in the hall without a pass. I remember her asking me, "What is your name?" I nervously replied, "Widdie Dean." Incredulous with my response, she retorted in her monotone voice, "Your name is W-i-l-l-i-e Dean." Looking back for more than 60 years, I am grateful that this little old lady took the time to correct my speech. Who knows, without her intervention, I might still be referring to myself as "Widdie Dean," oblivious to my poor enunciation. I developed a penchant for proper pronunciation and grammar that has carried me throughout my life, thanks to this harsh but caring, diminutive old lady.

My second-grade teacher, Mrs. C.W. Young, realizing that I was left-handed, assigned me a lefthanded desk. As I was larger than typical second graders, my desk was also larger than those of my classmates. The desk gave support to my left hand and arm and improved my penmanship; however, it wreaked havoc with my right-handed classmates when we stood in the aisle to recite the Pledge of Allegiance. I invariably blocked students who stood next to me in the crowded aisle. This was just the start of my larger-than-life existence.

Mrs. Young special ordered a pair of left-handed scissors so I wouldn't have to use scissors designed for right-handers. It took six weeks for the scissors to arrive, during which time I was exempted from activities that required cutting. When the scissors finally arrived—much to my teacher's chagrin—we learned that I didn't use my "left" hand for cutting. In fact, we learned that I'm semi-ambidextrous. I use my left hand for most fine motor skills like writing, drawing, etc., and I use my right hand for most gross motor skills like batting a baseball and shooting baskets. My ability to use both hands, and to see both sides of issues, would become a hallmark of both my sports and human relations skills.

Lack of access to routine health and dental care caused a number of problems during my formative years. I experienced frequent earaches, which caused multiple absences from school. This went on from the first through third grades before my parents found an otolaryngologist who diagnosed and treated me for ear infections. I missed so much of the third grade that I fell behind in my schoolwork. When I returned to school, I had to learn how to write cursive, and I never really learned phonics. Because my family didn't have much discretionary income, we only sought medical and dental care in emergencies. I had poor dental health, resulting in multiple untreated cavities as a child and teenager, requiring a partial denture by age 19, and periodontal disease in my twenties. Thank goodness basic vision screenings and vaccinations were provided at no charge throughout my grade school years.

I started third grade at Dunn Avenue Elementary School in September 1959. I loved my teacher, Mrs. Van. I didn't realize it then, but I was assigned to classrooms from the first through sixth grade (1A, 2A, etc.) that placed gifted students in advanced cohorts. I benefited from this advanced system; however, I don't know that it was fair to students who were placed in classrooms not so designated.

One day Mrs. Van handed out order forms for the *Weekly Reader*, a subscription newspaper with current events that helped round out our education. I don't know how or if our teachers made accommodations for students whose families were less fortunate and perhaps couldn't afford subscriptions. More than likely, students were asked to share their newspapers with classmates. One evening my father and I argued late into the night about the instructions on how to fill out the *Weekly Reader* subscription form. My father had one interpretation, and I had another. My refrain over and over again was, "Mrs. Van said!" This was frustrating for Dad and me, but it was emblematic of my confidence in believing I knew what my teacher said.

Much to the surprise and delight of my classmates and me, Mrs. Van moved with us when we were promoted from third to fourth grade!

My father and I had an agreement where he rewarded me with five dollars for each "A" that I received on my report card. This "stick and carrot" incentive system motivated me to perform at a high level and let me know that my parents—despite their limited education—understood the value of a good education for their children.

I enjoyed school and was especially good at spelling. This became the foundation for my success in writing and public speaking in later life.

Early Academic Achievement

Caring teachers and my yearning for knowledge gave me a pathway to success in school and in life. My sixth-grade teacher, Mrs. Fairy P. Austin, made an indelible impression on me. It was clear that she really cared about her students. I had 29 "A's" and one "B" on my final sixth-grade report card. I was elated having received so many "A's!" However, I never quite understood why I got that one "B."

Learning and good grades came easy to me. In junior high, I was named salutatorian—the number two ranked student—of my ninth-grade class, and I received the award for "Academic Excellence for an Athlete." In high school, I was a member of the *National Honor Society* and ranked in the top 25 students of my 500-member senior class. Looking back, I realize that had I applied myself more, I could have been an even better student. If I had taken advantage of an invitation to attend a college preparatory school (that my parents turned down) while I was in junior high, or if I had attended schools that were not bereft of resources because of discrimination, I might have achieved even greater heights.

One of my elementary school classmates, Beverly Baker, a petite girl with pigtails and eyeglasses—who was smart as a whip—was my frequent opponent in weekly schoolwide spelling bees. Beverly and I invariably would be among the last students standing around the cafeteria at the end of each spelling bee. I could never manage to beat her, and each year she would represent our school at the citywide spelling bee.

I was often distraught with classmates who sought to cheat off my test papers. I never let them; however, I faced considerable peer pressure to do so. I knew it was wrong, and I didn't want to be caught by my teachers. I don't know if these students were lazy, lacked moral fiber, or needed additional instructional support. Looking back, some of them may have suffered from inequities in the educational system. Learning disabilities were rarely diagnosed or attended to in those days. Could this have contributed to the "failure" of some students who were attending under-resourced schools? Did they lack access to the best teachers and curricula?

I'm blessed to have had a successful early learning experience. I can't help but think that if there had been preschool or kindergarten available to me, I could have achieved even greater success in school.

Athletic Prowess at a Young Age

When I was in elementary school, I was bigger and more agile than most of my peers. I was always picked first for dodgeball, relay races, and other sports. I didn't understand how it felt to be picked last or not picked at all. I could throw harder and more accurately than most everyone else, making me a formidable player. I also enjoyed basketball, although the playground at our under-resourced school didn't have a basketball court.

A Harlem Globetrotters' film, shown at my elementary school, showcased the team's trademark *Sweet Georgia Brown* theme song and the fancy ball work of the legendary Curly Neal and Meadowlark Lemon. This experience made a tremendous impression on me and cemented my lifelong love of basketball. It's amazing how even small experiences can excite a young person and provide the motivation to achieve a goal in life.

As I was larger and more agile than most other students, I was able to outrun and outplay most of my classmates. Recess was one of my favorite periods of the school day (perhaps a harbinger of my yet-to-come professional career in recreation). I enjoyed playing dodgeball and relished my ability to throw accurately to get other students out. Everyone wanted to be on my team. (I never experienced the disappointment of being picked last, or not at all, until much later in life when age caught up to my athletic abilities.)

Being larger than other kids my age had its downside, as it was difficult for my mother to find affordable clothes for me. She often had to shop for me from the more expensive "husky" clothing lines. And because I was tough on clothes as well, Mom almost always bought pants with "double knees," recognizing that I was likely to tear out the knees of my pants! (Now, as an adult at six feet, 256 pounds, and a size 15 shoe, finding stylish, reasonably-priced apparel is still a challenge.)

My father erected a basketball goal in our backyard, where I spent countless hours playing with my brother, Joe, and friends. The regulation basketball hoop and a crude plywood backboard were mounted on a metal pole. If you drove too hard to the basket, you ended up with whelps on your backside from grazing the top of the picket fence that separated the "basketball court" from the section of the backyard where my father's hunting dogs had free range. Often, errant balls wound up over the fence. Timeout was called so my brother or I could retrieve the ball, for no one else dared to enter our dogs' domain. I often shot hoops to hone my skills, well after dark. My mother would turn on the porch light so I could see.

Playing in our backyard, I developed defensive, rebounding, and shooting skills, and by the time I got to junior high, I was a pretty good basketball player. But, as I later learned, junior high was to be about much more than basketball. I would have to overcome my fear of getting hurt performing tumbles in physical education class, walking across the gym floor to ask a girl to dance, and being mugged by a neighborhood thug. However, through it all, God sustained me.

My time in elementary school was truly wonderful, as it was foundational to my success in junior high, senior high, college, and life.

Junior High
Age of Discovery

"Hear, my son, your father's instruction, and reject not your mother's teaching."
Proverbs 1:8 (Revised Standard Version)

Entering junior high is a challenging time for many young people. It's the same today as it was more than a half-century ago when I entered the next phase of my education. In addition to the stresses of a new school, new teachers, and new classmates, students also encounter temptations to smoke, use drugs, drink, gamble, have sex, and even fight to establish dominance or protect themselves from bullies. It is oft said that "an idle mind is the devil's workshop." I thank God that He—along with the love and the guidance of my parents, teachers, and a very special coach—occupied my time and my mind and kept me away from such evils and from running with the "wrong crowd."

Robert Terrell, Teacher, Coach, Role Model

I first met Robert Lewis Terrell in the fall of 1963. Mr. Terrell, as we called him, was a physical education teacher, an assistant football coach, and the head basketball coach at Corry Junior High School in Memphis, Tennessee. Known to his friends as "Bobby," Mr. Terrell was respected by faculty, staff, and students alike. It was perhaps fate that brought us together because I didn't want to attend Corry Junior High School.

Willie Dean

I had just completed the sixth grade at Dunn Avenue Elementary School and wanted to follow in my older brother's footsteps and attend Hamilton Junior High School, which was a 15-minute walk from my home. However, Corry was a new school that needed to increase its enrollment. The Memphis City Schools Board of Education decided, in their own wisdom, to redraw district attendance lines just as I was entering the seventh grade.

With redistricting, my residence would be in the Corry attendance area. This meant I would have to travel nearly two miles to school rather than attend the nearby Hamilton Junior High, which was only eight-tenths of a mile from my home. My parents and I worried about the long traverse and how I would get to school. It seemed too far for a 13-year-old to walk. What to a seventh-grader seemed like a five-mile journey, "uphill both ways," was actually less than a 1.5-mile trek. (I didn't learn this fact until age 50 when driving with my father, who pointed out the actual mileage.)

If going into junior high was not traumatic enough, the school board would have me walk a longer distance to get to a new school and tackle seventh grade in one fell swoop. To a seventh-grader on his own for the first time—changing classes, not having the supervision and nurturing support of a classroom teacher, and navigating a new environment—was a daunting and unrealistic expectation. My parents agreed and went to the school district office and applied for a transfer; however, it was denied. After exhausting appeals to the decision, they reluctantly registered me, and I prepared to attend my first day of class at a school that seemed like it was on the edge of nowhere.

When I arrived at Corry, I found a school building that was relatively new, so new in fact that it only went to the eighth grade, rather than grades seven through nine like other junior high schools, and it didn't have a gymnasium (a point that became poignant when I went out for the basketball team). Most of my classmates from my elementary school seemed to also be enrolled; a small consolation for a teen who was dealing with a new environment, a growth spurt, hormonal changes, and the discovery of girls!

While I went kicking and screaming, my years at Corry Junior High were some of the most rewarding and consequential of my life. I didn't recognize it then, but going to Corry was one of the best things that happened to me because there, I achieved academically, shone athletically, and learned to be independent. Our principal, Mr. Joseph P. Atkins, and the faculty and staff at Corry Junior High cared about us. They worked hard to educate us and to help us succeed.

Because our school didn't have a gym when I arrived in seventh grade, we had to use an all-purpose room that was outfitted with portable stanchions that held the basketball hoops and volleyball nets we used during P.E. classes. Students didn't seem to mind having to help put up and take down the equipment at the beginning and end of classes, for we were eager to help our teachers. In retrospect, we were learning teamwork even when preparing for classes.

Size Advantage?

I've been above average stature since I was a boy, which has aided me in excelling in sports and in life. I wore men's size 12 shoes, stood 5 feet 8 inches tall, and weighed 170 pounds when I entered seventh grade. I would soon learn that being larger than my classmates would not always be an asset. However, for most of my life, being physically larger than my peers was an advantage. I could rebound and block shots better than most of my pick-up game teammates, and I could throw a dodgeball harder and more accurately than most of my classmates.

However, being husky was a detriment when I attempted to dive over more than eight classmates during stunts and tumbling in P.E. class. I was terrified when the teacher had us jump over one, then two, and more and more classmates who were positioned on their knees on the tumbling mats. My smaller peers seemed to glide with ease as they jumped over other classmates, tucked their heads, and rolled upon touching down softly on the mat. But for me, at 170 pounds, I was afraid I might break my neck if I landed prematurely, as I frequently did, crashing onto the backs of my nervous classmates near the end of the gauntlet.

On the days when I knew I would have to jump over my classmates in P.E. class, I literally felt sick, and for one of the few times in my life, I dreaded going to school. Looking back, I believe the feelings I felt were akin to how youth who are bullied or have other traumas affecting their school achievement feel today.

Many factors contribute to low school attendance (and low achievement), including fear of something, or someone, on or off the school campus. Bullies, fear of failure, learning disabilities, poor nutrition, hunger, instability in the home, poverty, etc., make it hard for students to excel in school. By the grace of God, I was blessed to have two parents who nurtured, cared for me, and encouraged me. My mother and father ensured my siblings and I were well nourished and well rested for each school day. As I look back at some of my peers and their life circumstances, I realize how blessed I was then and continue to be today.

My fear of stunts and tumbling was equaled only by the fear and trepidation I felt with having to cross the gym floor to ask girls to dance during P.E. class. The latter fear I carried with me into high school and later into adulthood. Part of my fear was borne out of not wanting to look silly and embarrass myself with awkward, gangly movements on the dance floor. But in reality, it was just as much the fact that I never learned to dance. (Partying and dancing, like playing cards, were not done in my household.) This fear would follow me throughout my school career as I was a timid dancer and shy about talking to or approaching girls.

The enjoyment of dancing was foreign to me. No one in my home danced, and I only saw dancing on a few TV shows like *American Bandstand*. It was years later when I saw Black people dancing with feeling on shows like *Soul Train* or in movies like *Cooley High* that I began to yearn to do what other healthy boys and girls were doing on the dance floor. I didn't attend my senior prom, partly because of my fear of dancing and my discomfort in asking a girl to accompany me to the dance. I had recently broken up with my longtime girlfriend, the girl I thought I would eventually marry, and I used this as justification for not going to the prom. Dance partners have attempted to teach me how to swing and slow dance; however, I think I don't have the rhythm needed to dance smoothly. It was not until I took a required dance class for my recreation major at Memphis State University that I learned to clog, waltz, and square dance. I did manage to do the "bump," a dance that was popularized in the 1970s. However, as accomplished as I am in many facets of my life, I still feel awkward on the dance floor.

While I loved playing basketball at home and wanted to try out for the school team, I was wooed to go out for the football team. Looking back, given my size and agility, I can see why the head football coach, Robert Ledbetter, wanted me to try out for the team. However, after just one day of practice, I went to Mr. Ledbetter and informed him that football was not for me. I left the team but not without peer pressure from teammates to "stick it out." But I made the decision that I felt was best for me.

Later that fall, I went out for the basketball team, the sport that I had been in love with since third grade when my school showed that memorable filmstrip about the Harlem Globetrotters! I was enthralled with the wizardry and ball-handling skills of Curly Neal and the rest of the Globe Trotters and wanted to be just like them. (Years later, at a retirement dinner for my basketball coach, several of my brief football teammates reminded me of my short-lived experience on the football team. They implied that I didn't have what it took to play football! I never imagined that peer pressure would still be happening after more than 40 years. Apparently, peer pressure has no expiration date.)

Making the Team

I went out for the basketball team in the fall of 1963. I credit Mr. Terrell's discipline and physical regimen for getting me into shape for the team and helping me slim down from a "husky" 13-year-old to become a budding athlete. The physically demanding after-school practices helped discipline me physically and mentally and served to channel my raging hormones. I had little time to think about getting into trouble. Juvenile delinquency, drinking, smoking, drugs, and sex weren't on my mind. I did, however, begin to develop a healthy appreciation for girls.

I rode my bicycle daily in my neighborhood, and on weekends I rode two to three miles from my home and back without my mother knowing I had left the neighborhood. I never stood up on my bike, even when pedaling up hills. Mr. Terrell said my frequent biking was perhaps the cause for the massive development of my thigh muscles, which contributed to my leaping and rebounding ability. Biking would become an interest of mine throughout my life.

Looking back, going out for the team involved more conditioning and endurance than actually playing basketball. I think Mr. Terrell was trying to gauge which of us who had gone out for the team had the perseverance to keep going when the going got tough. He had us start every practice with laps around the 440-yard outdoor track. Then we went into the multipurpose room for calisthenics. We did lots of wind sprints, sit-ups, push-ups, and jumping jacks. With my size, I had difficulty with conditioning. My sides ached when running long distances.

Finally, we got to hold a basketball and began our journey to become basketball players. Each day after school we ran to the locker room to change into our practice gear and assembled on a makeshift court in the multipurpose room that was fitted with portable basketball goals. Mr. Terrell was relentless in teaching us the fundamentals of the game. He taught us how to dribble, shoot, and make layups. He also taught us how to keep a wide stance, with one foot in front of the other and our center-of-gravity low when on defense. He showed us how to put our butts on our opponents when rebounding, "boxing out," so they had no chance of jumping over us to get to the ball. He taught us to follow our shot to the basket, so we would be in a position to rebound the ball should we miss our shot. Occasionally we were allowed to scrimmage among ourselves and experience running the length of the makeshift court.

Then, one day Mr. Terrell posted the names of the individuals who had made the team on the bulletin board in the hallway outside of the multipurpose room. As we scrambled to see who had made the cut, I saw that my name was on the list, and before I could celebrate, I realized simultaneously that my best friend and next-door neighbor, Rufus Pulley's name, was not. Rufus was an exceptionally fast runner; however, he lacked the agility and finesse needed for playing basketball. I was saddened that Rufus would not be joining the team, and we would not be walking home together after practices and games. It was hard and hurtful that he had not been selected.

With my size, I was particularly good at rebounding, playing defense, and the forward and center positions. However, I realized quickly that my size would be problematic for playing guard as smaller players were often thought to be more adept at dribbling and running the floor. This would be a continuing truth throughout my life; bigger is not always better.

Since our school didn't have a gymnasium, Mr. Terrell had my teammates, and I travel two miles across town to South Side High School to practice. Southside, a new school building with a new gym, allowed our team to practice in their old gym. Mr. Terrell, a master of logistics, had half of our team start running from our school while he piled what seemed like ten others of us into his compact car and took us halfway to the old Southside gym. From there, we ran the rest of the distance to the gym. He then drove back and picked up the group that was running toward our destination and delivered them to our practice site. By that time, those of us in the second group had made it to the gym. We reversed the process at the end of practice and repeated this procedure daily until our gymnasium was completed.

Looking back, not having a gym of our own and having to run and be shuttled to and from our practice site enhanced our fitness and camaraderie and molded us into a stronger team. (Later, Mr. Terrell bought a 1965 *Ford Thunderbird*. He never piled us into that beauty.)

Finally, our new gymnasium was finished. We were excited to have P.E. classes and our first basketball team practice in our new home! I remember the smell of fresh shellac, the shiny hardwood floor, and the spacious locker rooms. The gym was a source of pride for the whole school. It became a welcomed site for basketball practices, pep rallies, games, student assemblies, and P.E. classes. We took pride in having our own gymnasium.

Basketball practice was like "boot camp" that prepared us mentally and physically for the season ahead. I remember the scent of liniment in the locker room, the feeling of exhaustion during practices, and the unbearable heat during the summers when we practiced twice daily in our un-airconditioned gym. I remember that we took salt tablets to combat muscle dehydration and cold showers to try to cool off after physically demanding practice sessions. I remember that we practiced at 3 a.m. on Thanksgiving morning, a test of our fortitude, which helped us bond and become a stronger team. This boot camp experience enhanced my cardiovascular endurance and taught me basketball fundamentals and resilience, all of which made me a better man later in life.

I was taller and bigger than many of my peers and was blessed with superior athletic abilities, especially rebounding and tipping. I was unselfish to a fault and would often pass the ball to a teammate when I had an open shot myself. The irony was that had I been a selfish "ball hawk," I could have been a top scorer in addition to having been a top rebounder. However, sharing and teamwork are qualities that I treasured then and value now. I believe fervently in the cliché, "There's no 'I' in TEAM."

The basketball team became my surrogate family and provided me with a network of friends who had interests and values that were similar to mine. The discipline and camaraderie I gained from playing basketball for Mr. Terrell gave me the skills and confidence to be successful in school and in life. Through athletics, I learned the importance of working together as a team to accomplish goals that enhanced my leadership in sports, church, my career, and raising my family. I never had the time, or the inclination, to join a gang or a clique or to run with the wrong crowd.

ACADEMIC EXCELLENCE

My transition from elementary to junior high school nearly 60 years ago was not much different than it is for students today. Many students of my era felt anxiety moving from elementary school, where their classroom teacher provided instruction and guidance throughout the day, to junior high, where they were responsible for finding their way to multiple classes. In junior high in my day, students experienced anxiety over many changes, not the least of which included a new school, changing classes, puberty, and peer pressure to smoke, use drugs, drink alcohol, engage in sexual activity, or join a gang.

(These pressures faced by students of my generation are similar to students today.)

The one thing that was a constant for me was the values that my faith and family had instilled in me from a very young age. My parents showed me love and ensured that my brothers, sister, and I went to church regularly. I had been a Sunday School student, and by age 13, I was even teaching an adult class. By age 16, I was named the Assistant Superintendent of my Sunday School and even had a key to the church.

I was a high achiever and had been placed in the top classes throughout my six years at Dunn Elementary. Looking back, I realize that students were assigned to classes based on their aptitude. I received a "Perfect Attendance Award" for not missing a single day during the 1963-1964 school year. Regular school attendance contributed greatly to my academic achievement. I realize now that students can't learn if they are not in school. Regular attendance is key to school success. Irregular school attendance results in far too many youths from disadvantaged communities falling behind and eventually dropping out of school.

With my elementary school success and focus on academic achievement, tackling junior high was not foreign to me. I did well in my classes. I especially liked English, history, physical education, and art. Mr. Terrell followed the academic performance of all of his players to ensure we were on track. When I was promoted from the ninth grade, I was named the salutatorian of my class and received the award for "Academic Excellence for an Athlete."

The Thrill of Victory – The Agony of Defeat

Mr. Terrell was a firm but caring coach. Unlike another more famous coach, also nicknamed "Bobby," Mr. Terrell never threw chairs or tirades. He had high expectations for his players both on and off the court. He worked us hard, sometimes holding two-a-day practices in the summer and even at 3:00 a.m. on Thanksgiving morning. However, we never practiced on Sundays as Mr. Terrell felt that the Sabbath was sacred.

Mr. Terrell and my father were two of the most influential men in my life. They were kind, nurturing, and God-fearing men who held themselves and others accountable for their actions. I believe in the adage, "You have to see a man in order to be a man." I am blessed to have had both these men in my life.

Mr. Terrell's diligence paid off. By my ninth-grade year, our team was a basketball powerhouse. We beat every team we played. I remember the score of one game that we won was 93-13, and another was 108-8. Lest you think that we were uncaring and took advantage of lesser skilled teams in our league, we even beat the "B" team from Hamilton High School, the school that I would enter the next fall. Looking back, I don't know why they agreed to play us. For them, it was a lose-lose situation. If they beat us, they would have been seen as a group of upperclassmen who had beaten up on junior high boys. Or, if they lost to us, they would have been seen as losing to a group of young kids. The latter ended up being the case.

We were a scrappy group of players who didn't know the meaning of defeat...until we met a team that was equally talented. I remember going to the citywide junior high basketball tournament (for Black schools) in ninth grade, my final year at Corry. The team we met from Porter Junior High School had an identical 30-0 record in their division...both our teams were undefeated. Everyone knew it was going to be a tremendous contest.

The game was hard-fought and went down to the final buzzer. Playing center, I—along with our forwards—had the primary responsibility for guarding against layups and grabbing rebounds. You could feel the tension in the air when—with the score tied—an opposing player tipped in an offensive rebound just as the final seconds ticked off the clock. Our hearts sank like lead balloons as the referees' whistles signaled the end of the play. We were devastated. My teammates and I cried as our opponents jumped for joy, hoisting their first-place trophy. It seemed unfair; we had worked so hard and achieved so much. However, that night we had to settle for second place. For the first time in my life, I felt dejected and forlorn.

We were playing at our opponent's gym and had been harassed on our bus upon arrival. We had been threatened through the windows of the locker room at halftime when someone yelled, "You better not win this fucking game." We wondered about the integrity of the officials and the fairness of the final call. Had the time expired before their player tipped that final shot? We were undefeated. We had beaten teams by up to 100 points. How could the last game of the final year at our beloved junior high school be marred with a defeat?

Regardless of what he might have thought, Mr. Terrell took the high road, congratulated the coach of the opposing team, and told us to hold our heads high as we had nothing for which to be ashamed. Mr. Terrell wouldn't let us wallow in our sorrow. His demeanor made a profound impact on me. I learned a number of valuable lessons that night. I learned how to handle adversity and how to lose with humility. I learned that I wouldn't be successful in every endeavor in life. Equally important, I learned that failing at something doesn't make me a failure. I have always tried to give my best at whatever I do. Mr. Terrell taught me how to overcome obstacles on the basketball court and in life.

CHALLENGES AND OPPORTUNITIES

I had many challenges and opportunities during my junior high years. I had to navigate a new school, make new friends and deal with the uncertainties of adolescence, all while competing on the basketball team, studying, and making good grades.

During my final year at Corry, the head basketball coach at Central High School, an all-White, Memphis City School, visited my family. He wanted to recruit me to play for him. My parents expressed concern about the distance from our home across town to Central. The coach said that some of his older players who had their driver's licenses would transport me to and from school daily. Looking back, I believe my parents' reticence, and the reason they turned down the invitation, was not just the distance to Central High School. It was more about my personal safety and "fitting in," given the racial climate in Memphis and most U.S. Southern cities in the 1960s. This opportunity, however, would not have happened had it not been for Mr. Terrell's coaching and honing of my basketball skills.

Looking back, I realize that my invitation to attend Central High in 1967 came only ten years after President Dwight D. Eisenhower had sent federal troops to Little Rock, Arkansas, to ensure the safety of nine Black students who had enrolled at the all-White Central High School. The invitation for me to attend Central High in Memphis would not have happened had it not been for Mr. Terrell's coaching and the vision of the liberal White coach at Central High School. It also would not have happened without the tireless work of civil rights workers throughout the South. The similarities between the integration of Central High School in Little Rock and the invitation for me to play for, and integrate, the basketball team at Central High School in Memphis were not lost on me.

The skills I developed under Mr. Terrell's guidance prepared me to make the varsity basketball team at Hamilton High School as a sophomore. In fact, there were four players from my junior high team who made the varsity, all of us bypassing the junior varsity squad. The discipline, teamwork, and leadership skills I learned playing basketball for Mr. Terrell also prepared me to do well in high school, becoming a member of the *National Honor Society*, President of the Student Council, and President of my school's Hi-Y Club!

My family also turned down an invitation—for a variety of reasons—for me to attend a college preparatory school at the end of my ninth-grade year. Additionally, I felt the need to work over the summer to help support myself. In retrospect, I don't think my parents and I understood how much attending a college preparatory school could have helped to further prepare me academically for college. However, I have no regrets about the course my life took or the decisions my parents and I made.

Remembering Mr. Terrell

Mr. Terrell was more than a teacher and a coach; he was a role model. He ensured that players on his team behaved properly both on and off the court. We always knew he was keeping an eye on us in the hallways or in his P.E. classes. Looking back, Mr. Terrell's guidance mirrored that of my father. Mr. Terrell set the example. He was intelligent, physically fit, well-dressed, and a caring family man. I admired Mr. Terrell and wanted to be like him. I owe Mr. Terrell a tremendous debt and pray that I can pay it forward by being a good role model for my sons and young boys and men wherever I go.

I remember Mr. Terrell's 1965 *Ford Thunderbird* and its sequential turn signals! It was the coolest car, one that players rode in only once or twice. He took such good care of this car and did not use it to haul the team around as he did with his compact. Years later, in 2003, I added sequential turn signals to my 1997 *Ford Mustang Cobra*. Once again, I was emulating Mr. Terrell.

In 2003, upon receiving my Ph.D., I looked up Mr. Terrell's number in the phone book. To my surprise, his address and phone number were the same as when I was in junior high. Because it had been 37 years since I had seen or spoken with Mr. Terrell, when I called him, I said, "I don't know if you remember me. This is Willie Dean. I'm a former student and player on your basketball team at Corry Junior High School..." Before I could finish, Mr. Terrell said, "Of course, I remember you, Willie! You and your teammates were a special bunch!" After I told him about my life and my accomplishments since junior high, he said, "I always knew you would do well!" What affirmation; the man who had made such an impression on me was telling me that I had made an impression on him!

A few years later, in 2006, when I was living in Cleveland, Ohio, I got a call from Mr. Terrell. He asked me to speak at his retirement dinner, which was to be a few weeks later, in Memphis. I told him I was honored and looked forward to the occasion. My father, who lived in Memphis, and I went to the dinner together. This was fitting to have the two most influential men in my life in a room together. I saw former classmates and teammates who also benefited from Mr. Terrell's tutelage. That night, just as during my junior high days, Mr. Terrell was well-groomed, caring, and circumspect. Speaker-after-speaker related how Mr. Terrell had given support to students and athletes who were privileged to labor under his caring yet demanding guidance. One of the speakers with whom I talked that evening was Dr. Carol R. Johnson, Superintendent of Memphis City Schools, who unbeknownst to me would become my wife a dozen years later, in 2018. (More on this blessing in a later chapter.)

Mr. Terrell taught my teammates and me basketball skills like shooting, rebounding, dribbling, playing defense, and running a fast break. But the most important thing that he taught us was the esprit de corps that he demonstrated during team huddles before the start of every quarter of every game. This moment of solidarity, symbolic of the teamwork needed to achieve shared goals in life, made an indelible impression on me.

Mr. Terrell passed away in March 2008, when I was living in Mansfield, Texas. His wife phoned to tell me the somber news. She said that Mr. Terrell always held me in high regard and often praised my accomplishments. Mr. Terrell had retired as the Principal of Cummings Elementary School, and a year after his death, the street on which his school was located was renamed "Robert L. Terrell Boulevard." A fitting tribute to a remarkable man.

I didn't know in junior high—five decades ago—that Mr. Terrell's guidance on and off the basketball court would help shape and mold me to be the man that I am today. Mr. Terrell personified the values of caring, honesty, respect, and responsibility. I thank God for bringing caring and supportive adults like Mr. Terrell into my life!

Junior high, characterized by my success in academics and athletics, were pivotal years in my life.

THE TUMULTUOUS SIXTIES

"When the architects of our republic wrote the magnificent words of the Constitution and the Declaration of Independence, they were signing a promissory note to which every American was to fall heir.... It is obvious today that America has defaulted on this promissory note as far as people of color are concerned. Instead of honoring this sacred obligation, America has given the Negro people a bad check ... which has come back marked 'insufficient funds.'"
Rev. Dr. Martin Luther King, Jr. "I Have a Dream" Speech, August 1963

THE 1960S WERE VIOLENT, bloody years in our country's history. Much of the tumult was fueled by racism and hate, a legacy of slavery, our nation's original sin. Medgar Evers—an American civil rights activist in Mississippi, the state's field secretary for the *NAACP*, and a World War II veteran who served in the United States Army—was assassinated in the driveway outside his home in Jackson, Mississippi on June 12, 1963. While the murder occurred more than 200 miles from my Memphis home, the realities of racism and hate were brought into our living room daily via the nightly news on television. I didn't understand the significance of Evers' murder or the rash of other high-profile political and racial assassinations that were to follow.

A few months later, on November 22, 1963, I was in a seventh-grade classroom at Corry Junior High School in Memphis, Tennessee, when we got word that President John F. Kennedy had been assassinated in Dallas, Texas. Conspiracy theories abounded. Many people believed that President Kennedy's death was connected to disaffected Whites who didn't like his support of Blacks and the Civil Rights Movement. The hate and disdain for Black people during this ugly period in American history, relics of slavery and Jim Crow, became the forerunner of White supremacy and police brutality in later years. (It was reported that threats of violence against a sitting U.S. President increased dramatically after the election of Barak Obama, in 2008, the nation's first Black president. Making it politically or financially does not inoculate Blacks from the evils of racism, for White supremacy and hate affect the poor and powerless, and the prominent and powerful alike.)

On February 21, 1965, Malcolm Little—better known as Malcolm X, an African American Muslim minister and human rights activist who was a popular figure during the Civil Rights Movement—was assassinated in New York City. Best known for his time spent as a vocal spokesman for the Nation of Islam, Malcolm X espoused a philosophy of Black pride, Black nationalism, and Pan-Africanism. His often-radical rhetoric made many in our nation uncomfortable. He later traveled internationally and espoused a more inclusive Muslim religious doctrine that some thought alienated him from the Nation of Islam.

A few years later, on April 4, 1968, Dr. Martin Luther King, Jr., a Baptist preacher and civil rights leader, was assassinated on the balcony of the Loraine Motel near downtown Memphis, Tennessee. I was a junior at Hamilton High School in South Memphis when Dr. King was assassinated. Although later I saw National Guard troops riding around in their Jeeps with their weapons at the ready, I didn't process the gravity of the situation and the violence that was about to befall our city and our nation.

Before the decade of the sixties ended, U.S. Attorney General Robert F. Kennedy, a candidate for president and brother of the late President John F. Kennedy, was assassinated at a campaign rally in California on June 5, 1968. That year, one of the darkest in our nation's history, was also the year that a man walked on the moon. What an incredible juxtaposition of events.

Any one of these assassinations was horrendous; however, when taken together, it seemed like a coordinated attack on the civil rights of a people and invariably an attack on our democracy. While these traumas did not affect me directly, they began to make me aware of the racism in America that I would face for years to come. Many believed these leaders were murdered because of racial hatred promulgated by White supremacy and systemic racism, problems that continue to exist in our country to this day.

The attack on the U.S. Capitol on January 6, 2021, by thousands of Donald Trump loyalists, was reminiscent of the attacks on our democracy that occurred during the Civil Rights Movement of the 1960s. I watched in horror as the mostly White mob breached police lines and forcibly entered the capitol, broke in and desecrated the House chamber, and went about declaring they were going to assassinate members of Congress and "hang Mike Pence," the Vice President of the United States. I believe these actions were stoked by the "Big lie" that former-President Donald Trump had won the 2020 presidential election and that President-elect Joe Biden was not legitimately elected. The irony is that had this been a group of African American or Latino protesters, they would likely have been met with bullets, tear gas, and bloodshed, as has often been the case in our country. They would never have been presumed to be peaceful protestors and allowed to storm our capital and threaten our democracy.

While Barack Obama became our nation's first African American president in 2008 and was reelected in 2012, many have realized that we are not living in a post-racial America. If anything, some in the majority are now more uncomfortable with the "browning" of America and fear loss of power, jobs, status, and other changes that may occur when the majority becomes a minority in a few years. They see a world that is framed by "winners and losers," not one that allows everyone to thrive. If life is better for some, they fear that they must have lost. They prefer a world that continues to provide them preferential benefits versus a world where we share equally.

The 1960s were turbulent years in our nation's history. Many strides were made towards achieving civil rights for Blacks; however, it was at a tremendous cost. Our nation lost a number of leaders and ordinary people simply because of racial hatred. Millions of Blacks, and other people of color, have benefited from the sacrifices of thousands of freedom fighters, some of whom were White. I was able to achieve much in my lifetime and overcome many obstacles because I was able to stand on the shoulders of those who preceded me.

Trauma, Violence, and Bullying

"But I tell you, love your enemies and pray for those who persecute you, that you may be children of your Father in heaven. He causes his sun to rise on the evil and the good, and sends rain on the righteous and the unrighteous."
Matthew 5:44-45 (New International Version)

I EXPERIENCED A NUMBER of traumatic and violent events while growing up in Memphis and pursuing my career around the nation, ranging from an encounter with a deranged man on a neighborhood street, an assault by a school dropout, oppression by a sadistic high school basketball coach, and bullying by a *YMCA* board chair. It is difficult to forgive those who persecute us and to do as the Bible directs us to "turn the other cheek." (Matthew 5:39). I pray for strength to forgive those who have trespassed against me.

One day while walking home from junior high school, I encountered a crazed man who took a football from my friends and me. Holding an ax, the man demanded the football that I was holding. I gave him the ball without resistance and scurried home. I didn't report this incident to my parents, school officials, the police, or anyone.

On another occasion, when walking home from junior high with a group of my friends, we stopped at a neighborhood sundry, and just as I stepped off the sidewalk and onto the plaza in front of the store, a neighborhood thug known as "Firebug" accosted me. He stuck his left hand into my pocket, punched me in the mouth with his right fist drawing blood and demanded money. Afraid and tasting blood and salty sweat from my lip, I was in disbelief. I told him I didn't have any money to give him. Although I wanted to cry, I dared not, sensing that it would be a sign of weakness and would only embolden him further. Rather, I held my ground. Firebug scowled at me and removed his hand from my pocket. I hurriedly left the store, wondering why my "friends" had not come to my aid.

Once again, I learned that my size would not always be an advantage. I also learned that you can't always depend on others—even friends—to have the courage to stand up and do the right thing. I hurried home, alone. Firebug was a grown man and, as I learned later, a high school dropout who lived in a house that was on the route to my school. Out of fear, I subsequently walked blocks out of the way to avoid another confrontation. This assault made me fearful of walking home from school along the route that I normally took; however, it did not dampen my excitement about school and playing basketball.

One day, some weeks later, I saw Firebug in front of the sundry where he had assaulted me. There was no other way to get home but to pass this location. I didn't know what to expect. With fear and trepidation, I proceeded. As I approached him on the other side of the street, he nodded his head to me in a twisted display of respect. He never bothered me again after that horrific first encounter. "Did he respect the fact that I didn't cower to him?" "Did he want to lessen the chance that somehow, I might muster the courage to inform my parents or the police that he had assaulted me?" I believe this thug never bothered me again because, while I felt fearful, I mustered the courage to stand up to him. Had I caved in when he tried to rob me, he would have bullied me again and again. Nevertheless, this experience was traumatizing.

I never reported the assault by the ax-toting man or the mugging by Firebug to my parents, the police, or anyone else. Not reporting troubling incidents that happened to me became a habit of mine. I don't know if it was out of fear, immaturity, naiveté, shame, machismo, or something else. I see now, however, how vulnerable individuals—children, women, or anyone who is different—can be traumatized by bullies who they encounter and not know if, how, or when to seek help.

In retrospect, I should have told my parents, Coach Terrell, or another trusted adult about these traumatic events. These experiences, however, taught me how to deal with bullies, a skill I would use numerous times in my life, including with my high school basketball coach and a *YMCA* board chair. Standing up to bullies helped me to overcome unfair treatment from numerous individuals and go on to achieve success.

Senior High
Caring for Others,
Discovering Self

"And you shall love the Lord your God with all your heart, with all your soul, with all your mind, and with all your strength. This is the first commandment. And the second, like it, is this: "You shall love your neighbor as yourself." There is no other commandment greater than these." Matthew 12:30-31 (New King James Version)

My high school years were a period of growth and discovery, when I deepened my love of God, my involvement in my church and caring for others, and I continued my quest to discover who I was. I began to appreciate the needs of others and worked to advance social issues by advocating for fairness, raising funds for the less fortunate, and assisting a family facing catastrophic loss from a house fire. A part of discovering myself included playing on the varsity basketball team, membership in the *National Honor Society*, and serving as president of both the Student Council and the Hi-Y Club at my high school. I was also recognized as a "Teenager of the Week" by the *Memphis Press-Scimitar*, one of the city's two major daily newspapers at the time.

Social activism and concern for my fellow man became a hallmark of my existence. From a biblical context, I believe that I am my brother's keeper. I led a boycott at my junior high school lunchroom because of a mean lunch lady. The lady, who was the cafeteria manager, was rude and treated students with disrespect. Following the model of nonviolent protest that was a sign of the times, several classmates and I encouraged students to bring their lunches to school daily. I had witnessed nonviolent resistance—utilized by Mahatma

Gandhi in his campaign for Indian independence and later deployed by the Rev. Dr. Martin Luther King, Jr. in the Civil Rights Movement—almost daily on local and national television news. After a while, with declining lunch sales, the cafeteria manager relented and became more hospitable and welcoming to students.

My concern for social issues, and empathy for my neighbors, continued into high school, where I led a campaign to raise money for a family whose home had burned. My classmates and I raised more than $500 to help the family during their time of need. These experiences led to future fundraising success in my *YMCA* career, including raising more than $500,000 to help *YMCA*s that were devastated by the flooding of the Red River of the North in North Dakota in 1997 and raising more than $5 million to update facilities and build a new Y in the urban core of Omaha, Nebraska in 1994. I also organized a bike-a-thon that raised more than $50,000 to assist the Sioux *YMCA* in Dupree, North Dakota, the only Y specifically organized to serve Native Americans.

My faith was strong, and the friendships I developed with classmates and colleagues alike helped me overcome various challenges in my quest to serve others.

MAKING THE VARSITY

After settling into my classes at Hamilton High School, I soon looked for extracurricular activities. At the top of my list was to go out for the basketball team. I tried out and made the varsity squad, something that was unusual for a sophomore. With the skills I learned playing in my backyard and on my junior high team, I continued to grow as a basketball player. It was an honor to put on our team's uniform and to represent my school on the hardwood.

There was a certain amount of pride and notoriety that came with being a varsity athlete. Other students, especially girls, seemed to take notice of skilled players. Like in junior high, I continued to be an unselfish player, often passing the ball rather than taking shots myself. I lived on the backboards, daring anyone to attempt a layup or to get around me to try and get a rebound after I "boxed" them out underneath the hoop.

Game days were special. Our coach required that players wear a dress shirt and tie, signaling to the student body that there was a game that day. I waited with bated breath to participate in a brief mid-day pep rally in the gym to pump up our classmates and our teammates. When it was finally game time, we were almost euphoric. With adrenaline flowing and the anticipation of the challenge that lay ahead, we entered the locker room to put on our uniforms and white *Chuck Taylor All-Star* tennis shoes. We only got to wear these special shoes for games. For home games, we wore our white uniforms, signifying we were the home team. Our team definitely lifted the school spirit.

I enjoyed playing on the team during my sophomore and junior years. I eventually became a starter, and my leaping abilities continued to improve. At six-foot-one-inch tall, I was able to outjump a six-foot-six-inch senior on our team, who played back-up center to my position. Like LeBron James, I took pride in running down opponents on fast breaks and pinning their ball against the backboard before it made contact.

I was jubilant during the warm-up before one game when I tried and succeeded at dunking the ball. It was exhilarating to be able to do something that few people can do. After that first dunk, five or six of my teammates and I lined up and dunked in succession. Our fans were ecstatic with each thunderous dunk! This practice became a ritual that would pump us up and make our opponents think twice about the challenge that lay ahead.

The second fistfight of my life occurred during an intense basketball game during my junior year. Playing center, I was trying to dominate the backboard and rebound the ball; however, an opposing player who was guarding me kept holding me down by grabbing my trunks out of the sight of the referees. Although I was a mild-mannered and nonviolent person, I lost my cool when the player continued to taunt and impede me from rebounding. Finally, I turned and belted him. We tangled, and both got thrown out of the game. My coach scowled at me from the far end of the bench. He said that I was a better player than the opponent who had goaded me into a fight. He asked me, "How does your being on the bench help our team?" I learned a painful lesson. You can't help your team if you're not in the game. Violence is not the answer to conflicts.

Amid my excitement about playing basketball, I discovered that our coach was a bully who motivated players by intimidation. He was often brash and threatening. I didn't mind the physical challenges—running wind sprints and enduring long practices—but I took umbrage to his constant, verbal berating of players. He would also paddle our behinds when we missed free throws during practice. Cheerleaders told us that during games they could hear him at halftime paddling us from the locker room if we were trailing the opposing team. Coach even paddled players who had poor grades at report card time. Because I was an honor student, he would lament, "I never get to paddle that damn Dean!" Rather than celebrate my academic achievement, he attempted to belittle me.

Coach was a lanky man, about six-foot-five inches tall, with eyes that were almost always bloodshot. He would often scrimmage with our team and seemed to take pleasure in getting physical on the court and putting us down when he made a shot or out-rebounded us. He often got up into our faces when criticizing us for not hustling, missing shots, or playing poor defense. Years later, I realized that his style was more like Coach Bobby Knight of Indiana University, who threw tantrums and chairs, than Coach Bobby Terrell of Corry Junior High (my junior high coach), who gave praise and encouragement. I responded better to the latter.

While I wasn't a star player, I had solid skills that helped our team win. Just like in junior high, I was a superior rebounder and defender. I wasn't a high scorer, in large part because I was unselfish in sharing the ball with my teammates rather than shooting every open shot myself. I thought I had the potential to obtain an athletic scholarship upon graduation. In the fall of my senior year, all of that changed.

During the fall of 1968, an event happened that ended my basketball career. The football team was using the boys' locker room, so the boys' basketball team used the girls' locker room to change into our practice gear after all the girls had exited. The last girl using the locker room was supposed to canvas the area, ensure it was unoccupied, and give us the all-clear. On one occasion, the last girl missed someone who was still in the shower. When my teammates and I entered the locker room, the girl who had been overlooked screamed. We backed out of the locker room immediately. When Coach learned what had happened, he decided to punish us. It appeared he felt—even though we had done nothing wrong—he needed to make an example of us and exert his power. I never understood why.

Coach resorted to his sadistic tendencies, telling us we had to endure a paddling for our alleged misdeed. I explained that we had done nothing wrong; it was a misunderstanding, and it was unfair for us to suffer punishment for something we didn't do. Coach told me, "You can take the whipping or give me my shit (practice jersey, *Converse Chuck Taylor All-Star* tennis shoes, and jockstrap)!" It felt like the thug, Firebug, had his hand in my pocket and was attempting to mug me again. After thinking about it, and as painful as leaving the team was, I decided to give him his shit.

This was one of the most difficult and consequential decisions of my young life. My burning desire to play basketball, an idea that was kindled in elementary school, was now fizzling before my eyes. I was giving up my prestigious position as a varsity basketball player and likely a chance for an athletic scholarship to a college or university upon graduation. Subconsciously, I knew I was standing up to a bully—just as I had to the neighborhood thug when I was in junior high. Upon reflection years later, I realized that had I allowed my coach to bully me, I likely would compromise my principles for the rest of my life.

Somehow, I thought that my teammates would join me in my protest of Coach's sadistic, unfair behavior. But just like outside that sundry when the would-be robber, Firebug, stuck his hand into my pocket and assaulted me, I found myself standing alone. My teammates—just like my "friends" in junior high—didn't come to my aid. To add insult to injury, an assistant coach implored me to take the whipping so I could return to the team. Coach told my teammates that my girlfriend had my "nose wide open," and that was the reason I didn't come back to the team. Naively I thought that he might reconsider and ask me to come back because of my athletic prowess and value to the team; however, he didn't. He never talked to me again. Instead, he scowled at me every time I encountered him in the hallway when passing classes. He always had to be the alpha male, even if it was to the detriment of the team and to his young players. For him, it was about power.

Although I had lettered on the varsity basketball and track teams since my sophomore year, my basketball career at Hamilton High School was over. Strangely, my parents never asked, nor did I tell them, why I left the team. And, I never appealed to the principal about what had happened. Nor did I think to call Coach Terrell at my former junior high to ask his counsel and advice. I continued the habit of keeping my hurts to myself. My decision likely cost me athletic scholarships upon graduation. I also lost the opportunity to play basketball, the sport I had loved since elementary; however, I don't regret having stood up for my principles. Leaving the team was painful; however, the experience prepared me to overcome future challenges involving bullies in my life.

LIFE AFTER BASKETBALL

After leaving the team, I sought afterschool employment to help pay some of my expenses. I worked one day in the stockroom at *Kent Dollar Store*, in the Lamar-Airways Shopping Center near my home, before being hired as a salesman at *Shainberg's*, a local department store owned by the same parent company in the same shopping center. The dollar store manager was irate that

Willie Dean

I left after such a short tenure; however, I did what I thought was best for me. I preferred talking with customers and selling clothing at the department store over marking merchandise and taking out the trash at the dollar store.

At *Shainberg's*, I had a more professional position where I learned how to wait on customers, sell goods, and ring up sales on the cash register. A classmate and friend, William Henry Tate, Jr., and I worked in the Men's Department. Our department manager, a White woman named Mrs. Hodge, taught us the ropes. She was a whiz with waiting on customers and ringing up sales. She taught us how to visually size up customers to estimate what size pants or suits they needed and how to match shirts and ties for dress ensembles. She also taught us how to recognize shoplifters and to always watch suspicious individuals' eyes because their hands were too fast to observe when they were slipping something under a shirt or blouse.

William and I often worked together on nights and on weekends. One day we witnessed a shoplifting suspect being chased through our store by a retired police officer who served as the security guard for the shopping center. The guard yelled at us to stop the female suspect as she began removing stolen merchandise from beneath her garments and waving her hand as if she had a knife or razor. As the guard yelled to us that the woman didn't have a knife, he collapsed and died on the floor in our department. It was later determined that he had suffered a massive heart attack. This was the first time I witnessed someone dying. It was a sad and somber experience. I don't remember what happened to the suspected shoplifter, as the loss of stolen merchandise paled in comparison to the loss of human life.

One night William and I—dressed alike in pink shirts, pink and gray striped neckties, and gray sharkskin suits—followed a shoplifting suspect out of our store toward the *Katz* drugstore next door. William followed the suspect out the back door, and I went out the front. We accosted the thief in the breezeway between the two stores and recovered the merchandise. All we got from the store manager was a thank you. We had a clear sense of right and wrong. Looking back, it was foolish and dangerous for us to have risked our safety and our lives to recover the stolen items. But we were young, and we felt invincible.

I continued to work at *Shainberg's* for the balance of my senior year and into my freshman year at Memphis State University. The job provided a modicum of income and a 10 percent discount on clothing for my family and myself.

Although I was no longer practicing or playing basketball for two hours daily, I continued to eat a high-calorie diet. I went from my playing weight of 190 pounds to 225 pounds in less than one year. This unhealthy trend continued throughout most of my life. At my heaviest weight, I tipped the scale at 297 pounds in 1981. I was age 30. It was not until I started working for the Y in St. Louis that same year that I began a healthier lifestyle. Through a combination of diet and exercise, I lost 80 pounds and got down to 217 pounds in the course of about one year. I owe much of my weight loss success to Carla Giles, physical director at the Monsanto *YMCA*, who encouraged me to eat a healthy diet and exercise regularly. At my best, I was eating a maximum of 2,000 calories per day and jogging up to a mile at a time, lifting weights, and participating in aerobic exercise classes almost daily.

Obesity, high cholesterol, hypertension, and other maladies have troubled me most of my life. While some of my health issues may be hereditary, others are likely the result of the poor lifestyle choices that I made. While I didn't smoke or drink, I loved to eat—sometimes to excess. Many African Americans may be predisposed to some ailments because of heredity; however, life choices and life circumstances (poverty, lack of access to healthcare and nutritious food, etc.) have a tremendous impact on individual and community health. If I had my life to live over again, I would make healthier choices about diet, exercise, medical and dental care, and stress management.

With the extra time I had after leaving the basketball team, I learned how to make plaster of paris plaques from my high school art teacher. I have always been industrious, and I enjoyed the creativity and the extra income I made from selling my creations to family, friends, and other customers. After more than five decades, some of my work still hangs in my family members' homes.

I took typing and was one of only a few boys in my high school to do so. This was one of the most consequential classes I took, for it gave me keyboarding skills that would prove invaluable later in my life.

I was shy and introverted in high school, yet I managed to excel. It was only due to the assertiveness of my girlfriend, who served as my campaign manager, that I was elected President of the Student Council. We plastered our school with handbills and posters and raised my profile with our classmates, winning me the office. I knew little about parliamentary procedures and learned as I went along. This was one of my early leadership development experiences. Later, I served as captain of the Hi-Y team of the Glenview Branch *YMCA*. (I would later be hired as program director for this Y before graduating college.) I was a member of the *National Honor Society* and was listed among the 25 top students in our graduating class of more than 500. I was named "Teenager of the Week" by the Memphis Press-Scimitar, in recognition of my outstanding character, leadership, and scholarship, during the 1968-69 school year. I regret that I didn't attend my senior prom; I was still skittish about asking a girl to dance. I graduated in May 1969, becoming the second in my family to earn a high school diploma and beating the odds against Black students of my generation.

I received a $200 scholarship from the James R. Hoffa Scholarship Fund from my father's pension fund that helped with my college expenses, yet it wasn't enough. Dad was a teamster whose truck driver salary allowed us to live a modest middle-class lifestyle; however, money was tight, and I don't know how Dad and Mom managed tuition and other expenses in order to have three children in college over a 12-year span. That's one reason I worked full-time during my undergraduate days at Memphis State University (MSU). Had I played basketball my senior year in high school, I probably would have gotten a full-ride scholarship to play basketball at a small college or university.

My nose was broken while playing basketball during the summer after high school when an older player elbowed me in the face. I was playing in a pickup game in Lincoln Park near my home when the player carelessly flung his elbow and flattened my nose, causing blood to gush from my nostrils. The park director took my brother, Bug, home to tell our mother. She called my father's job to let him know what had happened. The dispatcher radioed my father, who was making deliveries in the city, and told him he needed to phone home. An ambulance took me to the emergency room at *John Gaston Hospital*, the public hospital near downtown Memphis. I don't remember how my mother got there; I suspect she took a taxi, as she never learned to drive, and we knew few neighbors with cars who would have been home during the day.

While Mom and I were waiting to be seen, we saw many poor Black people come through the ER, including a boy who had a dog bite on his hip and a man who had a wound on his foot that had become infected. When the healthcare workers removed the bandage covering the man's wound, maggots fell to the floor. My mother was sickened when she saw what had happened. Oddly enough, this site didn't bother me. Looking back, it was disheartening to see so many indigent Black people who were suffering from both their maladies and the indignities of poverty.

We finally got to see the emergency room doctor. He examined me, determined my nose was fractured and straightened it with a screwdriver-like device. I remember the fear I felt as he stuck a needle up my nostrils to numb my nose. He then inserted the instrument into my nasal passage. Although he had administered a local anesthetic, I still felt pain as he moved my nose back into place. I heard the grizzle in my nose move as he finished the procedure and packed my nostrils with cotton to prevent them from collapsing during the healing process. I had to breathe through my mouth for weeks until the cotton was removed. This was the first of two times that I broke my nose while playing basketball. I also would break a bone in my hand while playing basketball as an adult. So much for basketball being a non-contact sport!

The sport of basketball had been good to me since I was an adolescent, playing on the makeshift court in my backyard, playing on our elite junior high squad, and as a varsity player in high school. I had learned the fundamentals of dribbling, shooting, rebounding, and playing defense. More importantly, I learned about teamwork, camaraderie, and esprit de corp., values that would help me overcome bullies and tragedies throughout my life.

YOUNG, GIFTED, AND BLACK

Many of the lessons I learned in school and from church were reinforced by my parents and other family members with whom I came in contact. I was fortunate to be told that "I am somebody." I understood that "Black is beautiful" and that we are all God's children. By virtue of these teachings and the love and grace of our Savior, I learned to cope with adversities and learned how to overcome many challenges, even though the odds were against me.

My education and church involvement during the 1960s caused me to realize that I am endowed with certain gifts from God. I was blessed to have been placed in advanced classes in school and was able to achieve much as a student and as an athlete. Along with my public education, I was blessed to have the opportunity to learn more about my faith through my church and Sunday School. I also was blessed to graduate from high school because data from the 1970 U.S. census show that nearly one out of three (29.4 percent) Black male students dropped out of high school the year after I obtained my diploma.

I felt that I was "blessed." I also felt valued and perceived myself in a positive vein, like the lyrics to soul singer Nina Simone's iconic 1970 song, *To Be Young, Gifted and Black*, I knew I was gifted.

Looking back, I realize that—as a Black male of my generation—I had only a 70 percent chance of receiving a high school diploma. But, by the grace of God, I not only graduated from high school, but I also earned bachelor's, master's, and doctoral degrees. Thanks to my faith, my family, and my friends, I was able to overcome significant challenges that could have easily derailed my education and my future.

St. Peter's AME Church in Minneapolis, Minnesota, was my place of worship for two stints when I lived in the Twin Cities.

Members of the St. Peter's AME Church ministerial team, Rev. Gerald Garth, Pastor Carla Mitchell, and Rev. William Jackson, ministered to our spiritual needs.

I served as Steward Pro Tem for the Steward Board of St. Peter's after I returned to the Twin Cities for a second time.

My maternal grandmother, Mama Rea, became a storekeeper later in her life.

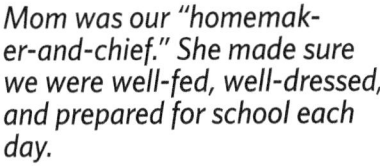

Dad was a positive role model and my hero.

Mom was our "homemaker-and-chief." She made sure we were well-fed, well-dressed, and prepared for school each day.

Willie Dean

Joe earned a bachelor's degree from the University of Tennessee in Knoxville and master's and doctoral degrees from Princeton University. He worked professionally as an architect.

Chris earned a bachelor's degree from Boston College and a master's degree from American University. She has spent many years in law enforcement and probation with the state of Maryland and the federal government.

Bug volunteers with the security team at his church and is active with his Masonic Lodge.

Overcoming

I admire strong Black men like Dr. Harold Massey, with whom I became friends through church.

Family friends, Dr. Karen and Bill Wells supported us after the death of Pam, my broken ankle, and other challenges.

Regenia Anglin served on the Steward Board with me and has been a dear friend of our family.

PART TWO:

YOUNG ADULTHOOD MAKING MY WAY IN THE WORLD

Boy to Man – My Transition to Manhood

"When I was a child, I spake as a child, I understood as a child, I thought as a child: but when I became a man, I put away childish things." 1 Corinthians 13:11 (King James Version)

Graduation from high school and enrollment in college signaled my transition to manhood. Although there was not a formal rite of passage, I knew I had to grow up fast. Looking back, I realize that I was being pushed from the safety and security of the "nest"—the watchful eye of my parents and my high school teachers—and had to "learn to fly on my own." When I became a man, I had to put away childish things. I had to learn painful lessons about using credit cards wisely, not selecting ping pong over Spanish class, choosing friends with similar values, and communicating my feelings clearly to love ones, friends, employers, and employees. While I never smoked, drank alcohol, or used illicit drugs, the temptation was always there from peers who sometimes pressured me, put me down, and called me a prude.

Campus Life? – An Oxymoron

I matriculated at Memphis State University (MSU) in the fall of 1969. Immediately, I went from being a well-known honor student and varsity athlete at the all-Black Hamilton High School, with a senior class enrollment of 500 students, to just one of 1,500 Black students in a student body of 15,000 that was 90 percent White at MSU. In the three months following my graduation from high school, I went from being a "big fish in a little pond" to being "a little fish in a very big pond." I felt anonymous and alone, isolated, and an introvert. I didn't realize how my life was changing. I had to "put away childish things" and act like an adult. I got married, had a child, and started working full-time before graduating from college. I had to become an adult at an early age, even before I fully knew or understood myself.

College seemed like an extension of high school because I lived at home and worked after my daily classes. Initially, I didn't participate in on-campus activities. Later, I took part in a judo club and an outdoor recreation club. I didn't get involved in the Panhellenic Council or the Black Student Association. Years later, when I attended my wife Carol's 50th-anniversary class reunion at Fisk University, I saw the friendships and bonds she had formed during her undergraduate days at Fisk on full display five decades later. I felt I had missed forming similar relationships by not living on campus. I also saw how attending an HBCU (Historically Black Colleges and Universities), as she had, helped to forge lifetime friendships with other Black students with similar values.

I registered for the draft with the Selective Service System as required by law. I declared myself a conscientious objector as I objected to killing on the grounds of my religion. When I registered at MSU and indicated my desire not to participate in Reserve Officer Training Corp. (R.O.T.C.) classes, I had to meet with the campus commandant to explain my request. When the commandant learned my denomination, he said, "Hell, I'm Baptist!" I told him I objected to killing and that if drafted, I would be willing to serve as a medic, but I would not carry a weapon. I eventually was exempted from R.O.T.C. At the time, America was involved in the Vietnam War. Many felt the war was unjust, and student protests of the war abounded on many college campuses nationwide. Perhaps because I was a conscientious objector and in college earning acceptable grades, my draft number was never called, and I didn't serve in the military. Looking back, I regret that I did not serve my country as a member of the military, even if as a medic, because I felt it was my duty to contribute to our nation's safety and security.

Being an introvert, it was not easy for me to make friends in college. I went from class to class in relative obscurity. My favorite period of the day was the lunch hour when I went to the University Center and played ping pong. I had learned to play the game as a youth in my family's garage, on a makeshift table that my father made from two sawhorses and a sheet of plywood. (My father had a penchant for making items for us at home: basketball hoop, ankle weights with BBs, and the makeshift ping pong table.) At MSU, I learned from the best players on campus and soon ordered a sponge-centered paddle to improve my ability to put English on the ball.

I got to be an excellent ping pong player and could compete with the best players. On Friday nights, I went to community centers in the city, seeking out and beating their best players. However, my penchant for ping pong became an obsession. On several occasions, I played ping pong in the University Center until 1:00 p.m., the start time for my afternoon classes. I would continue playing until 1:10 p.m., the grace period allowed for a timely arrival in class.

After missing the grace period on several occasions and not going to class, I got behind in my Spanish class and ended up receiving a failing grade. I learned a tough lesson about setting priorities and taking responsibility for my own actions. I felt bad and ashamed of my predicament. I didn't feel like I wanted to end my life...but I failed myself and wished I had never existed. Looking back, I realize how devastating failure can be to some individuals. (I would have the same feelings years later when I got a "C" in an economics course while working on my Executive MBA. More on that later.) I also did poorly in my freshman English class and had to take it over. This was the best thing for me, as I learned to be a better writer after suffering this setback. My second English professor was skilled and caring, and I learned a lot from her.

I had been a good student during the first 12 years of my education, yet I found myself being challenged in college. In retrospect, some of my challenges were my lack of discipline. I didn't have a classroom or homeroom teacher encouraging me to work hard. I didn't have the watchful eye of a school secretary or coach to keep me on the straight and narrow. My parents didn't give me rewards for every "A" I brought home at the end of semesters. And I didn't have time to adequately devote to my studies as I took a full-time, 15-hour class load and worked a 40-hour workweek on my job at a local community center.

After I got married and became a father, I had to work eight hours on Saturdays and eight hours on Sundays, in addition to my full-time—40-hours-per-week—job to make ends meet. My father helped me get hired to work on weekends at *ETWNC (East Texas West North Carolina) Trucking Co.*, the company where he worked at the time. I was pressed for funds, raising a young family and attending classes full time, and this extra income was critical to my family. My father, however, worried that I would become enamored with the $6.50 hourly wage and I would not want to finish college. However, I was determined to complete my degree. The addition of this part-time job meant that I was working seven days a week—for a total of 56 hours per week—while also taking a full class load in college. I had to do what I had to do. Lessons learned from Mr. Terrell helped me to be resilient and to overcome the fatigue that I experienced.

I majored in biology and thought I wanted to become a teacher. Unfortunately, my undergraduate days occurred during a period of unrest on many American university campuses. Several students were killed by police at Kent State University in Ohio, students at the University of California Berkeley protested the university's restriction on students' free speech, and there was unrest on many other campuses. The violence and unrest, in part, caused me to rethink becoming a teacher.

The Great Outdoors – Discovering Nature and Myself

One day I saw a flier on a university bulletin board advertising the formation of an outdoor recreation club on our campus. I was intrigued by the opportunity to enjoy the outdoors with like-minded students. I attended the meeting and became a charter member, and the only Black member, of the club. We learned outdoor skills—from our advisors and those among us who had camping experience—such as how to dig a latrine, start a campfire, use a compass, and read a map.

My positive experience in the Outdoor Recreation Club caused me to change my major to recreation, which was found in the Department of Health, Physical Education and Recreation. One of my professors, Dr. Mel Humphreys, was a rotund, affable man who loved to dance. It was in his survey dance class that I learned how to waltz, clog, and square dance. I also was enthralled by his love of the out-of-doors and his unambiguous acceptance of me without regard to my race or ethnicity. I always felt welcomed in club activities. Everyone was genuine and accepted me, the only Black student in the club. This was true as we traveled locally and when we drove across the country on camping trips to the Ozark Mountains in Arkansas, the Great Smokey Mountains in Tennessee, and the Snowmass Wilderness in the Rocky Mountains of Colorado.

Once, while on a backpacking trip to the Ozark Mountains, I had a flat tire on the Interstate at 75 m.p.h. I was driving my father's 1968 *Buick Electra 225*, known in the vernacular as a "Deuce and a Quarter" (the second prized Buick that my dad owned), the lead car in a three-car caravan. Those riding in the middle car said they saw what looked like a cloud of black smoke billow from my right rear tire. My signal light came on, and I got off onto the shoulder of the highway. I don't know how I controlled the vehicle at that speed. I believe it was God protecting me, just as He has done on multiple occasions in my life.

Learning to orienteer—using only a map and a compass—finding shelter, starting a fire, cooking meals, working as a team, and exploring the out-of-doors were new skills that aided me in my maturation. Camping also taught me a lot about life and myself. I learned to be resilient and to appreciate nature. My views on conservation were solidified as I learned how to pack light, reduce waste, and leave the environment as good or better than I found it, which included digging latrines for our toilet needs and burning leftover paper wrappers.

Initially, we took short trips to local and state parks. I remember one of our first overnight camping trips to Chewalla Lake Recreation Area in Mississippi. We arrived after dark, pitched our tents, cooked dinner, and retired to our sleeping bags. The next morning, with the benefit of daylight, we realized—much to our chagrin—that we had camped in a cemetery. Not to be outdone, we quietly and respectfully packed up our campsite and continued our camping trip.

On a subsequent trip, we went to the Ozark Mountains in Arkansas. As it happened, all of the men in our club, save me, were unable to go on this trip. So, I, the lone man, was accompanied by 10 White women. I felt the stares of Whites as we drove across the state of Arkansas, stopping in small towns for gas and supplies. Looking back, this was a potentially dangerous trip for a Black man in the South in the early 1970s. The movie *Deliverance*, starring Burt Reynolds and Ned Beatty, which had been released in 1972, portrays the stereotypical antipathy between city and country residents, which should have given me pause about camping in the remote Ozark mountains.

The next year we took a trip to East Tennessee to hike the 70 miles of the Appalachian Trail (AT) within the Great Smoky Mountains National Park. I remember being in awe of the blue haze that hung over the mountains as we approached Gatlinburg, Tennessee. We met two local university students with whom we had pre-arranged to take our cars and supplies and leave them at a designated halfway point.

The experience of hiking up the mountain and the view from the trail was breathtaking. We had been warned to avoid encounters with bears, and other wild animals, by hanging our food in trees at night; it was imperative that we kept no food in our sleeping bags or tents. We were also advised to stay overnight in log cabin shelters along the trail that had a chain-link fence front wall and latching gate to protect us from wild animals. I remember hiking up what seemed like an unending section of trail, all the while expecting to come upon a bear around the next bend. I was amazed upon stepping into a fog bank, which actually were clouds. We heard the sound of what we surmised were hooves pounding against the earth and later saw tracks of what we believed were wild boars.

As neat as the AT was, it paled in comparison to our trip the next year to the Snowmass Wilderness in Colorado. Our club traveled by car from Memphis, Tennessee, to Aspen, Colorado. We stopped for the night at a state park in Kansas. The wind blew fiercely across the plains, which had only a few trees or changes in elevation to provide relief. Although we saw signs that said, "No Overnight Camping," we unrolled our sleeping bags in the men's and women's restrooms to provide protection from the biting wind. Shortly after we retired, we were awakened by the yell of an angry park ranger who exclaimed, "What the hell is going on here?" I thought we were going to jail, or at the least, we would all be ticketed.

Our advisors scrambled to explain we were college students and faculty advisors from Memphis State University. They went on to plead our case by saying we were en route to Colorado for a two-week camping trip and had sought relief from the wind. Fortunately, the ranger was sympathetic. He bent the rules and allowed us to camp outside the restrooms until daylight.

We arrived in Colorado and could not resist getting out of our vehicles to see the Continental Divide, the area where the U.S. terrain and drainage slope east toward the Atlantic Ocean and west toward the Pacific Ocean. We had been cautioned not to run as our lungs were not used to operating in the rarefied air at the 14,278-foot elevation. The elevation even affected our vehicles. Locals told us they could tell we were "flatlanders" as our cars, which weren't tuned for high-altitude driving, drove slowly up the mountain. Although my brand new 1972 *Dodge Demon* had a 340-cubic-inch, high-performance engine, it too started sputtering while we were going up the mountain.

We reached our drop-off point in the Snowmass Wilderness near Aspen and hiked the final distance to a U.S. Park Service ranger station. (Some 30 years later, while attending a conference in Aspen, I drove past this same ranger station, complete with paved streets and cement sidewalks that I had to hike to in the 1970s. That's progress…I think!) When we made it to the wilderness, we saw small animals, including beaver and birds, and open areas with fields of wildflowers. The sights, sounds, and sensations of the city were left far behind. No billboards, honking car horns, or even aircraft were present. The sun at high elevation was especially intense; I learned a painful lesson that Black people could indeed get sunburned.

I remember hiking above the tree line, stepping onto a carpet of snow, and trekking through the snow so deep that it was hard to move. Once I fell into a deep snowbank; I was covered up to my armpits and unable to move. I was humbled when the "women" in our group helped me—a big burly man—get out of my predicament. Heretofore, I had been chivalrous, extending my hand to help the women cross streams and other difficult situations, not realizing that my actions might have been viewed as patronizing. I had an epiphany.

Helpless and requiring assistance, I realized that women are capable of doing anything that men can do. This lesson informed my thinking and was the beginning of my growing acceptance of women as equals. This experience helped mold me to be a better husband, colleague, employee, and supervisor. It made me a better man, one who appreciates and values the contributions of women in our society.

I didn't see another Black person for two weeks. In fact, the first Black I saw was "myself" in a mirror when we checked into a hotel in Aspen. Throughout my camping experience, I was treated equally and with dignity and respect. This was not to deny my race; rather, it was a recognition that we are all the same on the inside and that we have more things in common than we have differences. My camping friends and I shared similar values, aspirations, a love of nature, and the need for acceptance.

Laughter and storytelling around the campfire were just two of the camping experiences that I grew to love. I also treasured singing along the trail when the going got tough. Traveling up a steep incline was difficult but worth the reward of seeing the vista at the crest of the trail. We enjoyed coasting as we descended into the next valley, crossing cold mountain streams with algae-covered rocks and duckweed, often peppered with beaver dams that rivaled those of the best human engineers. Even collecting branches for kindling to start a campfire, digging a hole and lining it with rocks and twigs to make a latrine, and washing dishes after meals were enjoyable tasks that we ticked off the group caper chart daily.

My camping experiences taught me a lot about nature and myself. I learned to appreciate all that God has created and given man dominion over, and I came to understand my responsibility to be my brother's (and sister's) keeper. I know now that the out-of-doors is a microcosm of man's experience on earth and that we have a responsibility to care for the environment. Our blatant disregard for climate change is heartbreaking for anyone who loves the out-of-doors, but it should be a wake-up call for everyone.

On the way home from Colorado, the clutch in my car failed, and I nearly drove off the side of a mountain trying to maintain control. For the remainder of the trip home, I shifted without a clutch, remembering a lesson from my truck-driver father that you can accelerate to about 2,500 RPM and shift without a clutch. Once I got to fourth gear, I wasn't downshifting for anything but a stoplight! This was one of many lessons that I learned from my father that got me out of numerous predicaments.

The Outdoor Recreation Club was a wonderful experience for me during my undergraduate years at MSU. It provided me with wholesome relationships and taught me about the joys and beauty that can be found in nature. My camping experience helped me overcome my patronizing view of women and further helped me understand that not all Whites are racists. I wouldn't have traded the experience for anything. It also led me to my future career as a *YMCA* executive.

BACHELOR'S DEGREE – A SOURCE OF FAMILY PRIDE

I earned my Bachelor of Science degree in Education, with a major in Recreation, from Memphis State University, in December 1974. Becoming only the second person in my family to complete a college degree was a proud moment for my parents and me. This was especially poignant as my parents had limited education themselves and sacrificed much so that my siblings and I could get good educations.

With a college degree in hand, I was ready to conquer the world. But this was just the beginning of numerous formal and informal learning experiences that would help me overcome personal and professional challenges for the rest of my life. Finally, I felt like I had become a man.

Grad School – Age of Enlightenment

"And be not conformed to this world: but be ye transformed by the renewing of your mind, that ye may prove what is that good, and acceptable, and perfect, will of God." Romans 12:2 (King James Version)

MY GRADUATE EDUCATION WAS a period of enlightenment. I sought to not be conformed to my life circumstance—coming from an inner-city neighborhood with less than adequate resources for housing, education, and healthcare—and worked to renew my mind through Bible study and graduate education at several major universities. I learned about new subjects and new situations that would prove instrumental to my continued growth and development as an academic, employee, supervisor, father, son, and faith leader. I had one epiphany after another that served to strengthen my appreciation for my faith, my family, and my friends.

I attended the University of Texas at Arlington (UTA) when I lived in Texas in the 1970s. There I earned 12 credit hours towards a master's degree in Urban Affairs. I accepted a Y job in St. Louis and relocated to Missouri before completing my degree. The courses I took while at UTA helped to inform my understanding of urban issues in cities where I later worked. I learned how the urban core of many American cities deteriorated following the development of the interstate highway system, which facilitated family movement to newly created housing developments in the suburbs. I also learned that interstate highways decimated many thriving inner-city neighborhoods as they winded their way through cities to deliver suburbanites to their downtown jobs, with little regard for the poor, powerless, and often minority residents who lived there.

In some cities, interstate highways—like I-35W in Minneapolis, Minnesota—severed thriving, often poor, working-class, and minority neighborhoods when they were built. A similar battle is brewing in Houston, Texas, where the state and federal governments are seeking to expand I-45 to accommodate the burgeoning growth of urban dwellers and suburban commuters. According to a December 7, 2021, Google article:

> *Critics argue the expansion of I-45 will negatively impact local air quality and displace communities in the surrounding neighborhoods, many of which are historically Black. Community advocates say the project would displace more than 1,000 homes and more than 300 businesses as well as schools and places of worship.*

The experience of building I-35W in cities like Minneapolis is contrasted with the fight mounted by a group of activists and environmentalists that prevented the construction of I-40 through Overton Park—a 342-acre wooded refuge with mature oak trees, a zoo, a nine-hole golf course, and other assets—in Memphis, Tennessee in the 1960s and 1970s. This group saved the surrounding urban neighborhoods as well as the park.

History shows us that many urban landowners, who were mostly White, left inner cities, leaving behind less affluent, often minority residents who rented properties from Whites who still owned them. As history reflects, some of the movement from the inner city to the suburbs was fueled by "White flight," a desire by White residents to distance themselves from Blacks and other people of color, school integration, and poverty.

Today many inner-city communities are being revitalized, which tends to displace the people who live there. You see, higher-income homeowners, wealthy investors, and developers are moving back to inner-city neighborhoods. This trend is gentrifying urban communities, driving up costs, and displacing poor and minority landowners who cannot afford elevated property taxes, rents, and mortgages brought on by newly remodeled homes and, in some cases, totally redeveloped urban neighborhoods. I have witnessed gentrification in numerous cities where I have lived. The irony is that many of these neighborhoods just a few decades ago were blighted, and no one lived there except the poor, the disenfranchised, and a few Whites who chose to remain or couldn't afford to leave. Now, many Whites, and other higher-income individuals who are seeking to live closer to their work, the arts, and cultural attractions, are desiring to live in the urban core.

My understanding of urban affairs helped to inform my work through the *YMCA* and other nonprofits. I was able to develop policies and programs and raise millions of dollars to better serve youth and families. Through my efforts, we were able to overcome many of the challenges facing urban communities and give young people opportunities that would not have been available to them.

University of Nebraska at Omaha – Executive MBA

I moved to Omaha, Nebraska, in 1989, and as fate would have it, the Board Chair of the Omaha-Council Bluffs Metropolitan *YMCA*, Dr. Larry Trussell, was Dean of the Business School at the University of Nebraska at Omaha. Dr. Trussell approved my enrollment in the Executive MBA program at the university. The *YMCA* paid my tuition as part of my training and development, a blessing that ensured my continuing education.

My Executive MBA cohort met for two years on Tuesdays and Thursdays from 6-9:00 p.m., except for Thanksgiving and Christmas. The program included business coursework, books, snacks, and a two-week overseas practicum.

My background in education and recreation included no formal business classes. The Executive MBA curriculum helped to broaden my business skills with courses that included: accounting, business management, strategic planning, economics, human resource management, business law, strategic marketing, and continuous process improvement.

The Executive MBA curriculum was demanding. Students were required to earn no less than a "B" in all classes. Much to my dismay, I struggled with an economics course from which I received a "C." I was distressed, feeling I had embarrassed my family and myself, as I would have to withdraw from the program. How would I explain to the Y board, the staff, and others that I was no longer in the program? I felt forlorn and alone. I didn't know what I was going to do. I thought there was no way out of my predicament. Again, my faith was strong, and I prayed that God would make a way.

I met with the Executive MBA Program Director to see if there was a way for me to remain in the program. He recommended I meet with my economics professor. I met with my professor, who was sympathetic but said the only way for me to remain in the program was to enroll in two regular graduate economics courses (microeconomics and macroeconomics) and earn a grade of "B" or better in both. This meant I would have to attend two regular graduate classes during the day and continue my Executive MBA coursework at night. In addition, I continued my leadership of a major *YMCA* and performed the duties of husband and father to my family. Although this was a daunting undertaking, I had no choice but to attempt this arduous schedule.

With hard work and by the grace of God, I earned "A's" in both economics classes. When I met with my economics professor and shared my results, he said my first economics grade must have been a "mistake," as a lighthearted way to congratulate me. This experience taught me that when life circumstances seem impossible, lean on the everlasting hand of God. Reliance on God's grace would become a mainstay for me for the rest of my life.

My study team, which included three other male students and me, decided to research a robotics prototype from a Nebraska company as the focus of our overseas practicum. We planned to travel to Sweden, The Netherlands, and Germany to assess the robot's potential for introduction into the European market.

Our eight-hour trans-Atlantic flight landed after midnight in Stockholm, Sweden, the "Land of the Midnight Sun." Since it was June, it was still daylight when we arrived at our hotel. We were advised to draw the heavy drapes to our room in order to get to sleep as our biological clocks were off, and we would likely experience jet lag.

The next day we went sightseeing, and I observed the narrow cobblestone streets and many ornate buildings that had been around for centuries. We took an excursion on a harbor tour near the hall where Nobel Prizes are awarded. I was impressed and humbled that many Europeans were multilingual and spoke three, four, or more languages. I thought how arrogant many Americans must have seemed, being monolingual and expecting the rest of the world to speak English. As we now live in a multicultural, global economy, the least we can do is strive to appreciate other cultures through language, the arts, etc.

We met with local business executives in Sweden, The Netherlands, and Germany to assess the potential use of the robotics technology that we were researching in their manufacturing processes.

Late one night, while touring Amsterdam, we got lost trying to find our way back to the *Hilton Hotel* where we were staying. Not wanting to look like tourists and draw attention to ourselves, we asked a little old lady (who looked to be in her 80s) for directions. To our surprise, she said, "You young men shouldn't be out here this late!" She then directed us to our hotel, which was just a stone's throw away. I realized that I had made assumptions about this elderly woman that were unfounded. She was more at ease in her community than I assumed. I continued to grow in my understanding and appreciation for others who may not be like myself.

We traveled by train to Düsseldorf, Germany, where we were met by a contact who drove a *Buick Opel* instead of a big *BMW* as I had dreamed. We traveled on the Autobahn, which seemed like a glorified superhighway. I had hoped to experience a ride at 150 m.p.h. and had to settle for half that speed.

We ended our research in Germany and had a chance to ride the train and see the dichotomy of East Berlin and West Berlin. We toured a centuries-old castle and realized the young age of most American cities compared to their European counterparts.

We finished our trip and wrote our report to the company that we were representing and our final paper for class. In addition, I brought back the requisite souvenirs, including miniature Dutch shoes, Swedish crystal figurines, and pieces of the Berlin Wall for my curio cabinet. I also brought home a greater appreciation for America's place in the world community. Although we may think we live in the greatest country in the world, we should be humble, for there are many other countries that feel the same way.

I was honored to have my family attend my graduation, where I received the Executive Master of Business Administration Degree from the University of Nebraska at Omaha in May 1993.

My graduate education continued to expand my knowledge and expertise and helped me to overcome a number of challenges. I became adept at conducting strategic planning and developing and managing organizational budgets.

UNIVERSITY OF MINNESOTA – DOCTOR OF PHILOSOPHY DEGREE

I enrolled in the doctoral program in the College of Education and Human Development at the University of Minnesota in the fall of 2000. When I applied to the program, I was informed that grades from some of my lackluster undergraduate classes would need to be elucidated. I explained that I had been a new husband and father and had worked two jobs, all while taking a full-time college load as an undergraduate. I also asked Dr. Mel Humphreys, one of my undergraduate professors and the Chair of the Health, Physical Education and Recreation Department at the University of Memphis (formerly Memphis State University), to write a letter on my behalf. In his letter, Dr. Humphreys stated he was confident I could handle the rigors of the doctoral program. With Dr. Humphreys' letter and by the grace of God, I was admitted into the program.

I wanted to go back to school to further my education and round myself out as a person, although it would have little impact on my salary and career trajectory. This was during the time that my wife, Pam, was in a chronic vegetative state at the *Masonic Home* near my residence in Bloomington, Minnesota. She had suffered oxygen deprivation following surgery in 1998. (More on this later.) My doctoral studies were cathartic as they gave me a focus and little time to dwell on the hardship that had befallen my family and me.

I was blessed to have caring faculty in my doctoral program. Dr. Leo McAvoy was chairman of my department and Dr. Corliss Outley, a young Black assistant professor, became my graduate advisor. As with most of my professional and graduate experiences, I was the only Black in my doctoral program.

I served as a Teaching Assistant in the Sports Management Department and had the privilege of teaching a Sport Management class for undergraduate students. One of my most distinguished students was Lindsay Whalen, who played for the University of Minnesota's Women's Basketball Team. Lindsay went on to have a stellar career with the Minnesota Lynx of the Women's National Basketball Association (WNBA) and later served as the head women's basketball coach at the University of Minnesota. It was a pleasure watching her academic and professional career develop over the years.

My next-door neighbor sometimes cut my lawn or shoveled my snow when he felt I was under pressure to complete a paper or other assignments for my studies. What a loving gesture from a kind man. Many of my other neighbors brought over meals and cleaned our house for almost a year following Pam's accident. It was a real relief not to have to worry about these things during a very trying time in our lives. Dad flew up from Memphis when I had to travel out of town for my job until my son, Cedric, relocated to live with us and serve as a surrogate parent. Thank God that I was able to count on caring family, friends, and neighbors.

I graduated in May 2003 from the University of Minnesota with a Doctor of Philosophy degree in Education. I was proud to have my father, Cedric, and the president of the *YMCA* of the USA, Dr. Kenneth L. Gladish, attend my dissertation defense. Receiving my doctorate was one of the highest achievements of my life.

My dissertation research, entitled "Barriers to Upward Mobility for African Americans in Leisure Services: A Case Study of the *YMCA*," was a clarion call to the Y and a guide to recognizing and addressing systemic racism in the organization. I felt my research would be a lasting legacy to an organization that I love dearly and wanted to see it continue to grow and serve all people equitably.

I could not have overcome the challenge of countless hours of classroom instruction, conducting research, and writing my dissertation without the aid of many people. I owe a lot to Dr. Outley for her support and guidance as my graduate advisor. I could not have accomplished this milestone without the support of my family and friends. Most importantly, I could not have done it without the grace of God.

Receiving my Executive MBA was one of the high points of my education.

When I received my doctorate, I became the second offspring of Eddie and Mattie Dean to earn a terminal degree.

PART THREE:

MIDDLE AGE - GOD'S PURPOSE FOR MY LIFE

The Great Commission and My Role in Discipleship

"Therefore, go and make disciples of all nations, baptizing them in the name of the Father and of the Son and of the Holy Spirit, and teaching them to obey everything I have commanded you. And surely, I am with you always, to the very end of the age." Matthew 28:19-20 (New International Version)

As I continued to mature, I began to discover God's purpose for my life. Attending and becoming a leader in churches in communities where I lived, helping to make disciples of men, women, boys, and girls, embarking on a rewarding career, and maturing as a husband and father became critical to me. I had always been a "bench member," a member who attends church but does not get involved in leadership or does not tithe. I am proud that I have reversed that trend with the help of God. I have served in a number of leadership roles in churches where I have been a member. I also prayed to God to increase my desire and ability to tithe. I am now a regular tither; however, I had to get my personal finances in order and pay off some bills that I thought were inhibiting my ability to tithe. Now, I give of my "time, talents, and treasures" to help further the Kingdom. I want to overcome my reticence (actually shyness) about proclaiming the Good News and witnessing to everyone, not just to Christians.

My spiritual journey started early. I was a member of Baptist Hill Missionary Baptist Church, Potts Camp, Mississippi, the church where I confessed religion as a young boy. I learned to appreciate preaching and singing and began to understand lessons from the Bible. My early church experience at Baptist Hill laid the foundation for my future church involvement.

Willie Dean

I taught the adult Sunday School class at age 13 and was Assistant Sunday School Superintendent at age 16 at the Cane Creek Baptist Church in Memphis, Tennessee. My church activities gave me valuable learning experiences outside of my community. While at Cane Creek, I was selected as one of two youth delegates to the National Baptist Sunday School Convention held in Omaha, Nebraska, in 1967. The next year, 1968, I was selected as a youth delegate to the National Baptist Sunday School Convention held in Miami, Florida.

I rode down to Florida with the Reverend Bobbie Brooks and two of his friends in a 1968 *Dodge GTX*. I enjoyed driving this sporty car. I slept with my wallet under my pillow as I didn't feel totally safe in our hotel room. I remember feeling uncomfortable going into gas stations and restaurants as we traveled through Mississippi. Only years later did I realize that my discomfort was because some White patrons were probably displeased that I had the gall to come into "their" spaces through the front rather than the back door.

When I moved to Texas in 1975 to lead the McDonald Branch *YMCA* in Fort Worth, I joined and later became the President of the Congregation of Community of Hope Lutheran Church in Fort Worth. In this role, I provided leadership to the Church Council and worked closely with the pastor, the Reverend Gordon A. Roesch. Pastor Roesch and I became good friends and often met—after a long day of work at the office or at the church—at a tennis court in neighborhood parks in the community. Gordon's family invited me to share dinner with them on a number of occasions. His counsel and support proved invaluable when I went through the trauma of divorce and the loneliness that followed.

I became a member of West Side Baptist Church when I moved to St. Louis, Missouri. While I didn't assume a leadership role, I was a dedicated "bench member." I attended Sunday service regularly and provided financial support to the church.

My family and I became members of St. Peter's AME Church in Minneapolis when I moved to Minnesota in 1994. I was active in the Brotherhood Ministry and was invited to serve on the Steward Board. However, because of my extensive travel schedule for my job, my family and I attended service sporadically. Looking back, this was a mistake as my sons were in their formative years and could have benefitted from regular church attendance. The other thing is that the church did not have a functioning Sunday School, which would have benefitted my family and me.

St. Peter's AME Church supported my family and me when my wife, Pam, suffered oxygen deprivation following surgery and lapsed into a chronic vegetative state. Church members prayed for my family, and choir members visited Pam at the *Masonic Home*, where she spent her final days, to sing to her and pray for our family.

I became a member of the Olivet Institutional Baptist Church in Cleveland when I moved to Ohio in 2005. I attended service regularly; however, I never found my place in this 2,000-member congregation. Although it was the church where the Reverend Jesse Jackson and the Reverend Dr. Martin Luther King, Jr. had preached when they visited Cleveland, it seemed somewhat bourgeoise and impersonal. I felt uncomfortable when tithers were asked to march to the altar to give their contributions, as the practice seemed to ostracize those of us who weren't tithers.

I joined the Bethlehem Baptist Church in Mansfield, Texas, when I returned to the Lone Star State in 2007. My pastor, the Reverend Dr. Michael A. Evans, Sr., was a dynamic leader within the church and the local community. (Dr. Evans was elected mayor of the City of Mansfield in 2021). I had the honor of serving as Assistant Teacher for the Men's Sunday School Class and President of the Brotherhood Ministry. I also took thousands of digital photos of church ministries and activities.

I was honored to serve as a mentor for Pastor Evans' son, Michael A. Evans, Jr., affectionately known as "Tony." I recommended Tony for a job with the Cooper Street *YMCA* that was near his home. Tony and I keep in touch via Facebook. He is now married and has graduated with a bachelor's degree from Morehouse College and a master's degree from Howard University. Tony is now also an ordained minister. I am privileged to know and continue to connect with Pastor Evans and Tony.

Brother Rodney Kase Tyrone, a man whose deep bass voice is surpassed only by his deep love of God, sang in the choir, served as a deacon, and became one of my friends and mentors. We still converse via text, usually on holidays and special occasions. Rodney is a man who turned his life around and dedicated himself to Christ. Deacon Tyrone, or "Deac" as I call him, taught me a lot about accepting people where they are, regardless of their background.

I rejoined St. Peter's AME Church in Minneapolis when I returned to Minnesota in 2011. I rejoined the Steward Board and was selected to serve as Steward Pro Tem. In this role, I led the congregation in the replacement of a polarizing pastor and facilitated a successful capital campaign that raised more than $40,000 to replace our antiquated air conditioning system, upgrade our technology, and repair our roof.

Willie Dean

I will forever cherish the fellowship and support I received from my St. Peter's friends, including Jon Anderson, Bill and Regenia Anglin, Ajani Boganey, Curt and Carolyn Boganey, Cardell Boganey, Levi Brady, the Reverend Richard Coleman, the Reverend Archie Criglar, the Reverend Gerald Garth, Valton and Wilmetia Henderson, the Reverend William Jackson, Dr. Harold E. Massey, Harriet Solomon, Bill and Karen Wells, Jerry and Gloria Withers, and the Reverend Carla M. Mitchell, my pastor at the time.

I now attend St. Andrew AME Church in Memphis, where my wife, Carol, and I participate in the Digging Deeper Adult Sunday School Class. I am proud to have my pastor, the Reverend Dr. Byron C. Moore, Senior Pastor, write the foreword to this memoir.

The church has been the cornerstone of my life. I don't know where I would be without being spiritually centered. I have been privileged to know many strong Black men and women who are also devout Christians. I will always cherish their friendships and the values we share about our faith. I am also proud to have known many persons of different faiths or no faith who share a respect for humankind.

Giving Back – Service Beyond Self

"I have shown you in every way, by laboring like this, that you must support the weak. And remember the words of the Lord Jesus, that He said, 'It is more blessed to give than to receive.'" Acts 20:35 (New King James Version)

I HAVE PROVIDED SERVICE through community-based organizations and given my time, talents, and treasures through my church in every community where I have lived. I believe that community service—serving others—is one more way that I can serve the Lord. I have given back through service clubs and through nonprofit organizations.

At the age of 21, I was appointed an Auxiliary Probation Officer for the Juvenile Court of Memphis and Shelby County, Tennessee. My first case was a White adolescent boy who had stolen money from vending machines in his community. I visited my charge at his home at least once a week to check on his behavior, school attendance, and whereabouts. He had a nightly curfew and had to get permission from me to travel. I was a sworn officer of the court, carried a badge, and had arrest power with a second officer present. I volunteered for this position initially because of the allure of carrying a badge; however, once involved with the young boy, I saw the importance of providing structure and accountability that might help keep youth from progressing deeper into the justice system. This connection with youth became a hallmark of my 35-year career in youth development with the *YMCA*. I didn't realize at the time how fortunate I was to have had two loving and responsible parents who provided love, structure, and discipline in my life when I was growing up in my household.

Willie Dean

Later in life, when I lived in the St. Louis, Missouri area, I served as a member and president of the Jennings-North St. Louis *Kiwanis Club*. When I lived in Omaha, Nebraska, I was a member of the *Rotary Club* of Omaha. When I lived in Mansfield, Texas, I was a member of the *Rotary Club* of Arlington-North. When I lived in Bloomington, Minnesota, I was a member of the Minneapolis-University *Rotary Club*, where I served on the Board of Directors and was chair of the Community Services Committee. My involvement in service clubs gave me opportunities to give back to my communities and to volunteer alongside some of the best and most generous people that I have known. Through these service clubs, I had the opportunity to serve my community through activities like *Meals on Wheels*, fundraising for college scholarships, and patriotic U.S. flag displays on major holidays.

I joined the Upsilon Omega Chapter of Omega Psi Phi Fraternity, Inc. in 1982 when I lived in the St. Louis area. Brother Joel Weathersby, a retired music educator, invited me to join the Epsilon Phi Chapter of Omega Psi Phi Fraternity, Inc. in Memphis. I joined the chapter in September 2019. "Friendship is essential to the soul," Omega Psi Phi Fraternity's motto, has been emblematic of my life. I have been privileged to help my fraternity provide scholarships for deserving youth, help stock food pantries, and to raise funds for the needy in our community. I am proud to serve on the Advisory Board of Uplift, Inc., a nonprofit organization affiliated with Epsilon Phi Chapter, where I use my grant writing and strategic planning skills to help serve our community

I was a member of the St. Louis chapter of 100 Black Men, Inc.—an organization that engenders Black leadership and Black pride—when I lived in the St. Louis area. I later joined the One Black Men, Inc. chapter in Cleveland, Ohio, where I met Dr. Charles S. Modlin, a nationally recognized urologist and kidney transplant surgeon who at the time was at the Cleveland Clinic. Dr. Modlin would later save my life by performing renal sparing surgery to rid my kidneys of malignant tumors.

God has a way of putting people in our paths who test our faith or serve as instruments of His healing power. My story is replete with both. I am proud to give back to my community through church, service clubs, and other venues, for God has been good to me.

A Rewarding Career – Self-Actualization

"The best social program is a job." Ronald Reagan, Former U.S. President

A QUOTE OFTEN ATTRIBUTED to U.S. President Ronald Reagan, "The best social program is a job," speaks to the heart of a strong economy and, more importantly, to strong individuals, strong families, and strong communities. While I may not agree with many of the late president's conservative policies; I do agree with this statement, with some very important caveats: 1) jobs should be available to all, without regard to race, ethnicity, country of origin, gender, sexual orientation, etc., 2) there should be competitive-wage jobs available for all (including women) with equal pay for equal work, and 3) job advancement should be based on experience, skills, and performance. Lacking these requirements, it is incumbent upon society (federal, state, and local governments; companies, unions; activists, etc.) to ensure equal employment opportunity for all. We must work to level the playing field and ensure bias does not disadvantage any groups of people.

In order to obtain this "jobs utopia," we must ensure equal education and training opportunities for all. We must also provide a livable wage, affordable childcare, adequate transportation, affordable housing, comprehensive healthcare, and access to healthy food for everyone in our communities.

I sometimes ask myself, "How did my father make the transition from his humble beginnings as a poor sharecropper in rural Mississippi with an eighth-grade education—who could barely feed his family—to become a professional truck driver and a middle-class homeowner in Memphis, Tennessee?" Or, "How did I overcome barriers to upward mobility, earn an Executive MBA and a Ph.D., become one of the most senior Black executives in the *YMCA*, be fortunate to have lived across the United States, and traveled to countries around the world?" It is clear to me that my family's socioeconomic transformation—from poverty to the middle class in one generation—was made possible by my father obtaining not just a job, but a "competitive-wage job with benefits" that became a rewarding career.

Hometown Boy Makes Good – YMCA of Memphis and Shelby County

During my final semester at Memphis State University, H. Kent Russ, Vice President of the *YMCA* of Memphis and Shelby County, shared with me a need to hire a program director at the Glenview Branch *YMCA*. This branch was an old Railroad *YMCA* that served Black youth in South Memphis. Ironically, the branch was located within a few miles of my home and my high school; however, I had never been there. The antiquated building included a small gym and several offices and clubrooms. The branch executive director had suffered a heart attack, and there was a need for leadership at the branch in his absence. I started my employment on January 4, 1974. One of the first things I did was to inventory the program equipment and supplies and find out from the staff about what programs were being offered.

Kent arranged for me to participate in on-the-job training at several branches, all of which served White communities. I spent the first two weeks of my employment shadowing and learning from program directors at the Abe Scharf, Mason, and Whitehaven branches. I learned how the program directors at these branches set up sports leagues, tournaments, and other programs. I also learned to drive a school bus. The staff at all of the branches were cordial; however, I soon recognized the disparities between their branch facilities and mine. Their branches were located downtown or in the suburbs and had large, modern facilities that included a full-size gymnasium, indoor swimming pool, game room, and offices. My facility, on the other hand, was an old building with a small gymnasium, a small game room, and small offices. While the facilities were not "segregated" in that they were open to anyone, few Blacks attended the other branches, and no Whites attended mine. Racial inequities would be a phenomenon that I would grapple with and study for the rest of my career.

Given my skill and penchant for basketball, I recruited kids from a nearby low-income apartment building for a boys' basketball team that I coached. I later added arts and crafts classes for youth. During the summer, I offered swim lessons, even though we didn't have a pool. We partnered with several neighborhood residents to use their backyard pools for instructions. I also offered day camp at the Y and traveled to a nearby park for field trips. I remember fondly hosting a *YMCA* team from Birmingham, Alabama, for a basketball game. My boys lost the game, but we were excited to participate in the competition. We later traveled to Birmingham to compete against our newfound friends. This was the first time many of my players had ever traveled beyond the Memphis area. In a small way, the trip opened up a whole new world for these inner-city youth.

In addition to strengthening programs, I worked with the Board of Management, a group of policymaking volunteers who were responsible for fundraising and community engagement. The board had minimal experience with fundraising and advocacy in the community.

I started a women's exercise class that was held in our gym. Women from the community brought their exercise mats and enjoyed instruction two times a week. We also used the gym for youth dances on Friday nights. It was gratifying to see youth from the nearby apartments come to the Y as I slowly established their trust, and they began to see the Y as a "cool" place to be.

One Friday night, while closing the Y after a teen dance, I noticed that my keys—that I had left in the lock in the front door as I was ushering youth out of the building—were missing. I went outside and asked several teens who were milling about the entrance if anyone had my keys. They all denied knowledge of their whereabouts. After talking with the teens for more than 15 minutes and explaining the seriousness of the situation, I finally said to them, "If I don't get my keys back in the next five minutes, somebody is going to jail." After a brief period of silence, a boy came forward and handed me my keys. I thanked him and proceeded to finish locking up the building. This was a valuable lesson for me on keeping better watch over the property in my care. I don't know what I would have done if they had called my bluff, as I really didn't want to call the police. I used this incident as a teachable moment to talk with the teens about honesty and integrity when they returned to the Y to play basketball and shoot pool the next day.

I had been told that the executive director was viewed as a "controlling person." I learned this fact firsthand when he stopped in on numerous occasions before his doctor had cleared him to return to work. When he officially returned to the office, he was confrontational and insecure about what I was doing with the programs and the board. He accused me of being disagreeable. I respectfully told him that I believed that one could "disagree without being disagreeable." I am sure he felt insecure because I had been hired while he was on medical leave and he felt threatened by my education and success working with the youth, adults, and board. Once again, I was dealing with a bully.

During my second year working at the Glenview Y, I inquired about attending the *YMCA*'s Career Development Program (CDP), a 10-day training event that was going to be held at the *YMCA* Blue Ridge Assembly near Black Mountain, North Carolina. My executive director told me, "We usually don't send staff to training until they have been here for at least three years because young staff get trained, they get seen, and they leave." I assured him that was not my intention. Reluctantly he approved my enrollment in CDP.

I attended CDP at *YMCA* Blue Ridge Assembly in the beautiful mountains of North Carolina, where each morning before breakfast, I heard "Nothing Could Be Finer Than to Be in Carolina in the Morning" blaring from speakers throughout the conference center. I met leaders like Del Kinney, one of the facilitators, and Dr. Paul Limbert, a pioneer and icon in the *YMCA* movement.

I learned that the *YMCA* (Young Men's Christian Association) was founded in London, England, in 1844 to address the needs of men and boys who were moving from rural areas to industrialized London. These new urban residents fell victim to gambling and houses of ill repute. The *YMCA* started as a Bible study group that met over a drapery (forerunner of the modern-day department store). I was intrigued that the Y invented basketball and volleyball and started the USO, swimming lessons, and day camping. The Y also was instrumental in the offering of adult basic education. But most importantly, I was heartened to know that the *YMCA*'s mission, "To put Christian principles into practice through programs that build healthy spirit, mind, and body for all," was in synch with my own.

I gobbled up information and demonstrated my enthusiasm during the group work sessions. In fact, I was recognized by Del as a promising young director and won a "one dollar" prize during one of the creative mock program development sessions. When I returned home from CDP, I shared what I had learned with my supervisor and set about improving the programs and administrative functions of our small inner-city Y branch.

Money was tight for my young family, and we tried numerous money-saving strategies. We rarely ate out and tried to cook meals at home whenever we could. I biked to work in order to save money and to allow my wife to use our family's sole car to drive to her part-time job and run errands. We had moved in to live with my parents after we got married. We later moved into an apartment that my cousin and his wife had inhabited for more than two decades in

Castalia, a neighborhood that was a couple of miles from my parents' home. The small, two-bedroom apartment was infested with roaches that would scatter whenever we turned on the lights at night. Sometimes, unfortunately, we would find them in Cedric's baby crib. This situation was untenable; however, every time we had the management spray our apartment, the roaches seemed to go next door and return when the pesticide had dissipated.

As a struggling young family, we had little choice but to endure the conditions of our apartment because we couldn't afford to live anywhere else. As a result of this experience, I have a greater appreciation for the poor and downtrodden in today's society who have few housing choices due to cost and long distances to job locations.

One day I climbed a ladder and got onto the roof of the Y to change a floodlight bulb. When I attempted to get down from the roof, I realized I should have ensured the top of the ladder extended well above the roofline. I was in danger of toppling from the roof and sustaining major injuries if I was not careful. After an agonizing amount of time trying to figure a way out of my dilemma, I finally got down. I learned a valuable lesson about climbing ladders, a lesson that I wish I had learned earlier in life.

I achieved a number of successes in my first job with the *YMCA*. I brought a lot of energy and new ideas. And I learned to work with youth, adults, and volunteers, plan sports leagues and tournaments, and operate a swimming program and a day camp. These skills would prove valuable as I moved up the hierarchy in the *YMCA*, locally and nationally.

One day I came across a national job vacancy list that was distributed by the *YMCA* of the USA, the *YMCA*'s national office. I realized that my supervisor didn't circulate the list within our branch, perhaps out of fear of losing staff to other *YMCA*s. I learned from the vacancy list that there was a job opening for Executive Director of the McDonald Branch *YMCA*, a branch serving a Black community in Fort Worth, Texas. I was intrigued by this opportunity. I submitted my resume and listed Del Kinney, one of my trainers from CDP, as a reference. I was invited to interview and was offered the job based on my skills and experience and the fact that Del personally knew the hiring manager and gave me a glowing recommendation. I began to learn the importance of networking and the truth of the adage, "It's not what you know, it's who you know." (In retrospect, I realize the fact that I was "Black" also played a part in my hiring. Later, this would become an issue when I applied for jobs located in more integrated communities.)

Although unintentionally, I made my supervisor's fear a reality—I got trained, I got seen, and I left. Years later, when I told this story to Y colleagues during a training session that I was conducting, I asked, "Would you rather have staff that get trained and leave or have staff not get trained and stay?" They invariably chose the former.

Looking back, I didn't think twice about relocating for a competitive-wage job and better opportunities for my family, just as my father had done for his family a quarter-century earlier. I was emboldened because of the people I met during the interview process who seemed genuine and of good character. I also felt confident because I had seen my older brother, Joe, go away to college in Knoxville, Tennessee, and later relocate to Princeton, New Jersey, after completing grad school. Once again, I was following a path that he had blazed ahead of me that gave me the courage to be a risk-taker.

Go Southwest Young Man – YMCA of Metropolitan Fort Worth

I was excited to start my second Y job as Executive Director of the McDonald Branch *YMCA*, a branch of the *YMCA* of Metropolitan Fort Worth, Texas. I loaded up my wife and two-year-old son, Cedric, and traveled to Fort Worth. I started my new job on April 1, 1975. In hindsight, I'm surprised that I moved nearly 500 miles to a city and state where I knew no one. I put my faith in God and the prospect of a better future for my family.

God blessed me to be successful in my first executive job. I managed the branch's budget and coordinated leadership, program, and membership development. I also increased the branch's annual support campaign from $12,000 to $20,000 and received grants totaling $120,000 to build a tennis court, renovate the gym floor, construct a playground, and build an outdoor swimming pool.

The McDonald Branch *YMCA* was located on a hill at 2400 E. Berry St. in a predominantly Black section of Fort Worth. The facility included a full-size gymnasium, locker rooms, multipurpose rooms, and small meeting rooms.

When I arrived, the branch was primarily being used to offer a licensed, before- and after-school childcare program called "Kinder Kamp." The popular program provided badly needed childcare for working parents in the community. Parents dropped their kids off before school, and they were transported by Y staff in a van to their respective schools. In the afternoon, Y staff transported the students from their schools to the Y in a van and a bus. At the Y, the kids enjoyed a snack, arts and crafts, homework time, and recreation in the gym or on the outdoor playground.

The before- and after-school program provided a sorely needed service to the community; however, the branch facility was being grossly underused. The building closed at 6 p.m. after students were picked up from Kinder Kamp, leaving no opportunity for neighborhood youth to participate at the Y.

Although the Y had a burglar alarm system, many break-ins occurred. The police speculated that neighborhood youth were causing vandalism and destruction of the Y facility. When I arrived, I recognized there was a pent-up desire among neighborhood youth to use the facility. I immediately hired part-time staff to keep the gym open until 9 p.m. daily and to 6 p.m. on Saturdays. In addition, I hired a full-time program director. Once again, I leaned on my basketball experience and started a youth basketball program. I also started t-ball and flag football programs to engage the youth in organized activities. I also recruited parents and other adults to volunteer as coaches, referees, and program aides.

I built upon an already successful summer day camp program that served more than 150 youth daily. We used a nearby park as our campsite and Y-owned vans and rented buses to take campers on field trips throughout the Dallas-Fort Worth Metroplex. Our campers benefited from creative programming that included: hiking, field trips, arts and crafts, drama, skits, and weekly trips to a city swimming pool. Without the *YMCA*'s day camp program, many Black youths would not have had safe opportunities to have fun and recreate during the summer months, and many parents would not have had a safe and affordable option for childcare for their children while they worked.

I hired Winnie R. Scott to serve as childcare director. She was responsible for directing the Kinder Kamp before- and after-school program and the summer day camp program. Winnie was the consummate professional who cared deeply about the kids and the community. (A few years ago, while touring the new McDonald Family *YMCA* with my wife, Carol, I bumped into Winnie, who was touring the branch prior to joining as a member. I had not seen Winnie in more than 40 years! I asked myself, "Was this a chance meeting, or was it providence?")

I wrote a grant to the *General Dynamics* Employee Con-Trib Club requesting funds to purchase a new school bus for our childcare program. Much to our delight, our request was approved. We ordered a bus that was manufactured in Indiana and driven by an employee of the manufacturer to our Y in Texas. We proudly had the bus, which was painted powder blue, emblazoned on both sides: "McDonald Branch *YMCA* – Courtesy of *General Dynamics* Employee Con-Trib Club."

We acquired the bus in 1976, during the period of high gasoline prices caused by market manipulation by OPEC (the Organization of the Petroleum Exporting Countries) and a rash of thefts of gasoline. Thieves in communities across America were siphoning gasoline from vehicles to sell or use themselves. One night someone, while attempting to siphon gas from our new bus, set it afire, and it burned beyond repair. We were devastated the next day when we learned what had happened. How would we transport our kids to camp, to school, or on field trips? Fortunately, our friends at *General Dynamics* helped with our insurance deductible, and we were able to order a replacement bus without delay. This, however, was a sad commentary on the lengths some will go to steal from others rather than to work or engage in legal enterprise.

I explored offering teen dances at the Y, although some thought it was a risky proposition to have hundreds of teenagers together in a confined space. I had done it on a small scale at my branch in Memphis and felt that with the popularity of disco music in the 70's, there was a market. I brought my stereo and turntable from home, printed some fliers, and distributed them to several area high schools. Much to my chagrin, almost no teens showed up, except a few who stayed in the parking lot as if to see who else would come.

I believe my failed attempt to offer teen dances got the attention of some teens, for soon, an enterprising student from a local high school sought to rent our gym for a dance. After completing the paperwork and paying a deposit, the student brought in his stereo, amp, and twin turntables on the night of his rental. By 10 p.m., we estimated that more than 700 teens had packed our gym. They "partied" so hard that the walls began to sweat as the air conditioning couldn't keep up with the body heat that was being generated. A staff member and I took turns checking the restrooms and locker rooms to ensure nothing untoward was occurring. Occasionally, we came upon boys trying to smoke marijuana or participate in a dice game that we quickly disbursed. We had no fights or serious altercations.

We later found out that the young man who rented our gym was popular at his school and had a huge following. He paid the Y $50 per hour for four hours to rent our gym and charged his guests a dollar each, giving himself a $500 margin. Quite the entrepreneur, he rented our gym on numerous occasions.

Later, I spent funds from the Y's budget to buy a professional amp, microphone, and twin turntables and had a set of custom speakers built (that stood five feet high) to enhance the dance experience. However, the most teens we attracted were about 200 on any given Saturday night. We were pleased, however, to provide a safe alternative to the streets by presenting teen dances on our own or by renting out our space so others could do so.

I learned a valuable lesson following one of our Saturday night teen dances. The gym would be littered with paper, pop bottles, and other trash at the end of our teen dances. The area wasn't cleaned up until the following Monday morning when our custodian returned to work. One Monday morning, our Y's president arrived with several funders for a planned facility tour to support a funding request. He was embarrassed and livid at the appearance of the facility. He had our Vice President of Operations, my boss, share his disgust with me. I revealed that we had kept several hundred kids off the street that Saturday night; however, he was not moved. I was in hot water. I learned that I should have had a plan to clean the facility on Sunday, knowing that guests would be coming in on Monday morning.

I remember a young man, probably in his early 20s, who was large in stature who sometimes came to the Y. When sober, he was amiable and played hard in the gym, although he wasn't a very good basketball player. One evening he came to the Y and I immediately realized that he had been drinking, was agitated, and from the imprint under his t-shirt was carrying a .45-calibre pistol in his waistband. I talked to him calmly and suggested that he leave the Y because he was in no condition to be there, and I didn't want to see him get into trouble with the police. I believe he left without incident because of my relationship with him and the respectful way I addressed him. A few days later, he returned to the Y and apologized for his behavior earlier that week. (This was the second time during my work experience that I defused a potentially volatile situation by talking calmly rather than being macho.)

I started a men's basketball league to involve older males in our community. The league attracted men from throughout the area. I coached one of the teams and became fond of its players. I contacted the Y in Birmingham, Alabama, with whom my team in Memphis had played, and arranged a road trip. My players and I piled into the Y's leased 15-passenger childcare van for our trip. I estimated the distance to be 500 miles; however, it was actually more like 700 miles. (This was before the age of *MapQuest*, navigation systems, or GPS technology) I allowed one of the men, the same young man from the pistol incident, to drive while I rested. Late that night, while he was driving, I was awakened to a rattling noise from the engine. The player, who was driving, had been driving at 90 m.p.h., the maximum speed on the speedometer. There we were, a group of Black men stuck on the side of the road late at night in rural

Willie Dean

Alabama. What else could go wrong? This was a period before cell phones, and we didn't have a CB radio. How would we call for help?

Soon I saw lights pull up behind us and realized that it was the state police. I thought to myself, "Now we can call for a tow truck or other assistance!" My relief turned to fear when the driver informed me that he didn't have a driver's license. The players in the rear of our van raised up to block the view from behind, and without thinking, I traded places with the driver. Fortunately, the officer didn't see what happened. I shouldn't have traded places. (I should have only let licensed drivers who were approved by our insurance carrier drive the van. I also should have inspected any approved driver's valid driver's license before departing on the trip.)

When the officer realized we were from the Y and our vehicle had broken down, he called for a wrecker. While against their policy, the officer allowed the wrecker to tow our vehicle, with us in it, to a local Dodge dealer. I didn't have a credit card to rent a van; however, because we were representing the Y, the manager let me borrow a 15-passenger van from the dealership so we could complete our trip and return home to Fort Worth while our van was being repaired in his shop. Our vehicle had thrown a rod and required major engine repair. Once again, the Lord was looking out for me. (To add insult to injury, after all we went through, we lost the game against the Birmingham Y!)

Continuing education and professional development have always been important to me. I was named a *YMCA* Senior Director by the National Council of Young Men's Christian Associations of the United States on December 16, 1976. The designation was in recognition of my fulfillment of prescribed organizational requirements, including my personal commitment to career-long educational and professional development.

It was during a childcare training program in Boulder, Colorado, that I met a branch executive from St. Louis, Missouri. He was impressed with me and asked if I would consider relocating to St. Louis for a job opportunity. I told him I was satisfied with where I was in Fort Worth. (This chance meeting would later prove key in my upward mobility in the Y movement.)

While having breakfast at a restaurant in Boulder, I made a faux pas by ordering an item I had never had. The dish was quiche; however, I pronounced the word phonetically. I asked the female server for a "quickie." My colleagues promptly informed me the word was pronounced "KEESH!" Embarrassed, I apologized to the server and bore the good-natured ribbing of my colleagues.

Almost as soon as I returned home from the training in Boulder, I got a call from Ted W. Hawkins, Senior Vice President for Operations of the *YMCA* of

Greater St. Louis. Ted said that the branch executive who had inquired about my interest in a job in St. Louis had told him about me. He invited me to interview for the executive director position of a branch in the association. I respectfully said I was not interested; however, he invited me to come and just tour the branch and the city. Reluctantly, I agreed.

OFF TO THE MIDWEST – YMCA OF GREATER ST. LOUIS

On the morning of my St. Louis Y interview, I overslept and missed my plane. Embarrassed, I phoned Ted to tell him what had happened. Undeterred, he had his office rebook my flight for later that day and arranged for a staff member to pick me up at the airport when I arrived in St. Louis. The staffer gave me a tour of the community on our way downtown, where I met with Ted and other corporate office staff. Later, I met with members of the staff of the new Monsanto Branch *YMCA*. (The Monsanto Co. had given the Y a $2 million gift to construct the new branch facility, located in the inner-city.)

The branch Y arranged for Charles White, a local school principal and real estate agent, to show me some homes that were for sale in the community. I was impressed with several houses that had finished basements, or "rathskellers" as they are called. Interestingly, I learned that Charles White was actually Captain Charles White, a former member of the "Tuskegee Airmen," a heroic all-Black flying unit that contributed much to the winning of World War II.

George Elliott, Chair of the Board of Management and a respected local school principal, gave me a tour of the branch service area. It was immediately apparent that the community near the branch was economically depressed and riddled with dilapidated houses. There seemed to be little hope for change.

The Monsanto Branch *YMCA*—a new $2.5 million facility that was to open later that year—was located on the campus of its predecessor, the City North Branch *YMCA*, at 5555 Page Blvd. The 35,000 square-foot facility was to include: a gymnasium, fitness center, indoor swimming pool, steam room, sauna, multipurpose rooms, men's and women's locker rooms, and staff offices. The branch was poised to become one of the premier inner-city *YMCAs* in the nation, but it needed executive leadership. The executive of its predecessor facility, the City North Branch *YMCA*, was at odds with the administration, which could have impeded a change of direction.

I met with Ted again the next morning. He laid out his vision for the Monsanto Branch and said the staff and volunteers concurred that I was the right person to open and lead this new branch. He said that if I accepted his offer, I would serve as Executive Director for the Monsanto Branch and District Director for the City North District, which included supervision of two other branch executives. After returning home to Texas, and careful consideration, I accepted the position of Executive Director/District Director of the Monsanto Branch *YMCA* and started my new job on July 6, 1981.

I later learned that a number of Black *YMCA* colleagues had interviewed for this position, and some had turned it down, including Harold Mezile, who later became one of my best friends, mentors, and staunchest supporters. In later conversations with me, Harold said he turned the job down for fear it would further stereotype him as only being capable of running inner-city Ys. Sure to form, his pursuit of non-traditional roles paid off. Harold was a National Field Consultant for the South Field Office of the *YMCA* of the USA. Later he was selected as President/CEO of the *YMCA* of Central Maryland in Baltimore, Maryland. Harold, one of the most respected Black executives in the Y movement, was later named President/CEO of the *YMCA* of Metropolitan Minneapolis. Harold worked with Tom Brinsko, President/CEO of the *YMCA* of Greater Saint Paul, Minnesota, to merge the Minneapolis and Saint Paul *YMCA*s. Harold served as President of the new *YMCA* of the Greater Twin Cities, a position he held until his retirement in 2013.

I bought my first home in Olivette, Missouri, a western suburb of St. Louis. It was a quaint three-bedroom rambler with a finished basement. I was so proud of my accomplishment. It was located in the Ladue School District, one of the best school districts in the St. Louis area. In a conversation with me, the Y's chief financial officer expressed surprise that I could afford to live in Ladue, one of the most affluent suburbs in the St. Louis area. I shared with him that Olivette was in the Ladue School District; however, it was separate and apart from the city of Ladue. I guess he had preconceived notions about where I should live.

As a single parent, I sought an after-school program for Cedric, who was by then age eight and entering the third grade. To my surprise, neither the *YMCA* nor his school district offered after-school care in our area. I enrolled Cedric in a program at the Jewish Community Center Association (JCCA) near our home, where he received affordable, safe, and quality care.

I worked for the *YMCA* of Greater St. Louis from July 1981 to October 1989. During this period, I was promoted from Executive Director/District Director to Vice President-Urban Services. With training, experience, mentoring from trusted colleagues, and most importantly, by the grace of God, I was able to make significant accomplishments. The Monsanto *YMCA* was recognized by the *YMCA* of the USA as one of the "Ten Model *YMCAs* Serving Urban Communities in the United States." I balanced the budget and met operating targets annually, increased membership from less than 100 to more than 2,200, increased the operating budget from $350,000 to $900,000, raised $383,000 in a capital campaign, and secured grants to build a parking lot and renovate a daycare center.

The Monsanto Y served North St. Louis, an area of widespread poverty and high crime. Many students faced challenges to their learning readiness, including unstable living arrangements, poor nutrition, and neighborhood violence. A number of families were transient, often living in rental properties until they could no longer afford the utilities and then moving, sometimes multiple times during a single school year.

Early in my tenure in St. Louis, I engaged a group of young kids who were sitting on a curb in the parking lot watching the construction of the new Monsanto *YMCA*. I described to them the amenities of the $2.5 million facility. They had no concept of the dollar value of the new building, so I asked how many had seen the recently released *Star Wars* movie. Almost immediately, a number of hands shot up. I said it probably cost about four bucks for admission to see the movie. Then I said, "The cost of this new Y building is like seeing 'Star Wars' 600,000 times." They replied, "That's a lot of money!"

Many of the youth, adults, and families who participated at the Monsanto Y were low-income or transient. Thanks to our volunteers and donors, we were able to raise scholarship dollars that allowed us to serve a very fragile community. One of our most successful programs was "Senior Fitness Morning," an exercise program for senior adults. For only a dollar per visit, ambulatory seniors could participate in chair aerobics in the gym and water aerobics in the swimming pool. Many area doctors referred their geriatric patients to the Y for social engagement and physical exercise.

We became known in North St. Louis as the place to be for wellness and aerobic dance classes. On any day of the week, except Sundays, we offered multiple aerobics classes where you could hear the constant beat of music blaring over amplified-tape decks in the gym, pool, or multipurpose rooms.

We had one of only a few swimming pools in the community. I remember being told that my boss said, when the building was being conceived, that it would be better to build two gyms rather than build a swimming pool. The assumption was that "Black people don't swim." My experience was that if Black people didn't swim, it was because they didn't have access to swimming pools and swimming lessons on par with their White peers. My personal experience growing up in the segregated South, where swimming pools were off-limits to Black residents, informed my thinking. I contend that if swimming pools were as ubiquitous in Black communities as gyms, playgrounds, and backyard hoops, there would be as many Black gold medal-winning Olympic swimmers like Michael Phelps as there are Black superstar basketball players like Michael Jordan. Sadly, many Black youths are at greater risk of drowning simply because they don't know how to swim.

When I had a vacancy for an aquatics director, I hired a White female, certified lifeguard and swim instructor who worked at our Southside branch. Some gave me flack for this decision. They maintained that many Black folk in our community needed jobs. My retort was I needed someone to teach children to swim, and the person I selected was the best candidate that had come forward. Some also expressed concern that Black men would "hit on" her. She responded by saying that White men hit on her; however, she knew how to deal with inappropriate advances. (It's unfortunate that women of all races and ethnicities still have to deal with sexism and sexual harassment.) My new aquatics director developed wonderful relationships with our members and participants, especially our youth and seniors, and taught many in our community to swim. It was important for me that we walked our talk when it came to diversity, equity, and inclusion.

I modeled the behavior that I sought but did not always experience from my superiors when I hired a diverse staff. When the White female aquatics director left our staff to become Executive Director of the Southside branch, I hired a White male aquatics director to replace her. Later, I hired a White male aquatics director from Arizona to fill another vacancy. Looking back, I was the only branch executive who had diversity among the senior staff in our association. There was no Black professional staff at any of the predominately White branches or at our corporate office.

I was promoted to Vice President-Urban Services for the *YMCA* of Greater St. Louis, in part to provide greater services to inner-city communities and to entice me to stay in St. Louis with an increase in salary. Later, when I sought to broaden my skills, I applied for the executive director position at the West County *YMCA*, a branch located in one of the most affluent suburban communities served by the *YMCA* of Greater St. Louis. The Y president told me I would have to take a $10,000 pay cut from my vice president's salary in order to take the suburban job. As the saying goes, "I might have been born at night, but not last night." I couldn't afford to take a pay cut. (Mama raised no fool!) Needless to say, I did not pursue the suburban job any further. I began to ask myself if my VP salary was competitive within the association or was it a means to keep me in my place, serving mostly Black folks in the inner-city.

I sought to learn the salaries of the senior Y staff because the Internal Revenue Service (IRS) had recently required Section 501(c)(3) nonprofit organizations, like the *YMCA*, to make the salaries of the five highest-paid staff available for public inspection on a new "Form 990." However, when I requested to see the Y's Form 990, including the list of senior staff salaries, the CFO placed tape on the report to allow me to see only my salary. Only after I cited the IRS requirement that Form 990 be available for inspection did he relent and allow me to see the whole report. The long and short of it, I learned from my inspection of the association's Form 990 that the salary of the West County Y executive, located in the affluent western suburb of our service area, was on par with and not $10,000 below my VP salary.

I felt typecast because of my race, which limited my upward mobility. Getting ahead in the Y was dependent on getting well-rounded experience with large membership branches and raising significant contributions, both of which were nearly impossible to accomplish working in small, inner-city branches. Like the adage: "You can't get credit unless you have credit," I couldn't get experience running a large membership branch because no one would give me a chance to get that experience. I believed that White managers didn't feel Black staff would be received well in affluent, mostly White communities. (This fact would be driven home by comments made by a White CEO of a large *YMCA* after I was hired as CEO of the Omaha-Council Bluffs Metropolitan *YMCA* a few years later. The White CEO was alleged to have asked during a staff meeting, "What's wrong with the folks in Omaha? Didn't they know they didn't have to hire a Black CEO?" It was further borne out by findings from my dissertation research on barriers to upward mobility for African Americans in the Y.)

Emblematic of how Blacks and Whites experience the world differently is a "funny" anecdote told to our staff by the President/CEO of the *YMCA* of Greater St. Louis. The president, an affable White man, said, "I came home the other day to find a St. Louis County police officer sitting in his squad car, that was backed into my driveway, to clock speeders on my street. I parked my car on the street, blocking my driveway and the officer's car, retrieved my mail, and spoke to the officer as I walked past his open car window and proceeded into my house. A few minutes later, my doorbell rang. When I opened the door, the agitated officer exclaimed, 'What are you some kind of a smart-ass?' To which I responded, 'No, there's some dumbass parked in my driveway, so I parked on the street!'" My White colleagues laughed out loud at the story as he proudly told how he had confronted the officer; however, I couldn't help but see the irony of the situation. I thought to myself that a Black man would never have done such a thing, certainly not without experiencing major repercussions.

Other examples that illustrate how Blacks and Whites are treated differently by law enforcement include the 1991 police beating of Rodney King in Los Angeles following a high-speed chase for driving while intoxicated (DWI) and the 2020 police murder of George Floyd in Minneapolis after a store clerk accused him of passing a counterfeit 20-dollar bill. Black people—Black men and boys in particular—have little leeway with Whites who are in power (police and the criminal justice system, teachers and school administrators, employers, etc.). Stories as innocuous as the one told by the St. Louis Y president are not funny when one thinks about the hundreds, if not thousands, of Black people in America who have suffered indignation, pain, and even death simply because of the color of their skin.

One day in 1986, Cedric, my oldest son, who was 13 at the time, was home alone after school in our Olivette, Missouri home. In a panic phone call to me at my office, Cedric said he thought he heard someone trying to break into his bedroom window. He was terrified. Rather than phoning the police in our suburban city, I ran to my car and sped the five or six miles from my Y office in inner-city St. Louis to our home in the suburbs.

When I arrived at our home, I called Cedric's name, retrieved my handgun from its storage place, and frantically searched for him. However, he was nowhere to be found. I looked in each bedroom, under the beds and in the closets, and in the finished basement. Just as I was about to exit the front door to look around outside, I saw a police officer standing on my front porch. Instinctively, I placed my gun in my pocket, knowing the police might not understand that I was the property owner. However, as the officer saw me, he also saw the handle of my .357 magnum sticking from the pocket of my overcoat.

The officer yelled, "Gun!" I immediately froze as I realized I was in mortal danger—my life was potentially in jeopardy. As the officer reached toward me—with his left hand and his right hand on his gun—he removed my pistol from my coat pocket. Over his shoulder, I could see my wife, Pam, Cedric, and our middle son, Jarrod, standing by one of several squad cars on the street. She was yelling, "That's my husband! That's my husband!" While standing there, seemingly frozen in time, I heard an officer ask her, "Are you two estranged? Does he have permission to be in the house?" "That's my husband," Pam continued to exclaim loudly.

After things calmed down, the officers realized what had happened. Pam and Jarrod had returned home shortly after Cedric had called me, and they all drove to the police department, which was less than a half-mile away, and told the police that someone had been attempting to break into our home. By the time the police, and my family, got to my residence, I had finished the interior search of my home and was confronted by officers as I was preparing to exit my front door.

After the police searched my home and examined the windows and doors, the officer who had taken my gun emptied it and handed it and my ammunition separately back to me. At first, I was irate. I was legally carrying my gun on my property to defend my family, and here I was being treated like I was a criminal. However, after the officer explained they had to exercise caution and ensure that I was not a threat, I understood their position. The situation was embarrassing as neighbors witnessed the scene and probably wondered what I had done. I wondered how differently I would have been treated if I had been White. I believe the officers' caution was warranted; however, I can't help but think that as a Black man, the margin of error for my actions during this encounter was slimmer than it would have been for a White person.

When I think about the tragic death of Breonna Taylor in 2020, at the hands of police in Louisville, Kentucky, during the serving of a no-knock warrant at her apartment in the middle of the night, I can't help but think, "There but for the grace of God, go I too." Or, I think of Amir Locke, who was killed by Minneapolis police after the serving of a no-knock warrant. Locke, who was not the subject of the warrant, was shot by police after he displayed a handgun because he was startled by police who used a key to enter his apartment in 2022. If I had acted in a way that they perceived as imprudent or erratic, I could have been assaulted or killed under the guise that I presented a threat to the police or others who were present. I thank God for my naturally calm demeanor, which probably saved my life, or at the least averted grave bodily injury to myself or my family.

When I started my employment as Executive Director of the Monsanto Branch *YMCA*, I realized that a separate 501(c)(3) nonprofit organization, named The Junior Kindergarten, that provided badly needed full-day childcare was located on our campus. What I didn't realize was that the organization paid no rent or fees to the Y for the upkeep of the carriage house where they had been located for decades. I also didn't realize the hornets' nest that I stirred up when I suggested that the Y shouldn't subsidize another nonprofit. I found that politics were deeply entrenched. There were some members of my board that also served on The Junior Kindergarten's board, representing what I saw as a clear conflict of interest.

When I recommended that our *YMCA* acquire The Junior Kindergarten and run the daycare center as a Y program and allow its executive director to be a program director within the Y, I got major pushback from my conflicted board members. And I learned later that the dissent that was created put in jeopardy a $25,000 capital campaign gift from a corporate donor who was influenced by one of the company's executives who served on The Junior Kindergarten board.

To add insult to injury, once the acquisition was finally approved and we merged The Junior Kindergarten into the *YMCA*, we got a notice from the City of St. Louis that major repairs and updates had to be made to the carriage house to meet the current building codes, as the facility had been grandfathered under its previous operators. In short, we had to expend major funds to update the building's fire and smoke alarm system, elevator, plumbing, and electrical systems and remove asbestos and lead paint in order to meet the current building codes and state childcare licensing standards.

While the change was a hassle, put a strain on the Y's budget, and ruffled feathers with one of our corporate donors, the children and families served by the program deserved to have an updated, clean, and safe facility. I learned a valuable lesson about how internal politics and long-held relationships can sabotage the best of plans and efforts to improve quality and service. (This would not be the last time that the enemy from within would attempt to crater my plans and my career.)

I was blessed to have inherited some talented and dedicated staff when I came to the Monsanto Branch *YMCA*. Carla Giles, Physical Director, and Beverly Dyson, Program Director, were among this group and part of my management team. Carla was responsible for fitness and wellness classes that used the gym, weight room, and multipurpose rooms. She hired and supervised part-time aerobics instructors and fitness trainers. She was very talented and admired by adults and seniors alike. (Carla worked with me to develop a workout and nutrition plan that resulted in my losing 80 pounds over a one-year period. I felt and looked great. My weight had increased to 297 pounds, and I wanted to ensure I lived to see my son grow up.) Beverly was in charge of youth programs, including before-and after-school childcare and summer camp. She also supervised youth overnights in our gym from time to time. She was skilled in working with the youth and their parents.

We had wonderful experiences with youth and adults from the area; however, sometimes, we saw the underbelly of the community. One day I had to ask an unruly group of youth to leave the building. I had caught one of the youths crouching down to sneak into the gym without paying. When I confronted the kid and placed my hand on his shoulder to counsel him, he told me to take my hand off him. I learned that touching people during a conflict—however well-intentioned—was not a wise thing to do and, in some cases, may seem threatening.

I told the youth and his friends that sneaking into the Y was not appropriate. I said that we offered membership scholarships to youth and families in our community. All they needed to do was ask their parents to come in and fill out a scholarship application. I asked them to leave and come back when they were ready to enter the facility the right way.

I watched the youth as they crossed the parking lot and as they walked past my car. Something told me to walk out and examine my vehicle. Much to my dismay, I discovered a long scratch along the side of my car where the youth had just traversed. I yelled to them and walked over to ask if they had scratched my car. Like the missing keys years earlier in my career at my first Y job, no one admitted guilt. This time, however, I called the police. Upon searching the youth, the responding officer found a non-functioning pistol—missing the barrel cylinder—on one of the youths. These were the very young people who needed the kind of programs and services that the Y is designed to provide.

On another occasion, someone entered our lobby one afternoon and used a hand truck to wheel a dollar bill changer out the front door. The front desk staff didn't notice anything was awry until our vending salesman reported that the machine was missing the next day. We could not believe the audacity of some individuals. It made me wonder, "Why do some people refuse to work for a living?" "Why do some people spend time plotting and stealing from others?" I surmised that perhaps they didn't have parents, and other adults, with strong work ethics as role models who nurtured and mentored them when they were young. They may not have had the benefit of studying the Bible and learning that one of the Ten Commandments given by God is, "Thou shalt not steal." And, they may not have had an experience like mine with "buffalo-catfish" bones. (I learned a painful lesson when catfish bones got lodged in my throat when I tried to swallow "stolen" catfish—that I had taken from my family's kitchen table without permission—to cover up my misdeed." Stealing is wrong, and it can be hazardous to one's health!)

Willie Dean

When we opened the new Y facility, we had to hire a number of new staff. Rev. Frederick L. "Fred" Norris, our new head custodian, was one of my most valued hires. Fred was a military veteran, a black belt in karate, and a minister. His knowledge and certifications in heating, ventilation, air conditioning (HVAC), and boiler operations proved invaluable. Near the end of my tenure at the Monsanto Y, Fred asked me to meet him at the facility on a Saturday night after the building was closed. We stood center court in the empty gym, where he grasped my hands and prayed aloud. He told me he had a vision that I would rise to a high position in the *YMCA* nationally. Soon after our prayer session, I was hired as the first African American president of the Omaha-Council Bluffs Metropolitan *YMCA*. Just four years later, I was hired as the National Field Executive for the Mid-America Field of the *YMCA* of the USA and was one of two high-ranking African Americans on the national Y staff. Fred's vision had come to fruition.

I remember Al Porter fondly, a young African American man who worked as a swim instructor and lifeguard at the Monsanto Y. Al told me years later that he had become a successful entrepreneur. He said that he had been an angry Black man when he was younger and that I had helped to save his life. He had observed the way I carried myself, which helped him develop a positive image of himself, his life, and his future. I was humbled to learn that I had had—without even knowing it—such a profound influence on Al's life. It affirmed for me once again that young people, eager to find role models, are watching what we do.

I am grateful to many volunteers who served on the Board of Managers of the Monsanto Branch *YMCA*, including Teri D. Bascom, Martha Perine Beard, Thelma Cahill, George J. Elliott, Maurice Grant, Ruby Hiram, McKinley "Mac" Johnson, Lt. Col. Clyde H. Orr, Lou Moore, N. Webster Moore, Charles Shelton, and others.

In 1982, I traveled with a group of volunteers and staff to Bogota, Colombia, to help strengthen the partnership between the *YMCA* of Greater St. Louis and the *YMCA* of Bogota (Association Jovenes de Bogota). N. Webster Moore, a retired teacher and a board member of the Monsanto Branch *YMCA*, and I were roommates during our weeklong trip. We were impressed by the hospitality of our hosts and the level of services they provided their community. They showed us a used passenger van that the St. Louis Y had donated to them several years previously, when it was essentially worn out, with in excess of 100,000 miles on the odometer. Our Colombian partners were still using the van, which at the time of our visit had been driven more than 500,000 miles.

We saw abject poverty almost everywhere we went in the city of Bogota, which had a population of about five million residents. While there was no public transportation, the city was estimated to have had more than 50,000 privately operated buses. These buses crisscrossed the city, picking up passengers, many with goods, including chickens and other small livestock in cages under their arms. Some residents would steal rides on the back of buses without the drivers' knowledge or ability to control this commonplace behavior.

Many people were moving from the rural countryside in search of employment and better opportunities in the city. Unfortunately, for many, this was not a winning strategy. The Bogota Y developed a youth outreach program called "Operation Gamines" to work with street children who resorted to crime to support themselves and their families. We were told that many poor fathers would put their older children on the street—some only five or six years of age—to beg or steal to help to support their families. We were advised not to give beggars money as this would only embolden them and invite danger. The Y's outreach program sought to provide the street children with food, shelter, basic education, and love. We were touched by the paradox these children faced, unable to grow up as children under the protection of their families; they were forced to grow up too fast on the dangerous streets of the city.

We were warned not to drink the water or eat fruit without rinsing it with bottled water. This was necessary because the area had bacteria with which our digestive systems were unfamiliar. We wanted to avoid Montezuma's Revenge (dysentery). Seeing fresh food, including fruits and vegetables in open-air markets was not uncommon to us; however, we couldn't understand how it was safe to cook and consume un-refrigerated meats that had been covered with flies at these markets.

There were some middle- and upper-class neighborhoods in the city; however, they were always surrounded by tall stone walls that were topped with broken bottles embedded in cement to prevent trespassing. We found this technique to be barbaric but effective. These neighborhoods were dramatically different from the poor neighborhoods of the city and served as a reminder of the dichotomy between the haves and the have-nots in the United States.

When we were given a tour of the countryside, we saw many shanties that were constructed of sheets of tin and, in some cases, cardboard. Hundreds, if not thousands, of these shacks had been erected on hillsides with electrical wires strung throughout by residents. Sanitation was poor as people often relieved themselves outdoors, and there were few places for handwashing and bathing. As we got farther into the countryside, we saw many trees and working farms. This was in stark contrast to the poverty we saw in many parts of the city.

Our trip to Bogota proved to be an eye-opening experience for those of us who traveled from the comfort of our middle-class homes in the U.S. We saw poverty and desperation that more than rivaled the situation in many cities in our country. We also saw youth, adults, and families that were striving to learn, grow, and survive in a culture that was much different than ours.

On the Road Again – Omaha-Council Bluffs Metropolitan YMCA

In October 1989, I was hired as the first African American CEO in the 123-year history of the Omaha-Council Bluffs Metropolitan *YMCA*. I moved my family to Nebraska, knowing no one in the entire state except for a few volunteers and staff who I met during the interview process. My hiring was made possible because of support from my Black Y friends (professional staff and volunteers) that I had networked with over the years.

I talked with local *YMCA* volunteers to understand what the board was looking for in a new CEO. When I interviewed with the selection committee, I asked them not to look at me as a Black man but rather to look at me as a talented professional who could do the job. My employment with the *YMCA* of Greater St. Louis—an Urban Group *YMCA*, one of the 30 largest Ys in North America—and my urban portfolio made me an attractive candidate to deal with youth gangs and violence that were beginning to plague Omaha and other midwestern cities.

Although I was qualified and had excellent references, there were still doubters, as evidenced by comments alleged to have been made by the White CEO of an Urban Group *YMCA*, "What's wrong with the folks in Omaha? Didn't they know they didn't have to hire a Black CEO?" It seemed he was inferring that *YMCA*s in primarily minority communities like Newark, New Jersey, had to hire a Black person in such a role. And conversely, *YMCA*s in predominantly White communities should hire White leadership. Notwithstanding these racist assumptions among some *YMCA* leaders, I was hired as one of the first African American Y executives to be hired in a large, multi-branch *YMCA* in the country.

I served as President/CEO of the Omaha-Council Bluffs Metropolitan *YMCA* from October 1989 to April 1994. During this period, I continued to develop my leadership skills and achieved a number of accomplishments. I increased the Y's operating budget, eliminated a $250,000 deficit, and brought the current unrestricted fund positive for the first time in 30 years; served 27,000 members and 97,000 program participants; collaborated with five nonprofits to implement a $250,000 multi-agency outreach program, called YouthNet, for at-risk youth; raised $5.3 million to improve branch facilities, collaborated with the City of Omaha to acquire the site for a new inner-city *YMCA*; and received gifts of land and grants totaling $500,000.

In the early 1990s, cities across the country were being plagued by youth gang violence, and Omaha was no exception. What seemed like a large-city problem was fast becoming an issue for small- and mid-size cities as well. Drive-by shootings and drug crimes were becoming commonplace. As promised during my interview, working with teens would be a hallmark of my administration.

I contacted H. Eugene Dooley, President/CEO of the *YMCA* of Greater Kansas City, Missouri, who had developed a multiagency program called "YouthNet," to address the youth gang issue in his community. Gene graciously drove to Omaha, along with his outreach director, to provide training and insights on how their program operated. A key component of the program included outreach workers who were assigned to a youth-serving agency but were stationed in schools to work with students and faculty. In addition, a master's-level therapist was available to counsel students on a variety of issues. Since this was at a time before cell phones were in widespread use, each outreach worker and the therapist were equipped with a pager to make them available, day or night, to respond to students' crises or just to talk when needed.

I assembled a coalition of Omaha youth-serving agencies to explore a possible multiagency collaboration to address the youth gang problem in our community. After several meetings, it became clear that we would have to find a way to take off our "individual agency hats" and think as "members of a collaborative." This was easier said than done. A number of questions and trust issues surfaced. "If we obtained program funding, which agency would serve as the fiduciary?" "To whom would the program staff report?" "Where would they be officed?" I had to ask the agency partners to "Check their egos at the door," just as Quincy Jones, music writer, singer, and producer, said to the large group of superstar singers and musicians before they produced the song "We Are the World," in 1985, to provide relief for Africa following a devastating drought. If the youth outreach collaborative in Omaha was going to effectively serve teens in our community, we had to start by working together.

After many meetings, phone calls, and informal discussions, the YouthNet collaborative was born. We received a $250,000 grant from the United Way of the Midlands to underwrite the project for one year. The Y was named the fiduciary agent. The collaborative included: Boys and Girls Club, Chicano Awareness Center, Family and Children Services, Omaha-Council Bluffs Metropolitan *YMCA*, and United Way of the Midlands.

Once when planning to meet with a group of teens who dubbed themselves "Teens Against Gangs" (TAG), I got a phone call a few minutes before the scheduled meeting requesting that I meet with the teens at our North Branch rather than at my Downtown Y office. Upon arrival at the North Branch, which was located in the inner-city, I got another call asking me to meet at a nearby public housing development. Upon my arrival at the meeting, I noticed youth who had congregated around the site. Later I learned from the TAG leaders that I had been tested to see if I was serious about meeting with them and about effecting real change. I passed the test. I also learned that some of the youth who had been watching me upon my arrival were gang members.

I was blessed to have inherited a group of dedicated professionals who were yearning for leadership. Louie Warren, who served as Executive Director of the South/Southwest Branch *YMCA* (our largest branch), was later promoted to Vice President-Operations for the association. Louie was one of the most dedicated, loyal, and trustworthy persons that I have ever known. He affectionately refers to me, even to this day, as "Chief." Jim Schuldt served as Vice President-Chief Financial Officer and did a marvelous job managing our finances. He and Louie worked closely to monitor branch performance and recommended adjustments to our overhead when we received a sudden reduction in local United Way funding following a scandal that befell the national United Way. Marsha Pope, who I hired as Marketing Director, worked hard to position our Y in the community and in the hearts of our members. Her writing and editorial skills were indispensable as we sought to upgrade our program guides, member newsletters, and campaign literature. Linda Butkus, who served as Executive Director of the West Branch *YMCA*, was also a skilled administrator. Stan Anderson, who served as the Downtown Branch Executive, had his finger on the pulse of our downtown branch members' needs. Margaret Reed served as the Executive Assistant to the President. Marge was a trusted and effective colleague.

Jim Beatty, an African American Board Member, and local entrepreneur, became one of my strongest advocates. And Rich Schoffelman, the National Field Consultant from the Mid-America Field Office of the *YMCA* of the USA, who was assigned to our area, provided excellent consultation and resources to our Y.

Money was tight in my household during my first year in Omaha. I went all winter without a functional car heater, only to learn all that was needed was a thermostat. Needless to say, I almost froze my buns off before I discovered what I needed to repair my car. As a "trailing spouse," it took my wife, Pam, a while to find employment. She eventually landed a job as a classroom teacher. We lived in a modest four-bedroom home in West Omaha, near Boys Town, the nationally renowned residential program for boys and girls.

My son, Cedric, was age 16 when we moved to Omaha. I didn't know until years later that he had to fight almost daily at school. I also didn't know he often had to fight on the campus of the Monsanto Y when we lived in St. Louis. I guess by not telling me of these problems; he was emulating my habit of not telling my parents about dangerous incidents that I encountered growing up myself. Parents must understand that our children watch us and often walk in our footsteps in ways that we might never have anticipated.

The house we rented in Sarpy County before moving into our home in West Omaha was in a predominately White community; we rarely saw other Black families. When we did see other Blacks at the mall, we felt relieved, and we almost wanted to go up to them and introduce ourselves. Omaha, which is located in Douglas County, had more Blacks but was by no means "diverse," except in North Omaha, where most Blacks lived.

Moving On Up: Mid-America Field – National Field Executive

My next move was from Omaha to Minneapolis as I continued to advance in my Y career. I served as National Field Executive for the Mid-America Field of the *YMCA* of the USA, based in Minneapolis, Minnesota, from April 1994 to June 2001.

Like when we lived in Omaha, as a trailing spouse, Pam had difficulty finding employment. She eventually was named Dean of Students at a Bloomington middle school, where the students affectionately called her "Dean Dean." She also worked as a teacher at Valleyview Elementary School, under the tutelage of the principal, Dr. Karen Wells (Karen and her husband, Bill, became some of our best friends. We all attended St. Peter's AME Church in Minneapolis.) Pam would also work in the administrative office of Hamline University in Saint Paul, Minnesota.

I was one of the most senior African American Y leaders in the national office and achieved a number of accomplishments. I managed four field offices and collected $9.7 million in local member dues, supervised 17 consultants and eight support staff, and provided consulting services to 700 *YMCAs* in 18 states. I also managed the National Crisis Team and raised $500,000 to assist *YMCAs* in crisis.

My job as National Field Executive required me to travel extensively; however, flying 100,000 miles per year to visit Ys and my staff was not as glamorous as it might seem. Sometimes I would catch a 6 a.m. flight and return home that same night. I remember flying to Dallas to perform a staff review, have lunch with colleagues and be on an evening flight back to Minneapolis. I banked a lot of frequent flier miles; however, it was at the expense of precious family time. I regret that I was away from home during some critical periods of my kids' lives, including regular church attendance.

Assisting local Ys to identify candidates for CEO vacancies and then helping newly hired executives with the transition to their new roles was among the most critical parts of my job. I believe that the value of my role and the image I portrayed—as a respected Black professional in a position where Blacks were not always visible—was incalculable. It changed the perceptions of both Black and White staff.

My employer, the *YMCA* of the USA, began to examine its service delivery system in the early 2000s. Until that time, services were provided via field offices located in four areas of the country: East, South, Midwest, and West. My peers, other National Field Executives, and I, along with our National Field Consultants and Management Resource Center (MRC) Directors (local Y employees who provided services to neighboring *YMCAs*) traveled from our offices to local *YMCAs*. After extensive study, we decided to close field offices, decentralize operations, and provide consulting services by consultants from their home-based offices. This new service delivery model brought services closer to local Ys. The new system also eliminated National Field Executive positions, closed leased office space, reduced travel costs, and saved significant overhead costs that could be used to enhance services.

With the closing of my office and the elimination of my job, I took a generous severance package that the *YMCA* of the USA offered to help with the transition to new employment. My goal was to find a CEO job with a local Y;

however, I couldn't consider relocating my family with my wife, Pam, being in a chronic vegetative state following a devastating surgical accident. Instead, I decided to go back to school to earn a doctorate, expand my knowledge and expertise, and enhance my prospects of landing a CEO job in the future.

After Pam's passing, I sought to reenter the YMCA, the organization that I loved and had worked for more than 25 years. I went on a number of interviews for president/CEO positions with Urban Group YMCAs; however, I was never offered a job. Disheartened, I looked for chief executive positions with other nonprofits in the Twin Cities and around the nation, all to no avail.

My dissertation, "Barriers to Upward Mobility for African Americans in Leisure Services: A Case Study of the YMCA," examined issues that keep minorities and women from advancing in organizations. My research found that organizational leaders tend to hire and nurture people like themselves. Invariably diversity is inhibited because those in power don't see the value of diversity and inclusion. Ironically, the barriers that I experienced in my job search paralleled those of the minorities and women in my study.

Years later, I learned from a colleague that one of the references I had been listing on my resume had been influenced by a national board member who falsely represented that I was hard to get along with and I was an ineffective leader. My own reference was giving less than a full-throated endorsement of me when contacted by selection committees. I had been sabotaged by "the enemy within." I also feel that some of the interviews that I went on were "sham interviews," interviews arranged to have a "token" Black candidate in the mix, but a preferred candidate had already been identified, or there was no real commitment to consider hiring a qualified Black candidate.

There I was, a talented Black man with 30 years of YMCA executive experience, a successful track record as a leader (Program Director, Branch Executive Director, District Director, Vice President-Urban Services, President/CEO, National Field Executive), an Executive MBA, and a Ph.D., and I still could not land an Urban Group YMCA CEO position. Intuitively, I believed something was wrong with the system. That something, I believed, included racism.

Additionally, I felt my attempt to reenter the YMCA at a senior level was hampered because people didn't know whether I could still lead, given that I hadn't been a CEO of a local Y for over ten years. I believe that managing a YMCA, or any organization for that matter, is just like riding a bicycle. It's a skill that you don't lose. Once you've learned how to manage, the skill stays with you. Since I hadn't been a CEO for a number of years, people assumed I could "no longer ride a bicycle." All I needed was a chance to demonstrate that I could still lead and contribute to the organization's success.

EASTWARD HO – YMCA OF GREATER CLEVELAND

I got the chance to lead again in September 2005. Glenn Haley, a colleague, and friend, who was President/CEO of the *YMCA* of Greater Cleveland, hired me as Chief Operating Officer for his 17-branch metropolitan *YMCA*, located in Northeast Ohio. Ironically, Glenn had been one of my mentees, proving that mentor-mentee relationships have value for both parties.

I worked with Glenn and our volunteers and staff to position the *YMCA* for growth. I was instrumental in developing the organization's five-year strategic plan and setting the course for the future. My tenure in Cleveland situated me to compete for CEO positions by giving me recent operational and leadership experience. Finally, I could demonstrate that I still "knew how to ride a bicycle."

I sold our home in Bloomington, Minnesota, and bought a townhouse in Cleveland, Ohio. Although I had relocated numerous times in the past—sometimes alone and sometimes with my family—this move was different. This time I was leaving a home that I had shared with my family for the past ten years and the memories of a beloved wife that I had lost to a terrible medical tragedy. I was also moving more than 700 miles from Matt, my youngest son—who had recently graduated from high school and had just turned 18—in order to pursue my career and to put food on the table.

I put on a brave face, but deep inside, I was crying at the sight of Matt in my rearview mirror as I drove away that September morning en route to a new life in Cleveland. Once again, I compartmentalized my feelings in order to cope with a difficult situation. I sometimes wonder if it would have been better if I had shown my sons my emotions so they wouldn't grow up thinking that "real men don't cry." I should have let them know they didn't have to be stoic in order to be "real men."

I moved to a section of Cleveland, which was part of the Ohio City neighborhood, just about a mile from downtown. I could see Lake Eerie from the fifth-floor balcony of my split-level townhouse. The neighborhood was in transition. Years earlier, it had been a grand neighborhood with large houses along tree-lined streets. In recent years, however, the neighborhood had lost its luster, and many middle-class families had relocated to the suburbs. The exodus of the middle class left behind many urban poor, a weakened tax base, and crumbling schools with inadequate resources. When I moved into the neighborhood, gentrification was beginning to happen with higher income, often White families moving back and renovating flats and multi-story homes in the neighborhood. And unfortunately, it would only be a matter of time before low-income and elderly residents would be pushed out of their homes because of increasing housing costs (mortgages, rents, and property taxes).

My home was a five-story, split-level townhouse with a postage-stamp-size front yard and a slightly larger fenced backyard. The backyard had a koi pond, and a trellis draped with grapes. My neighborhood included everything from abandoned or dilapidated buildings that were slated for rehab to recently modernized, tax-abated, multi-story homes with elevators. Ohio City, home to a wonderful farmer's market, also had a number of family-owned restaurants and boutiques.

I often heard the sounds of sirens in my neighborhood as crime in the area was relatively high. One night I looked out of my bedroom window, which was over my driveway in front of my townhouse, and saw an unfamiliar car in my driveway. Peeping through the shutters of my unopened blinds, I observed the vehicle for some time and decided to phone the police. After officers arrived and examined the vehicle, they told me it had been carjacked down the street and abandoned in my driveway. On another occasion, a technician who was cleaning my koi pond discovered two rusted pistols at the bottom of the pond. The police officer who responded to my call surmised that someone had likely tossed the weapons over my back fence while running down the alley to evade police. Both of these events were unsettling, to say the least.

I started as Chief Operating Officer (COO) of the Cleveland Y and was later promoted to Senior Vice President/COO. In my role, I managed operations of our $17-million urban *YMCA*; increased member retention and membership revenue; led Product Development Teams; standardized programs and increased program quality and innovation; improved the operating net by $555,000; led staff retreats, team building, diversity and inclusion training; provided programs through nine branches, four program sites and 19 child care sites, served 27,600 members and 10,800 program participants through 719,800 annual visits; supervised 500 full- and part-time employees; and led a 14-month planning process to develop our strategic plan.

Unfortunately, in late 2006 the Cleveland Y, like other organizations in our community, suffered from the economic downturn that was happening across the country as the nation reeled from the impending housing bust. Reluctantly, Glenn had to cut operating expenses by eliminating a number of jobs. I was laid off at the end of 2006. I was fortunate to have received a three-month severance package which helped sustain me during my search for a new job. I was undaunted and trusted that the Lord would see me through, just as He had done all my life.

In early 2007, I learned the *YMCA* of Arlington (Texas) was looking for a CEO. Having worked in Texas three decades earlier and knowing the management consultant assigned to the area from the *YMCA* of the USA and others familiar with the Arlington *YMCA*, I decided to submit my résumé. I conducted extensive research on the community and the organization. And after reference checking, a phone interview, and a personal interview, the selection committee and I felt that I was a match for the job. Once again, I thought, "God is good!"

Go Southwest Again – YMCA of Arlington

I was hired as President/CEO of the *YMCA* of Arlington, Texas, and started my new position on June 1, 2007. I was the first African American President/CEO in the Arlington Y's 49-year history. I worked hard to get involved in the community. I became a member of the Bethlehem Baptist Church in Mansfield and the Arlington North *Rotary Club*. Additionally, I graduated from Leadership Arlington and the Dale Carnegie Course. I also was involved as a member of the Arlington Independent School District's Community Gang Prevention Taskforce, the Success in School Summit, and the Mayor's SPIRIT Task Force. I was also appointed by the mayor to chair the Our Community, Our Kids Task Force.

Through the grace of God, and the help of a dedicated group of volunteers and staff, I achieved a number of accomplishments. I developed a five-year strategic plan; led program evaluation, marketing, membership development, and retention, managed a $7.7-million budget, supervised 365 employees; operated three branches, 20 program sites, and 21 child care sites that served 17,500 children. I also served 56,300 members and 36,000 program participants, including 11,200 kids in sports.

My team and I enhanced our Y's stature in the community and strengthened our financial development. Together, we raised $340,000 to provide financial assistance to youth and families in need; facilitated the donation of 200 bikes and gifts for youth to combat childhood obesity, improve wellbeing and build self-esteem; received $184,000 in grants to combat type 2 diabetes and to develop policies to improve community health and wellbeing, and developed an annual Community Prayer Breakfast that brought together more than 150 ecumenical leaders and individuals to pray for the youth and families in our community.

Two years into my job as head of one of Arlington's largest nonprofits, I paused to look back at my achievements and ahead at what the future would hold. I had turned 58 in March, had an earned doctorate, and had been described by one of my colleagues as a "renaissance man." I had been named by Arlington Mayor Robert Cluck, M.D., to chair "Our Community, Our Kids," a community-wide collaborative designed to respond to issues faced by youth, adolescents, and teens in our community. My hobbies included biking, sports cars, and photography. I had a first-degree black belt in Tae Kwon Do and was learning to play the guitar!

Upon reflection, I realized that I was truly blessed. I'm a Christian who embraces the teachings of Jesus to guide my life. I have been an overachiever all of my life. I give credit to God for all that He has allowed me to accomplish. All of my life, I've cherished the importance of "faith, family, and friends" and have benefited greatly from God's grace, family support, and friends' advice. Learning, teaching, and leading have always been important to me.

For 50 years, the *YMCA* of Arlington had enriched the lives of thousands of residents. We redoubled our commitment to serving kids and families in Arlington, Mansfield, and surrounding communities. Our goal was that by the year 2014, the *YMCA* would have made significant contributions toward the development of individuals and families in our community. The *YMCA* mission, "To put Christian principles into practice through programs that build healthy spirit, mind, and body for all," and our core values, "caring, honesty, respect, responsibility, and faith," would guide everything that we did. The *YMCA*'s mission and values are what differentiates it from other organizations. I had the best job in the world, one that provided gainful employment and, at the same time, allowed me to demonstrate my faith as I worked with hundreds of volunteers and staff to serve the community.

In developing our strategic plan, we conducted research using *United Way*, U.S. Census, university, and other data to determine the key issues facing youth, adults, and families in our community. Critical community issues were found to include: changing demographics, increasing numbers of economically disadvantaged, public safety and crime, latchkey kids, youth not participating in programs, youth gangs, challenging schools, lack of public transportation, lack of parenting skills, insensitivity to diversity and inclusion, lack of life skills education, need for neighborhood revitalization, and population growth. We developed "Vision 2014: Building Strong Communities," a five-year plan to respond to community needs that included: childhood obesity, youth values, teen programs, diversity and inclusion, and health and wellness programs for youth, adults, and seniors.

Studies found that unhealthy behaviors, sedentary lifestyles, and poor nutrition had led to an epidemic of obesity and related chronic disease in the U.S. Childhood obesity likely leads to lower life expectancy and chronic health issues. Children and teens were increasingly growing up in single-parent homes. Racial diversity was increasing, and the need for the teaching of values and the appreciation of diversity and inclusion was paramount. We believed that to effectively address these critical issues, it was imperative that organizations work collaboratively to maximize limited community resources. (Looking back now, one can see how the lack of appreciation for racial and ethnic diversity in the first decade of the 21st century should have been a harbinger of racial and ethnic insensitivity, xenophobia, and tribalism that we see on the rise today.)

Our *YMCA*'s vision was to be the premier human service organization in our community. To do that, we sought to dramatically expand our membership, programs, and facilities and focused on goals that would develop youth and teens, strengthen families, create health and well-being for all, connect members to one another and the community, and develop leaders for the future.

Our *YMCA* was the area's largest provider of before- and after-school programs. During 2008 we served more than 1,000 children at school sites throughout Arlington and Mansfield. Our summer day camps served nearly 635 children each week at our seven day camps and three teen camps. These programs focused on kids, ages 5 to 15, with working parents who needed a place for their children and young teens that was safe, fun, and productive. Many of the children would have been unable to attend if it were not for the financial aid they received from our Strong Kids Campaign.

Organized sports helped to provide valuable life skills for those who participated in them. Our *YMCA* served more than 14,000 kids in 2008 in sports like baseball, basketball, extreme track, flag football, soccer, softball, and volleyball. Through participation in team sports, kids not only have fun, but they build a base for health and well-being that lasts into adulthood. Additionally, at the *YMCA*, youth sports participants focused on character development along with skills development. Those who played at the Y learned teamwork, good sportsmanship, and respect, along with how to throw a ball or shoot a basket.

Through a partnership with the City of Arlington's Weed & Seed program, our Y learned of a group of kids who attended Hutchinson Junior High School who wanted to play soccer. They desperately needed something to do after school, but they were either ineligible for the school's organized sports programs or, for some other reason, were unable to play. During the 2008-09 school year, the *YMCA* continued the efforts started by Weed & Seed volunteers and organized an after-school soccer club for Hutchinson students. Gang problems were evident in this neighborhood, and we saw this soccer club as one way to address the issue. Our *YMCA* was an agent of change in order to keep kids safe.

One of our *YMCA*'s most successful teen programs was proven to be our Teen Leadership Council (TLC). We expanded this program to include youth ages 10 to 12 in a Tween Leadership Council. In 2008, 70 teens and tweens participated in this important leadership development program. TLC and TweenLC offered area youth the opportunity to learn about their community, become involved, and learn how to become a leader in effecting change. With community service projects, field trips, and educational components, our *YMCA* helped build our community's leaders of tomorrow. Each of our branch locations served their area's teens and tweens, and we worked to take this program "beyond the walls" of the Y as well.

In the spring of 2008, the City of Arlington was looking for a partner to work with the youth and families who resided at the Artisan at Rush Creek Apartments in South Arlington. The apartment community had a high incidence of calls to the police for help with issues like petty larceny, assault, and loitering. Police officials said many of the calls resulted from youth and teens having nothing to do.

We met with city staff to devise a plan. Lynn Frankenfield, Executive Director of the Cooper Street Branch *YMCA*, developed a proposal to serve the youth and teens in the apartment community. Arlington City Manager Jim Holgersson made a $5,000 Neighborhood Assistance Grant available, to which our *YMCA* matched $5,000 from our Strong Kids Campaign. Additionally, the apartment owners provided $5,000. With only $15,000 in funding, the *YMCA*, the city, and the apartment owners developed a partnership that changed the situation and ended up changing lives!

The partnership provided programs that included basketball, flag football, Safe Sitter classes, Tae Kwon Do, Teen Leadership Council and Tween Leadership Council leadership development activities, and monthly field trips to the *YMCA*. We also implemented a tutoring program at the apartment complex in collaboration with the Mansfield Independent School District.

As a result of the partnership and the Y's intervention, crime was reduced to virtually zero, and youth and teens were involved in positive activities. Our YMCA hosted a Christmas party at the Artisan apartments, where youth and their families received 90 bicycles and helmets, 140 Christmas baskets and turkeys, coats, and 42 pairs of athletic shoes and socks. I was honored to have been asked to dress up and play Santa Claus at the party for the kids.

The apartment program continued to grow and thrive, and the results were phenomenal! Youth from the apartments participated in Global Youth Service Day in April to create a flower garden at the Cooper Street Branch YMCA. Our Y provided lifeguards and taught swimming lessons at the apartment pool during the summer. Proudly, one of the teen residents, involved in the program since its inception, was hired as a lifeguard in her own community!

Our YMCA was able to make a real difference in this one part of the city. There was a significant decrease in vandalism and petty crime in the neighborhood and an overall improvement in the image of the community by those who lived there. Because of the positive results, we worked to expand our programming at Artisan to similar communities around the city.

The YMCA of Arlington was the largest provider of swim lessons in our area, with more than 2,500 youth enrolled each year. During the summer of 2008, we piloted a project called "The Urban Swim Program" and offered free swim lessons and water safety classes to youth who otherwise might not have had an opportunity to learn to be safe around water. Nationally, minority youth drowned at disproportionate rates because they didn't know how to swim or hadn't been taught how to be safe around water. Partnering with schools that we served through our afterschool programs and the leaders and volunteers of Arlington's Weed & Seed program, we hoped to serve up to 50 youth. We enrolled an astounding 76 youth and teens—proof for us that this program was sorely needed and should be offered each year. Our Y worked with the Parks and Recreation Department of the City of Arlington in order to expand the program. (The success of this program was especially gratifying to me, having grown up in the segregated South when swimming instruction, and access to public swimming pools, were limited for Black residents.)

The more than 60,500 members of our YMCA's facilities and the more than 36,000 program participants spoke to our organization's relevance. Through their participation in YMCA activities and programs, our members and participants knew the difference the Y makes. By providing a caring and nurturing place to work out, be cared for, play sports, or learn to swim, the Y became much more than a childcare center, workout facility, swimming pool, or gymnasium. For our members and participants, the Y became a community, family, social center, and much more. It was a place to learn, grow, become healthy, and become stronger in spirit, mind, and body.

None of the work of our Y would have been possible without the support of almost 1,700 volunteers and nearly 1,200 donors. These leaders helped make the *YMCA* in our community successful. They knew the importance of having youth sports, health and fitness, aquatics, and childcare programs with an emphasis on the core values of caring, honesty, respect, responsibility, and faith.

With the economic downturn during the Great Recession that came to a head in 2008, many individuals and families in our community found it difficult to make ends meet. A number of Y members suffered job layoffs, and many were concerned about their future. Our *YMCA* responded by making financial assistance available—nearly $600,000 in 2007—to members who couldn't afford memberships or programs.

During periods of uncertainty, organizations like the *YMCA* are needed more than ever. Individuals and families in our community needed safe, affordable childcare and accessible health and well-being programs to ensure good community health. Our *YMCA* had been part of the heart and soul of our community for nearly 50 years. We celebrated good times, and we supported those in need through child and youth development, family strengthening, and health and well-being programs. We were committed to helping all members of our community live healthier lives—in spirit, mind, and body.

Our focus didn't change because the economy changed; however, it had particular relevance in the moment. Our *YMCA* helped people focus on the important things in life: children, family, community, and personal well-being. Our *YMCA*, a charitable, nonprofit organization, was open to all, irrespective of income. We provided financial assistance to those in need.

My three-decade career with the *YMCA* was uniquely suited for my focus on faith, family, and friends. I learned how to serve youth, adults, and families in the communities where I lived. And, without preaching or proselytizing, I was able to demonstrate God's love and testify to His unmerited grace in my life's work.

I was optimistic about both my personal and professional life. My focus on "faith, family, and friends" continued to sustain me and allowed me to conquer the challenges that I faced. I was blessed, my faith was strong, and I had the love and support of family and friends. My health was excellent, and I had the benefit of working for an organization that prided itself in helping to improve the health and well-being of everyone in our community.

I looked forward to leading the *YMCA* of Arlington in accomplishing its five-year goals to reduce childhood obesity, enhance youth values, expand teen programs, improve diversity and inclusion, and make health and wellness programs more readily available for youth, adults, and seniors.

I believed our Y was vibrant and strong after 50 years of serving the Arlington and Mansfield communities because every day our members, volunteers, staff, and leaders lived our mission, "To put Christian principles into practice through programs that build healthy spirit, mind, and body for all."

Back to the Midwest – KFAI Radio and YouthCARE

After working in Texas for four and a half years, I sought to move back to the Midwest to be closer to family. On August 1, 2013, I was hired as Executive Director of *KFAI, Fresh Air, Inc.*, a nonprofit community radio station located in Minneapolis, Minnesota. At KFAI, I had a number of accomplishments. I managed this nonprofit community radio station that served 18,000 listeners through 89 on-air programs in 13 languages; supervised five employees; worked with a 16-member board of directors and 500 volunteers; received $25,000 in pro bono support through the Nerdery Overnight Website Challenge to update the organization's website; managed a $1.1-million budget, including a $100,000 federal grant and a $150,000 state grant; and developed the "Fresh Air Institute," a collaborative program between YouthCARE, Urban 4-H and KFAI, that provided training and orientation in radio broadcasting to 30 multicultural youth from the Twin Cities.

I later served as Executive Director of YouthCARE, a Twin Cities youth development agency, from March 1, 2015, to December 31, 2017, where I had a number of accomplishments. I managed this nonprofit youth development agency that annually served 600 urban youth; supervised 12 employees; worked with a 24-member board of directors and 200 volunteers; wrote a proposal, and received $25,000 in pro bono support through the Nerdery Overnight Website Challenge to update the organization's website; managed a $1.2-million budget, including a $480,000 state grant; managed a summer camp and city programs for diverse youth; developed a strategic plan to guide the organization; and facilitated the donation of 100 bikes for diverse youth.

During the summer of 2017, my father, at almost 90 years old, had a second stroke. I recognized the need to have greater flexibility to be available to respond to his changing health condition. I knew that it would be difficult to travel to Memphis at a moment's notice if I were working full-time. I had greater flexibility to travel on short notice than my siblings (Joe, in Princeton, New Jersey, and Chris, in Baltimore, Maryland.) After considering these critical issues, I retired from YouthCARE on December 31, 2017, in order to spend time with family, especially my ailing father, who lived in Memphis.

Health Challenges – The Patience of Job

"And the Lord said unto Satan, Hast thou considered my servant Job, that there is none like him in the earth, a perfect and an upright man, one that feareth God, and escheweth evil?" Job 1:8 (King James Version)

THE BOOK OF JOB describes how the angels came to present themselves before the Lord, and Satan was in their midst. The Lord asked Satan where he had been. Satan replied that he had been scouring the earth looking for someone to devour. The Lord asked Satan if he had considered his servant Job a good man. Satan told God that Job was good only because He had blessed him.

The Bible says the Lord gave Satan permission to strip Job of his material possessions (property and livestock), and even his servants and his children, but not to lay a hand on his person. After losing everything, Job refused to curse God and die as his wife admonished him. Instead, Job praised the Lord: "Naked I came from my mother's womb, and naked I will depart. The Lord gave and the Lord has taken away; may the name of the Lord be praised." (Job 1:21)

Well, I'm no Job; however, there have been times in my life `when I have felt the Lord had allowed Satan to test my faith. My wife's lapse into a chronic vegetative state following surgery and subsequent death and a number of serious medical conditions that befell me—obstructive sleep apnea, pericarditis, pituitary tumors, and bilateral renal cell carcinoma—unexpectedly and fervently tested my faith. There were times when I didn't see how I would survive. Through it all, however, I remained faithful and praised the Lord for His love and gave testimony to His amazing grace. I know now that without testing, there can be no testimony. I cannot fully understand God's will, but I trust His wisdom.

SLEEP APNEA – NOT JUST SNORING

I snored incessantly as a young man, which wasn't a problem at home in my own bedroom; however, when I got a job and attended conferences with overnight lodging, my snoring became problematic. In fact, colleagues unlucky enough to be assigned as my roommates would often relocate to other rooms before the next morning. I even won a "snoring award" at the 1981 *YMCA* of Greater St. Louis' staff retreat. This was a dubious honor that I didn't relish and one that I was not proud to receive.

A year later, I was dating a nurse who told me I had stopped breathing during the night and that she had pounded on my chest, performing CPR while I slept. Much to my dismay, I had no knowledge of this. Due to my condition, I could never get a full night of uninterrupted sleep. The situation was so bad that I was taking the over-the-counter medication, *No-Doz*, at the end of the workday in order not to fall asleep during my 30-minute drive home. I was also falling asleep in meetings. Needless to say, the situation was inconvenient, embarrassing, and extremely dangerous. Exhausted, I finally sought medical attention, and my doctor ordered a sleep study.

I reported to the sleep center at Barnes Hospital in St. Louis. After being hooked up to a web of wires and electrodes, I said to the technician, "I guess I can't get to sleep." She looked at me and said, "Mr. Dean, you've been asleep for 10 minutes." I realized then how serious my condition really was. I was falling asleep in meetings and while driving and often didn't even realize it.

I was diagnosed with obstructive sleep apnea, a condition where one stops breathing and awakens hundreds of times during the night. Sleep apnea is prevalent among overweight men. I was alarmed to learn that this condition, characterized by loud snoring, places a dangerous burden on one's heart and other systems. It also deprives sufferers of attaining restful sleep, no matter how long they are in bed. The fact that I could not achieve restful sleep was disheartening.

A sleep specialist prescribed a continuous positive airway pressure (CPAP) machine that keeps my airway open and allows me to achieve restful, restorative sleep.

Sleep apnea is a serious medical condition. According to the *Mayo Clinic*, "Complications from sleep apnea can include: daytime fatigue, difficulty concentrating, feeling quick-tempered, moody or depressed, increased blood pressure and strain on the cardiovascular system, increased risk of recurrent heart attack, stroke, and abnormal heartbeats, such as atrial fibrillation, type 2 diabetes, liver problems and more." The discovery by my nurse friend and the subsequent diagnosis and treatment for my sleep apnea likely added years to and maybe saved my life. Again, God was watching over me.

Pericarditis – Fluid Around My Heart

In 1996, I learned that my pericardium, the lining of my heart, had fluid that serendipitously appeared on a chest X-ray. I was at a Y meeting in Kansas City, Missouri, when my doctor's office contacted me on my cell phone with the alarming news. I went outside to the parking lot to take the call and preserve my privacy. However, a colleague who was arriving at the meeting came over and asked if I was alright because I looked like I had lost my best friend. If only he knew that I was shaken by the news and I didn't know the severity of the diagnosis. "Was the fluid life-threatening?" "Was my heart function compromised because of the fluid?" "What would be my prognosis?"

I underwent a biopsy after a few weeks—which felt like an eternity—that revealed that the fluid was benign. The fluid was drained and has not reappeared. Needless to say, this was a frightening experience. I credit my "faith, family, and friends" with helping me endure the anxiety created by this situation.

Chronic Vegetative State – Till Death Do Us Part

It was December 30, 1998, a day not unlike any other day in my Bloomington, Minnesota household. That all changed when I received a call informing me that my wife, Pam, was in the emergency room of a nearby hospital with excessive bleeding from fibroid cysts. The emergency room doctor, who happened to be our family physician, was doing his ER rotation. He concurred with a specialist's recommendation, "Pam needed a hysterectomy as soon as possible to stop the hemorrhaging." She was admitted to the hospital, and we prepared for surgery the next day. I arranged for our sons, 12-year-old Matt and 16-year-old Jarrod, to spend the night with their respective friends' families, thinking it would be for a day or two. Looking back, I never imagined that our kids would never be able to speak with their mother again.

Willie Dean

On the day of Pam's surgery, December 31, 1998—New Year's Eve—the hospital administrative staff told us that they needed signatures on some insurance forms before her procedure. Since Pam was being prepped for surgery, we decided that I would go and sign the documents. I held her hand and left her side to sign the forms. Little did I know that, like my sons, I would never be able to speak with my wife again.

The surgery went well, and after several hours the surgeon greeted me in the waiting room to share the positive results. I immediately phoned Pam's sisters and mother in St. Louis, Missouri to share the good news. An hour or so later, the surgeon reappeared in the waiting room. This time his face was gaunt, and his manner was somber. As he guided me to a private area, he said there had been a problem in recovery. Pam had experienced respiratory distress, and they had difficulty re-intubating her. She had been without oxygen for a period of time and had experienced oxygen deprivation to her brain. She had been moved to the Intensive Care Unit (ICU) and was being monitored.

In disbelief and in near shock, I called Pam's family again and shared this latest development, not wanting to alarm them and not fully appreciating how dire the situation was myself. The next day Pam's two sisters from St. Louis arrived at the hospital, and we maintained a prayerful vigil in the ICU waiting area.

The doctors determined that Pam had suffered hypoxia—the absence of sufficient oxygen in the tissues to sustain bodily functions—to her brain. It was not immediately known what damage had occurred. I prayed and asked God to heal Pam's body and to bring her back to me whole. Later, the doctors met with us to share their grim prognosis. Pam had experienced oxygen deprivation to her brain for a period of time sufficient to result in brain damage. While there was activity in Pam's brain stem, there was evidence of extensive damage. She was deemed to be in a chronic vegetative state from which she was not expected to recover. We were told that medical science knows little about the brain's ability to recover from injury. We prayed and held out hope for a miracle.

This news hit me like a ton of bricks. I asked myself, "How could this happen to my wife of 13 years?" "A beautiful young woman who was so full of life?" "How could the mother of my children not be coming home to care for them ever again?" I continued to pray for Pam's recovery. While on a break in the hospital cafeteria, a nurse who had been in the operating room came over to me and said, "I'm sorry. Something went terribly wrong." I thanked her for her consolation and continued to eat and pray.

My dad flew up from Memphis to help and give comfort at the hospital and to assist with my children. He and my sisters-in-law relieved me at the hospital while we maintained a 24-hour vigil in the waiting room. Friends from the Twin Cities, Bill and Karen Wells and Rich Schoffelman, visited and offered their support. My friend, and Y colleague from Omaha, Louie Warren, flew up to be with me during the most trying and painful time of my life.

After several days in the ICU, the doctors informed us that Pam had minimal brain activity and that it was unlikely she would recover from her injury. That night, my sister-in-law and I sat down at my home with Matt and Jarrod and shared their mother's prognosis. As delicately as I could, I explained that their mother had suffered an accident following surgery that left her with a brain injury from which she was not expected to recover. This was the most difficult conversation of my life, to tell my sons that their mother would never be coming home again.

Both their countenances were of disbelief. I can still feel the weight of Matt's limp body draped over my knee as he wept in sorrow. Although Jarrod said nothing, I could see both sadness and anger in his eyes. Little did I know that this tragedy would haunt our family for years to come, causing pain and requiring many hours of family and individual therapy. I know now that time does not heal all wounds, for even after more than 20 years, the pain of this tragedy still affects our family in subtle and sometimes unexpected ways.

Eventually, the doctors decided they could do no more for Pam, and a plan was devised to transport her to a long-term care facility. I chose the *Masonic Home* in Bloomington, Minnesota, just a few miles from our home.

The facility, while clean and orderly, was depressing upon entry. I couldn't help but think that Pam would never be able to leave. She would likely spend the rest of her life bedridden and unable to communicate. While the staff was cordial and professional, almost all of the residents were elderly Whites. I never felt uncomfortable having my wife as a resident or when visiting myself.

Matt and Jarrod visited the Masonic Home only once together. Jarrod would visit on his own after he got his driver's license; however, Matt couldn't bear to see his mother in her condition. Matt later expressed guilt for not being able to visit her. I assured him that his mother would understand how difficult it was for him and that she would always love him.

I visited Pam daily, sometimes twice daily. Often, I would ride my bicycle the three miles from our home to the Masonic Home. Other times I would drive and bring my acoustic guitar to sing to her. I was always hopeful that the music and my voice would provide some comfort to her and maybe even help her to recover. The *Masonic Home* staff told me they enjoyed hearing my singing up and down the hallway. Although Pam's eyes were often open, there was no indication she could see or hear what was being said. However, we were always positive in her presence and stepped into the hallway to discuss anything that might have been perceived to be negative.

Pam had many visitors, including her former colleagues from Hamline University and Bloomington Public Schools, sorority sisters from Alpha Kappa Alpha Sorority, Inc., friends, and neighbors. Our choir from St. Peter's AME Church in Minneapolis also visited and sang to her.

We received cards and letters from family and friends from across the country and from around the world. On Easter Sunday, I read Pam an email from colleagues at the Jerusalem International *YMCA* wherein a colleague said he had prayed for Pam at the Wailing Wall, the place where Jesus had stood. At that moment, I thought I saw Pam respond upon hearing the name "Jesus." It might have been just an involuntary twitch; however, I believe it was an embodiment of the Holy Spirit sent to comfort me.

Pam had suffered oxygen deprivation following her surgery, and it became apparent that she would never regain consciousness. I prayed for her recovery; however, it wasn't to be. I cared for my 12-year-old and 16-year-old sons during this difficult period in our lives. Prayers and gestures of love and support continued to pour in from family and friends. Neighbors brought over home-cooked meals and cleaned our home weekly for nearly a year. This tragedy helped me to understand what it means to have strong faith, a caring family, and true friends.

Here is an excerpt from a letter that I sent to our friends on April 8, 1999, to update them on our situation and to ask for their prayers:

> *Dear Friends:*
>
> *The past three months have been the most challenging period of my life. As you may know, my wife, Pam, my soul mate, has been in a coma since December 31. Pam underwent a hysterectomy and suffered oxygen deprivation following surgery. The doctors don't expect her condition to improve. I continue, however, to pray for a miracle.*
>
> *When I visit Pam, I try to stimulate her senses. The research I've read on coma recovery suggests that we only use a small part of our brain's capacity and that following injury, the brain may have the ability to regenerate itself. It may also be able to "reroute" information around damaged areas. I spray my*

cologne on my wrist and tell Pam that when she smells this scent, I'm with her. I pray, sing, massage, and encourage her each time I'm with her.

Pam was wearing a pulse oximeter when I visited her recently. When I walked into her room, I noticed that her pulse quickened. This was the second time this has happened. Later, I prayed with Pam and shared a fax from a colleague at the Jerusalem International YMCA. In the fax, my colleague said that he and his family had gone to the Church of the Holy Sepulcher to light a candle for Pam. They also said a prayer for Pam and my family at the grave of Jesus. When I said this, Pam's pulse quickened even more!

Our sons, Matt (12) and Jarrod (16), and I have been going to grief counseling to help us cope with our loss. We are doing reasonably well under the circumstances. We have wonderful support from our family, friends, and neighbors! Our 25-year-old son, Cedric, who lives in Memphis, is seeking a job transfer to the Twin Cities. If this works out, he will live with us and help serve as a surrogate parent.

I am planning a tribute to celebrate Pam's life and legacy to us all on Saturday, July 31, 1999. The tribute will be held in the Twin Cities...

Pam is in the Masonic Home in Bloomington, about 10 minutes from our home... Feel free to visit, read a favorite book, sing a song, or pray with Pam as often as you like.

Whatever happens, I know that Pam is in God's hands. She told me just a few weeks before her surgery that she is a child of God. I know that Jesus is looking after us. Thank you for your support of our family. We appreciate your love and generosity.

Sincerely,
Willie Dean

My employer, the *YMCA* of the USA, was very supportive during my family's crisis. They allowed me to care for my family, taking several months off without having to use vacation or sick time. When I returned to work, I was able to work from my Minneapolis office rather than having to fly one to two times a week as I had done prior to Pam's accident.

On occasions when I had to travel, I would fly my dad up from Memphis. We joked that he was one of the most-traveled babysitters in the country. While he was in town, I would outline a "to-do list" for him to tackle. On one occasion, he built shelves in our garage in a couple of days, a job that I thought would take him a week. The bonding between my dad and my sons during these visits was important and connected them to their grandfather in a nurturing way.

Cedric, my oldest son, was living in Memphis, Tennessee, after his discharge from the U.S. Navy. He had started his career in the information technology industry, had bought a car, and was renting an apartment. When he learned of Pam's accident, he offered to relocate to Minnesota to support our family. I told him I didn't want him to disrupt his life; however, he said, "That's the way you and Mom raised us." In a few weeks, Cedric quit his job, canceled his apartment lease, rented a *U-Haul* truck, and drove more than 800 miles, almost nonstop, from Memphis with his car in tow. He found a job fairly quickly and began to settle into his new life in Minnesota. Cedric's sacrifice was much appreciated. There were some bumps and bruises having a sibling serving as a surrogate parent; however, we survived them.

During this difficult period, my job was eliminated when the *YMCA* of the USA reorganized its national service delivery system. The *YMCA* was very accommodating and leaned over backward to support my family and me. However, I realized I couldn't continue to perform a job that required extensive travel. I took a severance package and left my job as National Field Executive for the Mid-America Field, one of only four such positions nationwide. Again, I was sustained by my "faith, family, and friends" during a very trying and unpredictable time.

In order to strengthen my reemployment possibilities and continue my education, I enrolled in the Ph.D. program in recreation administration at the University of Minnesota, from which I graduated in May 2003. In June of that same year, I received a first-degree black belt in Tae Kwon Do after studying the martial art for more than ten years. I found the academic rigor of my doctoral studies and the physical and mental demands of learning a martial art to be therapeutic as I dealt with my grief and the stresses of being a single parent once again.

In time my prayers changed from asking God to return Pam to me whole to asking Him to "let His will be done." I also asked God to give me the strength and fortitude to accept His will and overcome any challenges that lay ahead. When I thought it apparent that Pam's condition was not going to change, I prayed for guidance. With a heavy heart, I decided to remove Pam from life support. I made that difficult decision after she had languished in a chronic vegetative state for more than three years. This decision was one I prayed a lot about and discussed with my family and friends.

Overcoming

I had lots of questions about how to ensure compassionate treatment during the removal of Pam's life support. The nursing staff assured me they would keep her mouth and tongue moist and that pain medications would be administered as needed. There was no way to predict how long she would live once life support was removed; however, I was intent on being with her as often as I could. I spent hours on end at her bedside talking, singing, and reading the Bible to her. Then one morning, when I arrived, the staff said, "She's gone." I approached her bed, placed a kiss on her forehead, and said a prayer—just as I had done with my mother three years earlier. I asked God to receive her soul into His care and thanked Him for the opportunity to have had her in our lives.

I had Pam's body returned to St. Louis for her funeral and burial. Family and friends from the St. Louis area, my father and brother, Bug, drove up from Memphis, and a *YMCA* of the USA colleague, Carmelita Gallo, attended from Chicago, Illinois. Matt, who then was 14, became distraught and laid his head on my shoulder. His nose began to bleed, and we left the service so I could tend to him in the restroom. Carmelita took my suitcoat to clean the bloodstain, a caring gesture that meant a lot to me.

Our lives were hollow after Pam's death. My sons felt a pain that could not be soothed. Although I sought grief counseling for my sons and myself, we never really filled the void. The kindness and support of friends, neighbors, and church members were very much appreciated. However, no one and nothing could fill the hole that was left in our hearts and in our lives.

My colleague and friend, Rich Schoffelman, came over one afternoon to help me clean out my basement. I remember going through the motions as we discarded items that I no longer needed but, over the years, had accumulated. Later, I tackled one of the most difficult tasks, cleaning out Pam's walk-in closet. This was the most personal thing I had done involving her since her accident. It seemed I was discarding a part of her and, therefore, a part of me. The act of giving away her possessions evoked the pain of seeing her casket lowered into the ground following her funeral...she was gone.

In time I recognized the need to move on with my life; however, I was nervous about dating and bringing another woman around my sons. Eventually, I reached out to friends and was set up on a blind date. I was very particular about who I brought around my sons. While I didn't seek their approval, I did want their respect.

Willie Dean

Rathke's Cleft Cyst – First Brain Surgery

In March 2007, while living in Cleveland, Ohio, I experienced double vision. My physician ordered an MRI, which revealed a pituitary mass, a brain tumor. Although the tumor was believed to be benign, I was devastated. I had just a year earlier had a colleague in the Twin Cities who succumbed to a malignant brain tumor. I couldn't help but wonder, "Was I to have a similar fate?"

I looked for a neurosurgeon and discovered that some of the best in the world were at the *Cleveland Clinic*, less than five miles from my home. However, I could not find a surgeon there who could schedule an evaluation and surgery without significant delay. To complicate matters, I had just been laid off from my position as Senior Vice President/COO for the *YMCA* of Greater Cleveland—a victim of the slowing local and national economies—and I was in the process of looking for a new job. I had recently interviewed with the *YMCA* of Arlington, Texas, and had been offered the position of President/CEO.

Just when things were going right again, my world ground to a halt. I had a job offer to become a Y CEO again; however, my surgery and recovery might prevent me from reporting to the job on time. The Lord, as always, made a way. I called the chairman of the board, Terry Gaines, and asked if I could report to Arlington in six weeks, rather than the customary four weeks, because I needed to have some "minor" surgery. My request was granted, and I scheduled my surgery. I prayed that the mass wouldn't be malignant and that my surgery and recovery wouldn't jeopardize my ability to start my new job. I located a surgeon at *MetroHealth Medical Center*, the public hospital in Cleveland, who could see me right away.

In April 2007, I had brain surgery at *MetroHealth Medical Center*. My neurosurgeon removed most of a pituitary mass called a Rathke's Cleft Cyst that was benign. "God is good." During my time in Ohio, I would be fortunate to fall in love and get engaged. My fiancé and my father took care of me during my brief recovery. My father stayed with me at my townhouse after I was released from the hospital. When he had to return home to Memphis, I checked into an Extended Stay America hotel in Akron, Ohio, near where my fiancé lived, so she could care for me.

One afternoon after my fiance got off work and checked on me, we discovered my nose was bleeding profusely. Unsure if this was an emergency, we called my surgeon and were advised to go to the nearest emergency room. When we arrived at the ER at *Akron General Hospital*, the doctors there were reluctant to treat me as my surgery had been done at the *MetroHealth Medical Center* in Cleveland. They advised that we should drive the 45-mile trip to

Cleveland to be treated at MetroHealth. With fear and trepidation, we set out on the drive to Cleveland, not knowing whether the blood was seminal fluid leaking from my brain. In hindsight, we should have demanded to be treated or to be transported by ambulance or helicopter.

When we got to the *MetroHealth Medical Center* in Cleveland, the doctors there were able to stem the hemorrhaging. We drove back to Akron that night, albeit the worse for wear following this harrowing experience. To God be the glory.

My recovery took only six weeks, and I relocated to Texas, started my new job on June 1, and got married on June 23. My wife and I commuted between our homes in Mansfield, Texas, and Akron, Ohio, about one weekend a month for the next two and a half years. The distance didn't make it an ideal situation; however, we both had careers in different regions of the country. We hoped that, in time, we would be able to live together in one home.

I have had subsequent MRI imaging for the past 13 years to monitor any reoccurrence or growth of the vestiges of the mass. (I had a second surgery to remove a benign cyst from my pituitary gland in April 2022 in Memphis. More on this later.) The Lord is good!

Bilateral Renal Cell Carcinoma – Kidney Cancer!

In December 2008, while investigating whether the pain that I was experiencing in my upper abdomen was related to a previously diagnosed diastasis rectus—a tear of my abdominal muscles—an alarming discovery was made. An MRI ordered by my primary care physician did not show a diastasis; however, it showed that I had lesions—potentially malignant tumors—on both my kidneys. I was referred to Dr. David Rittenhouse, a urologist in Fort Worth, Texas, who practiced near where I lived in Mansfield. I shared the frightening news with my wife by phone, as she was living in Akron, Ohio at the time.

I also shared the grim news with my father, who, along with my wife, encouraged me to attend Watchnight Service at my church that night. Obediently, though reluctantly, I went to the service on December 31, 2008, at Bethlehem Baptist Church, in Mansfield, Texas, even though I didn't feel up to it at all. The ceremony opened with prayer, singing, and reading of the scripture. I felt forlorn and inspired at the same time. My faith has always been the foundation of my life, and the present challenge was no exception.

Willie Dean

I joined Bethlehem Baptist Church shortly after relocating to Texas in June 2007. I felt the warmth and love from my pastor, the Reverend Dr. Michael A. Evans, Sr., our senior pastor, and from the many members whom I had gotten to know. Pastor Evans had even invited me to give the keynote address at our church's Martin Luther King Celebration earlier that year.

During the Watchnight Service, Pastor Evans asked individuals who had received a bad medical report from their doctor and those with testimonies to stand together. I nervously but obediently rose to my feet. Members and guests whose prayers had been answered were asked to go and stand with someone who was facing a new challenge. Nervously, I continued to stand.

At that moment, Warren Davis, a member with whom I had briefly spoken with in the past, came over and took my hands, and we sat together. I shared my diagnosis with him. He then shared that a year ago, he had been diagnosed with stage III lung cancer, and thanks to God, he was in remission. Although the cancer was back, he said he was blessed. I cried. We had breakfast together a few weeks later, and Warren became an important part of my support system. Once again, God was busy in my life, bringing me comfort and support through my "faith, family, and friends." Warren's courage was palpable. His unmistakable faith helped me to renew my own.

Warren and I bonded and became friends. He invited me to his home to share meals with his family. Having the friendship of a Christian man who also was dealing with cancer was therapeutic for me. We shared similar values, and we both recognized the importance of faith, family, and friends in our lives.

Dr. Rittenhouse ordered a biopsy of my left kidney, which was scheduled when my wife was in town in January. I nervously spent the holidays not knowing the nature of the lesions or my fate. A few weeks later, when the results were available, my urologist's office phoned and informed me the tumor was malignant. I phoned my wife in Ohio and drove to my urologist's office alone, not knowing what lay ahead or my chances for survival. The 20-minute trip was the longest drive of my life. With my wife on speakerphone, Dr. Rittenhouse confirmed that I had bilateral renal cell carcinoma—malignant tumors on both my kidneys.

I didn't want to hear the diagnosis—bilateral renal cell carcinoma—cancer on both kidneys. I was devastated. I thought that my cancer was a death sentence and that my life was over. Dr. Rittenhouse said that my prognosis was good and that surgery was the recommended protocol for treating kidney cancer.

While I had prayed that the lesions would be benign, I also asked the Lord to let His will be done. The moment that I learned I had cancer, I felt afraid, angry, and hopeful, all at the same time. I was afraid, not knowing whether the cancer diagnosis was a death sentence. I was angry that my life—although a good one—already had been filled with many trials and tribulations. (Was God testing my faithfulness like he allowed Satan to do with Job? I felt cheated that time with my wife of fewer than 18 months was being cut short.) Yet, I was hopeful as I knew that God has dominion over all things. I prayed for guidance and strength.

I phoned my wife after returning home from Dr. Rittenhouse's office. She had already begun research on the Internet and was trying to understand the battle in which we were about to engage.

After further tests, I received some good news. A bone scan, chest CT and head CT revealed that the cancer was confined to my kidneys and had not metastasized to other parts of my body. Praise the Lord!

Dr. Rittenhouse suggested I seek treatment at a top cancer hospital. He wanted to refer me to specialists at the *M.D. Anderson Cancer Center* in Houston, Texas, to attempt renal sparing—removal of the tumors and salvage of my kidneys. I liked this strategy; however, I was concerned about having surgery in Houston, where I wouldn't have the benefit of the support system afforded by my church and friends in the Dallas/Fort Worth area. Dr. Rittenhouse then suggested the *Mayo Clinic* in Rochester, Minnesota, only 75-five miles from the Twin Cities, where two of my sons and their families lived. I thought about these alternatives. Then I asked Dr. Rittenhouse about the Cleveland Clinic in Cleveland, Ohio. He said the Cleveland Clinic was among the best hospitals in the world, and it would be an excellent choice.

I had lived in Cleveland previously and was aware of the world-class reputation of the Cleveland Clinic; however, the fact that my wife lived just 45 miles away in Akron, Ohio, made it an easy choice. I had no family in Texas; thus, surgery in Cleveland would make my recovery after surgery a lot easier. However, when we contacted the Cleveland Clinic, we discovered there would be a significant wait before I could be seen by one of their urologists. I knew I had to find a way to overcome this long wait.

The *Cleveland Clinic* was the obvious choice; however, after we learned there would be a significant wait—perhaps months before I could get an appointment to be seen—it was problematic. Also, the process would involve flying to Cleveland for an office visit and tests, flying home, and later returning to Cleveland for the surgery. I was worried that I didn't have the time for such an elongated process. Time was of the essence.

Then, as if God had sent a personal message, I remembered I had known Dr. Charles S. Modlin—a Black urologist and nationally renowned kidney transplant surgeon at the Cleveland Clinic—from when we both were members of 100 Black Men of Cleveland. Dr. Modlin had also been my urologist when I lived in Cleveland. I emailed Dr. Modlin, asked if he remembered me, and shared my diagnosis. Dr. Modlin wrote back the same day and said, "Yes, I remember you, Willie. Call my office next week and make an appointment for as soon as possible." The Lord works in mysterious ways!

I shared my diagnosis with other family members. My sons, Matt and Jarrod, offered to give me a kidney if I needed one. My sister, Chris, who is a devout Christian, told me (just as she did with my previous brain surgery), "We're going to give this to God and claim the victory!" I, too, am a devout Christian; however, I was fearful as to what might happen. I believed that God could heal me, but I wasn't sure that He would. "Was healing me going to be God's will?" "Could Dr. Modlin excise the cancerous tumors and save my kidneys?" "What if I lost one or both kidneys?" "Would dialysis be an option?" "Would I be a candidate for a transplant?" I was moved by the words of "Leave It There," a hymn by Charles A. Tindley: "...take your burden to the Lord and leave it there." I prayed and tried to leave my burden with God.

I shared my diagnosis and my need for surgery with my *YMCA* board and staff, neighbors, and church friends. I also shared that I would be away for three to four weeks. My board of directors, chaired by Terry Gaines, was very supportive. Bill Bowie, one of my board members, volunteered to drive me to the airport on the day I left Texas for my surgery in Ohio. My next-door neighbors had agreed to watch my house and water my plants. As much as I had faith in God, as I locked up my house, I couldn't help but think that it might be the last time I set foot inside it. As much as I tried not to, I began to doubt God's power. I arrived in Akron, and my wife picked me up at the airport.

I met with Dr. Modlin, nationally renowned and at the time one of only 15 African American kidney transplant surgeons in the United States, in his office for my pre-op visit on February 25, 2009. He had read the clinical notes and reviewed the images sent by Dr. Rittenhouse and others that had been ordered through the radiology department at the *Cleveland Clinic* after my arrival. Dr. Modlin had his office schedule additional tests and surgery. I was able to have my surgery in three weeks, not months. "God is good."

I went to surgery on March 2 at 6 a.m. A local pastor and my wife accompanied me to the hospital. The nursing staff wheeled me to the operating room. Dr. Modlin performed a left open partial nephrectomy to remove a malignant tumor from my left kidney. The surgery went well, and I was taken to the intensive care unit and then to a patient room.

I awakened in my hospital room to a sea of white coats. Someone was frantically asking, "Mr. Dean, can you hear me?" Someone else said, "Mr. Dean, squeeze my hand!" Yet another person exclaimed, "I can't get his blood pressure!" It felt like my head was sinking into my pillow. I sensed that something had gone horribly wrong and that I was in mortal danger. It became apparent to me that something was dangerously wrong. I later learned I had suffered a drop in blood pressure which sent me back to ICU. Over what seemed like hours, the medical team tried numerous strategies to raise my blood pressure.

The doctors thought that I was bleeding internally and feared I might bleed out. I heard someone say, "He looks as white as a ghost!" Someone else said that my epidural could have caused a drop in my blood pressure. Another said I had a low platelet count and that I was anemic and in need of a blood transfusion. I heard another person say that they were calling my surgeon back in to perform emergency surgery to stop the hemorrhaging. They prepared to take me back to the OR.

I could hear the doctors discussing what needed to be done. At one point, they prepped me for surgery to run a coil from my groin up to my heart and down to my kidney in an attempt to cauterize "leakers," areas of internal bleeding, in order to stem the hemorrhaging.

I was moved to the operating room prep area. The medical team asked my wife if she wanted to leave the room; however, she wanted to stay to see and hear everything that was going on herself. My wife, exemplifying her wedding vows, "In sickness and in health…," stood steadfast by my side throughout my life-threatening ordeal.

As the medical team was prepping me for surgery, I made my peace with God while holding my wife's hand. I asked the Lord to heal me and, more importantly, to let His will be done. I thanked the Lord for all He had done for me and for the things He had allowed me to accomplish in my life. I asked Him for humility. I repented and asked Him to forgive my sins. I acknowledged Jesus Christ as my Lord and Savior and asked Him to accept my soul. And I asked God to take care of my wife and children.

Every time I started praying, the technicians, who were prepping me for surgery, would stop their work. Finally, my wife said to them, "You're gonna have to keep working because he's not going to stop praying!"

The medical team had summoned Dr. Modlin in the event an emergency surgery would be necessary. In what I believe was the early morning hours. As I was being prepped for surgery, I heard a voice say, "Everything is going to be alright." I later told my wife that I didn't recognize the voice. I didn't know if it was Dr. Modlin's voice or the voice of God. Either way, I believe it was the Holy Spirit that was sent to comfort me!

Radiology images didn't reveal significant bleeding, and the doctors decided not to perform the emergency surgery. Instead, they gave me a blood transfusion and continued to monitor me closely. Why there appeared to be active bleeding from my blood pressure drop and no leakers seen on the CT imaging later was a mystery. Or was it a miracle?

I was moved the next day to a patient room where my roommate, a pastor of a Presbyterian Church in Erie, Pennsylvania, and I enjoyed talking about our surgical experiences and how our faith had brought us through. My recovery progressed well, and as with any major surgery, my first bowel movement was cause for celebration. My roommate and I laughed when we were able to break wind. Becoming ambulatory was also an important goal; however, a nursing assistant lightheartedly told my wife that I flashed the whole nursing staff when I took walks around the floor with my gown open behind.

The next day, I awakened in my room to the appearance of Terry Gaines, then-Chair of the Board of the Arlington *YMCA*. While on a business trip to Pittsburgh, Pennsylvania, Terry had rented a car and driven more than 130 miles to Cleveland to surprise me and deliver an oversized get-well card from volunteers and staff at our *YMCA* back in Texas. Terry's visit took me by surprise. I was elated that our friendship was so strong that he wanted to show his support for me in such a dramatic way. He told me later that he had been practically giddy the week before his surprise visit. The fact that he went out of his way to visit me meant the world to me. I cherish the support of friends like Terry in my life. God is good...all the time!

Thanks to God's grace, I was discharged after four days in the hospital and then recuperated over the next four weeks at our home in Akron. Thanks to my wife and her mother, I received tender loving care and was soon on the mend. I received lunch daily from the local *Meals on Wheels* program. When I was able to move about, I carefully descended the steps once daily to have lunch in the kitchen and then retreated to my bedroom upstairs. I spent a lot of time looking out the bedroom windows into the wooded area in our backyard. Seeing the trees and an occasional deer was cathartic; it helped me experience nature and enjoy my love of the outdoors, even though I couldn't easily go outside.

I had excruciating pain when walking or riding in a car. The rides to check-up appointments were nearly unbearable, as the slightest lateral movement during my recuperation caused excruciating pain to the area around the surgical incision near my left kidney. However, as the healing progressed, the pain subsided, and I was given clearance to return home to Texas.

My wife and I flew together back to DFW and took a taxi to our home in Mansfield. I was welcomed by my neighbors, staff, and volunteers at the Y when I returned to the office and by members of my church when we went to Sunday service. Contrary to my fears of just weeks earlier, I survived surgery and returned to my home. I was back in the office just one month following major surgery. Thanks be to God!

My healing continued, and in less than three months, I flew back to Ohio for my second surgery. On May 11, 2009, I underwent a right open partial nephrectomy at the *Cleveland Clinic*. Dr. Modlin removed a tumor and saved my right kidney! Unlike my first surgery, I had minimal pain and swelling and no unusual bleeding. Dr. Modlin said he did not find a one-centimeter spot on my left kidney that seemed to appear on CT imaging previously and that they would monitor my recovery from Ohio.

The pastor, who was my roommate from my first surgery, visited me at the hospital. My pastor, the Reverend Dr. Michael A. Evans, Sr., and the Reverend Leonard Hornsby, Executive Pastor of Bethlehem Baptist Church, phoned to check on me. I felt the love and grace of God all around me. I was elated to receive comfort from these men of God.

I was discharged from the hospital after four days following my second surgery. Dr. Modlin said, "Fifteen years ago, a person with a diagnosis of bilateral renal cell carcinoma would have had their kidneys removed and ended up on dialysis. We were able to remove the tumors, and Dr. Dean now has two healthy kidneys." I recuperated in Akron and returned to Texas and to work in a month.

I undergo blood work and CT scans every six months to monitor my kidneys and determine whether the tumors have returned. By the grace of God, I have been cancer-free for more than 13 years.

When I first learned I had cancer, I asked, "Lord, why me?" After experiencing God's awesome healing power, I asked, "Lord, why not me?" I serve an awesome God, a God that is capable of doing all things, and I am privileged to bear witness to His power and grace. I credit Dr. Modlin, an instrument of God, for literally saving my life. Dr. Modlin said of my witness: "This is a very powerful and important testimonial that will surely help others when they read it. I am moved, and I am in awe to have been a part of your journey. There must have been a reason that you and I met each other several years ago. Often, we doctors take care of patients and operate on patients without having the opportunity to learn about their personal experiences facing them. I thank you for sharing your story with me, and I am proud that you chose to come to me to participate in your care."

Perhaps Pastor Evans said it best, "My brother, we are calling out your name daily. Your church family is interceding on your behalf, and we believe in God for healing."

I'm convinced that my surgeries, support, and recoveries would not have happened as quickly or as smoothly without the influence of my "faith, family, and friends." God, the ultimate healer, made it possible; my wife and her family cared for me during my recovery, and my friend, Dr. Modlin, allowed the Lord to use his hands as instruments of His healing power.

Dr. Modlin not only saved my kidneys—thanks be to God—he saved my life!

Pituitary Adenoma – Second Brain Surgery

Since my pituitary surgery in 2007, I have been monitored by a neurosurgeon in every city where I have lived to ensure that the tumor I had earlier has not returned. In early 2021, it was determined that a mass that was visible on my MRIs had enlarged to the point that it was problematic. It was believed that I had a benign pituitary adenoma. I had a second pituitary surgery in April 2021. My wife, Carol, accompanied me to the hospital on the morning of my surgery. Her and my prayers and the prayers of family, friends, high school alumni, and church members from Memphis and Minneapolis were lifted in mass. Our prayers were answered. The surgery went well, the tumor was found to be benign, and my neurosurgeon felt he was able to remove it all...the Lord is good!

The Lord has carried my family and me through numerous health challenges. Each night before retiring, Carol and I pray for our children, our grandchildren, our siblings, and our extended family. We also pray for the health and safety of our friends, our church, our city, our state, our nation, and our world.

BEING BLACK IN AMERICA

"Say it loud. I'm Black and I'm proud!" James Brown, Singer, Songwriter, Bandleader, 1968

BLACK LIVES MATTER—A MOVEMENT and a mantra that vocalizes the need to recognize the value of Black lives—is not a new concept. "Say it loud. I'm Black and I'm proud," lyrics and title to a song popularized in 1968 by soul singer, James Brown, became an anthem for Black people in America who saw a need to shore up Black pride in the face of racism and segregation. I was a 17-year-old high school junior when this song debuted. The song's uplifting message is as salient today as it was then—for Blacks in this country face a resurgence of racism and hate. Being Black in America comes with a hefty toll on Black children, teenagers, adults, and families. They are often treated quite differently and more harshly than their White peers. The disparities are especially troublesome for Black males, as they are often feared and demonized as dangerous, lazy, untrustworthy, and incorrigible.

For more than 400 years, Blacks in America have been mistreated, dehumanized, and undervalued. Since 1619, when enslaved Africans were first delivered to Virginia in shackles and sold for supplies, people of African heritage in this country have suffered oppression and struggled to overcome racism, segregation, discrimination, and other atrocities.

I've worked hard all my life—in grade school, college, and professionally—and I have often felt that I had to perform at a higher level in order to be considered equal to my White peers. Likewise, I felt like I was stereotyped and relegated to working only in Black communities. But it wasn't until I was in my 50s that I began to realize the full impact of prejudice and racism on my country, my community, my family, and myself.

Whites are often clueless about the plight of Black Americans unless egregious racist behavior is displayed before them on national television, like the brutal police beatings of John Lewis and others on the Edmund Pettus Bridge in Selma, Alabama, in 1965; the execution of George Floyd by a police officer in Minneapolis, Minnesota in 2020; or the murder of Ahmaud Arbery by White vigilantes outside Brunswick, Georgia in 2021. "Why must acts of violence and racist behavior go unabated unless it is captured on videotape?" Even then, there are some Whites who attribute these kinds of brutal acts to the undertakings of "a few bad apples" rather than to systemic racism.

Comments from several respondents to a survey of a random sample of 50 Black and 200 White *YMCA* leaders, conducted as part of my dissertation research, highlight the situation faced by Blacks in America. A White male respondent from the Midwest said he was awakened to racial discrimination while driving with his Black friend, "We'll be driving around. You know, I've never been stopped when I'm by myself." When asked if by "stopped," he meant being pulled over by law enforcement, the respondent said:

Yes, "Driving while Black." But in my case, it's "Driving while [a] Black guy is with me." But when it [first] happened, I told him, "I don't think that's why we got stopped." But, by the third time, it was like, "I can't believe that this is still happening in our country."

When asked if a Black person would likely be hired to manage a *YMCA* in a service area that was predominantly White, a White male respondent from the Northeast said, "I have to answer that question speaking on the climate in [our city]. I would have to say no." When asked if there was something inherent in the organization's decision-making that might prevent it from hiring a Black executive in that scenario, the respondent said:

I think the things that exist are the external pressures, you know, to place an African American in one of our suburban sites is gonna put the suburban people a little bit ill at ease by saying, "Well, you know, they don't really know our community. They don't really belong here."

A Black male respondent from the South said he'd only gotten invitations to interview for jobs in minority communities. "I was applying at a suburban YMCA... And, it kept coming back and getting interviews... but the suburban Ys were not even bringing me to the table." When asked if racism was involved in his not being invited to interview for suburban jobs, the respondent said, "Yes. Being a young Black professional seeking to be an executive director with the suburban *YMCA*s was not in the cards. The thought process is that because you are African American, you can only supervise your [own] race."

There are numerous factors that disadvantage people of color in this country, including "White Privilege," "White Silence," "Systemic Racism," and "Homosocial Reproduction." White Privilege—a system that favors Whites, and disadvantages persons of color by devaluing or ignoring their contributions to society—affords the dominant group (Caucasians in this country)—opportunities not provided to other racial groups in numerous areas of American life. These include education, employment, housing, criminal justice, and healthcare, to name a few. White Silence, a term that has taken root recently, suggests that Whites are complicit in racism unless they actively work against it. Systemic Racism, which looks at racism on a macro level, is the result of a group of people who look down upon another group of people based on race. The concept of systemic racism refutes the notion that racist acts committed by single perpetrators are simply aberrations and the work of lone individuals. Finally, Homosocial Reproduction—a theory first postulated by *Harvard Business School* Professor Rosabeth M. Kanter to describe favoritism in employment—posits that those in power (in this case, Whites) tend to hire and promote individuals who are socially similar to themselves. This tendency puts women, Blacks, and other minorities at a disadvantage in the workplace and in our society.

I have experienced racism and hate firsthand during my three scores and 11 years. Unfortunately, neither the "Emancipation Proclamation"—issued by President Abraham Lincoln on January 1, 1863, declaring "that all persons held as slaves" within the rebellious states "are and henceforward shall be free"— nor the election of Barak Obama—our nation's first Black president, on November 4, 2008—signaled that we are living in a post-racial America.

OKLAHOMA ROAD TRIP – RACISM ON A TWO-LANE HIGHWAY

My earliest recollection of racism occurred at the age of ten, during a harrowing 1961 road trip. My family was traveling from Tennessee to visit family in Oklahoma. We often traveled by car, complete with food, water, and empty pop bottles (to use as urinals as public accommodations frequently weren't available to Blacks). When facilities were available, they often were labeled "Whites Only" or "Colored Only." (Although "separate but equal" public accommodations were illegal by this time, many White facility operators and patrons harbored animus against Black travelers.) At the time, I didn't understand what these signs and the larger issue of segregation meant for my family, me, or my country.

It was late at night, and we were driving on a lonely stretch of a dark two-lane highway when a driver sped up to prevent us from passing. I didn't understand what was happening; however, looking back, I realize now that we were in a life-and-death situation. I was seated in the passenger seat directly behind my dad, who was driving. As I looked into the face of the White man driving the other car, I was looking into the face of racial hatred and White Supremacy. (I ask myself now, "How could this man have hated us when he didn't even know us?" "Was he jealous that my father was driving a 1959 Buick Electra, a vehicle that was probably nicer than his?" "Did he think that we were uppity and out of our place; a Black family with the audacity to pass him in his America?")

Suddenly I felt my dad's seatback press against my knees as he punched the accelerator of our powder blue *Electra*. Our Buick's 325-horsepower engine and Dynaflow transmission combined to produce 445 lb.-ft. of torque that defied gravity and thrust my body into my seatback. Miraculously, we sped past the racist driver, narrowly avoiding a head-on collision with the oncoming traffic.

Normally a mild-mannered man not known for using derogatory language, Dad exclaimed, "That peckerwood (a demeaning term used to describe a White person, especially a poor one) sped up and tried to run us off the road!" But by the grace of God, our entire family could have been killed. Dad (and that big Buick) saved our lives that night; however, he never spoke of the incident to explain what had happened. Maybe in private conversations with our mother, other relatives, or friends, he was able to describe the fear he must have felt driving that night—and whenever we were traveling—or in today's vernacular, "driving while Black."

SEGREGATION – SEPARATION OF PEOPLE, HOARDING OF OPPORTUNITIES

The incident on a lonely stretch of Oklahoma highway was my first experience with racial hatred; sadly, it would not be my last. Until then, I didn't think of myself as being hated or being "Black." I didn't think that I was "White," but I believed that I lived in a world of idyllic White families that were portrayed in 1950s television shows like *Leave it to Beaver* and *Father Knows Best*. The families depicted in these shows had fathers who worked in white-collar jobs and mothers who were homemakers whose hair was never mussed. These families were loved, or at least accepted by society, and seemed to not have to worry about the adequacy of their employment, education, food, healthcare, or where they lived. The biggest challenges faced by these families related to whether Wally (the older brother of "Beaver") or one of his friends was late arriving home from school or to class. I later learned that life portrayed in these television series was in stark contrast to the reality faced by most Black families in America. I didn't know what segregation was or that it was more than the "separation of people." It was also the "hoarding of opportunities."

My father was a truck driver, and my mother was a stay-at-home mom. I assumed that all of my friends, neighbors, and classmates had stable, two-parent households, adequate housing, and food, just as we did. I did not know that my family and I lived in a segregated section of Memphis that was subject to redlining, segregation, and discrimination in employment, education, healthcare, and a host of other socioeconomic issues. In later years, Dad told me that a Jewish developer sold him and Mom a lot and built our three-bedroom, brick home, one of three new homes built on our block. Without this help, they wouldn't have been able to buy the home where they did. This was the beginning of my parents' accumulation of a modest amount of generational wealth and our family becoming part of the landed gentry.

Dad became somewhat of an entrepreneur when we moved to our new Memphis home in 1958. He rented out our West Memphis house and later bought, fixed up, and rented out two additional properties in Memphis that provided rental income to supplement our family budget. He also bought a 7.4-acre farm in Olive Branch, Mississippi, in 1986, where he raised beef cows and an occasional goat. He also grew vegetables such as turnip greens, sweet potatoes, corn, green beans, and purple hull peas. Little did I know at the time that my dad was an exceptionally industrious man who did everything necessary to provide for his family, all while accumulating a modest amount of wealth.

Just think: "If Blacks had come to this country as 'immigrants' in 1619 and had been given equal opportunities to attend school, obtain gainful employment, and acquire property, how much generational wealth could they have amassed?" Instead, Blacks were brought to this country in shackles, and more than 400 years later, many suffer from generational poverty.

Swimming pools in Memphis were segregated in the late 1960s, making it less likely that Black children would learn to swim. Our family had to take my brother, Joe, and me across town to the Orange Mound Swimming Pool to take swimming lessons. We were enjoying the water and learning to swim until a child drowned in the pool. Our parents never took us back. I would not have another swimming lesson until I was in college.

Sadly, minority youth die from drowning at disproportionate rates compared to their White peers, in part because they don't know how to swim. A June 18, 2021, Centers for Disease Control and Prevention (CDC) report, "Persistent Racial/Ethnic Disparities in Fatal Unintentional Drowning Among Persons Aged ≤29 Years - United States, 1999-2019," found that "During 1999-2019, the drowning death rate among persons aged ≤29 years was 1.3 per 100,000 population. The rate per 100,000 among American Indians or Alaska Native persons (2.5) and Black persons (1.8) was higher than among all other racial/ethnic groups and was 2.0 and 1.5 times higher than among White persons (1.2). The report went on to say:

Proven drowning prevention strategies include installing barriers that prevent unintended access to water, teaching basic swimming and water safety skills, using life jackets properly, active supervision, and knowing and performing cardiopulmonary resuscitation (CPR).

Unable to swim the width of Memphis State University's Olympic-size pool to satisfy the swimming requirement for my recreation major, my instructor referred me to the *YMCA* for swimming lessons. Unfortunately, the Y swim instructor looked at my 250 lb.-frame and said he wasn't sure he could save me if I got into trouble. While this didn't give me confidence, I learned enough to be able to traverse the Olympic-size pool at MSU. I subsequently took swim lessons at one of our Y pools in Arlington, Texas, where I greatly improved my swimming skills. However, I'm still not an excellent swimmer. Perhaps this would have been different if I had had a greater opportunity to learn to swim as a young child.

Not having access to swimming pools and swimming lessons, and other public accommodations violated the intent of the landmark 1954 U.S. Supreme Court "Brown v. Board of Education" ruling, which struck down the "separate but equal" practices that were common in public education. Learning to swim became another obstacle that I, and other Blacks, had to overcome because of systemic racism. Not knowing how to swim put many Blacks and other youth of color at greater risk in the water simply because they did not know how to swim. Teaching basic swimming skills could help prevent drowning deaths of many minority youths.

Looking back, I realize that road trips were necessitated not only by economics but by the racism of the era. There were few places where Black travelers could dine or stay overnight. My mother always packed sandwiches, and we always carried an empty soda bottle to use as a urinal. I remember seeing "Whites Only" and "Colored Only" signs posted above public restrooms and water fountains. Many stores even had separate lunch counters for Whites and Blacks. The Black lunch counters were always at the rear of the stores and were always smaller and more spartan than the ones for White customers. Traveling by bus was too expensive for a family of six, and air travel for Blacks was virtually nonexistent. Even when Blacks could afford to buy a ticket for the train or bus, they were relegated to sit in the back as they weren't allowed to sit up front with Whites.

I remember as a teen going to the movies at the Malco Theater in downtown Memphis, entering the theater from a side door, and climbing the stairs to the balcony. I thought the balcony was kind of cool. But in hindsight, I realize that, in years gone by, Blacks were relegated to the balcony because they weren't allowed to mix with Whites who sat on the main level.

Years later, after I joined the St. Peter's AME Church in Minneapolis, Minnesota, I learned that movie theaters were not the only places in American society where Blacks were previously required to sit in the balcony. According to the African Methodist Episcopal Church (AMEC), Richard Allen, Absalom Jones, and other African Americans established the African Methodist Episcopal Church after these Free Africans were pulled off their knees while praying at the altar. (Black members of the mostly-White St. George's Methodist Episcopal Church in Philadelphia, Pennsylvania, were required to worship from the balcony.) According to the African Methodist Episcopal Church website:

> *The AMEC grew out of the Free African Society (FAS), which Richard Allen, Absalom Jones, and others established in Philadelphia in 1787. When officials at St. George's MEC pulled blacks off their knees while praying, FAS members discovered just how far American Methodists would go to enforce racial discrimination against African Americans. Hence, these members of St. George's made plans to transform their mutual aid society into an African congregation.*

I recall walking into a restaurant in North Mississippi while en route to a Sunday School convention in Miami, Florida, in 1968. I felt the stares of people looking at me, but it was not until years later that I realized that they were not used to seeing a Black boy walking through the front door of a restaurant to use the restroom. Jim Crow, an era of legalized segregation and systemic racism, was rampant in the South. Although slavery had been abolished for more than a century, discrimination in public accommodations was still practiced. Racial disparities characterized by the lynching of Black people, voter suppression, redlining, acts of violence, and intimidation by White Supremacy groups like the Ku Klux Klan (KKK) made life difficult for Blacks in America.

Systemic racism—demonstrated by the horrific 2020 murder of George Floyd by a Minneapolis police officer, with three other officers looking on—still plagues our nation. According to a 2020 study by the T.H. Chan School of Public Health at Harvard University, "Black Americans are 3.23 times more likely than White Americans to be killed by police." Many fail to recognize that "White supremacy" is one of the greatest threats facing our society. "White privilege," sometimes unseen by the majority, advantages Whites at the expense of people of color. "White silence is White complicity," words often chanted by protestors in streets across America over the past few years, highlight the pain and degradation caused by White Americans who do nothing to right the wrongs that are perpetrated against people of color.

MEMPHIS PARK COMMISSION – TALE OF TWO CULTURES

I lost my Park Commission job at the Davis Community Center in Memphis because of my relationship with a White female colleague. The White director of the center where I worked hired her daughter's boyfriend; however, she did not approve of the friendship I had developed with a White female colleague. The director also didn't seem to like me roller skating and jumping on the trampoline with my White female colleague and the mostly Black kids from the community.

When I learned I would not have a job at the community center at the end of the summer; I didn't know what I was going to do. Fortunately, Madeleine Rawlings, the Black director of the Hollywood Community Center, located in the mostly-Black North Memphis community, hired me when she learned I was to be unemployed. "Sister," as she was called by her friends and colleagues, saw potential in me and understood the racist reason I was not going to be reemployed at my last job. Although I was appreciative of having a job, the change meant that I had a 30-minute daily drive after getting out of class at Memphis State, nearly tripling my commute. I also now had a 45-minute drive home each night, double the time to get home from my earlier job near the university.

I learned a lot at the Hollywood Community Center, my first full-time job in an all-Black setting. I observed Mrs. Rawlings' leadership style. She pretended to be tough, but she had high standards, and inside she was a caring, motherly figure for the staff and the hundreds of kids who came to the center each day after school and on Saturdays.

I used my athletic skills, especially basketball and ping pong, to engage the kids in physical activity and dialogue. I learned to play billiards; however, I was never really good at it. I had even less success with foosball, a game that the kids took pride in beating me. We occasionally roller-skated on the gym floor with younger kids or threw a dance for older youth. Whether playing a board game or simply sitting and talking, we kept kids occupied and off the streets. I learned to be both comfortable and confident working in the Black community and with people who looked like me.

During the summer months while in college, I worked as an assistant director and later director of a playground in East Memphis. The park where I was assigned served a neighborhood that had a pocket of Black families who, in years past, were domestic workers employed by the upper-income, White families that resided in the area. When I arrived at the park in the summer of 1972, the class differences between the rich White kids and the poor Black kids were evident in the clothes they wore and the houses where they lived. The Black kids always walked to the park, while the White kids were often dropped off in the mornings by their stay-at-home mothers.

I had a good relationship with my colleagues and the kids who came to our site. Each morning we would unfurl and raise the U.S. flag on the flag pole in the center of the park. Daily activities included singing, group games, arts and crafts, and sports.

I enjoyed giving the younger kids piggyback rides around the playground. One day, while giving a ride to a five-year-old, blue-eyed White girl, I noticed her mother getting out of her car and approaching the playground. Instinctively I assumed the mother might not approve of the bond I displayed with her daughter. I assumed that the proverbial "shit was about to hit the fan." Instead, the mother reached out her hand to shake mine and exclaimed, "You must be Willie! I've heard so much about you!" I learned a valuable lesson that day: don't stereotype people and assume how they will behave based on the color of their skin. This is true for minorities as well as for those in the majority.

Willie Dean

Assumptions and Fears About Blacks

Once when I was in St. Louis for an interview for the position of President/CEO of the *YMCA* of Greater St. Louis, I went for a walk downtown. This was a city where I had lived previously and was very comfortable taking an evening stroll. Shortly after leaving my hotel, I encountered a boisterous group of young Black men. Instinctively, I crossed to the other side of the street. Just as I did, I heard someone say, "Hey Willie!" Much to my chagrin, I recognized the voice as that of one of my nephews, who crossed the street to speak with me.

After my nephew and his friends departed, I could not help but feel ashamed. I had seen Whites cringe when encountering Blacks on the street. I had heard stories of White women clutching their purses when a Black man got onto an elevator. I had even been followed by security guards and store employees. Sadly, I realized I had done the very thing that I found abhorrent in others. I had assumed that this group of young Black men represented a threat. This assumption has played out time and time again across more than 400 years of our country's history. Even I, a Black man, was not exempt from this stereotyping behavior.

Once when driving back to my office at the Monsanto *YMCA* in St. Louis, I traveled through the heart of the "hood," an area that was all-Black and low-income. Much to my alarm, my car broke down. This was before cell phones were in common use. I had no way to summon assistance but to ask a resident to use their phone. I felt afraid. It was clear that I was in distress and vulnerable. Instinctively, I removed my necktie and began to speak in the vernacular of the neighborhood. I tried to fit into the surroundings. Finally, the tow truck arrived to take my car and me to "safety." My "fear"—an emotional response to an event that hadn't happened—was unfounded. Having lived much of my life in the suburbs, I had acquired a fear of being with my own people.

On another occasion, I was riding my bike in a public park in Edina, Minnesota, a posh Minneapolis suburb. I rode around the lake, as I normally did, and then followed the trail through a wooded section of the park that allowed one to get away from the noise and hubbub of city traffic. As I turned around a bend in the trail, I came upon a White female jogger who was approaching me. The woman seemed startled at "encountering" me in this remote section of the park. She froze in her tracks and immediately turned and quickly ran in the opposite direction. Instinctively, I stopped, got off of my bike, and allowed her to "retreat" away from me.

At first, I was appalled that this woman appeared to be afraid of me. "Was she afraid of me because I was a large Black man, and we were not in earshot of any other human beings?" Or, "Was she afraid because I was a man that she didn't know and didn't expect to encounter in such a remote location?" I rationalized the situation to myself by asking, "Would I want my wife or sister to use a similar tactic to remove herself from a comparable situation?"

Fort Worth Private Security – Rent-a-Cop Racism

Shortly after moving to Fort Worth, Texas, in 1975, my two-year-old son, Cedric, and I were driving in the all-White, upper-income Wedgewood Community in West Fort Worth. Soon a White "rent-a-cop" began following us as we drove through the neighborhood, on public streets, looking at the beautiful houses. When I realized we were being followed by the security guard, I turned my car around and left the neighborhood. I then became irate and turned my car around again and drove slowly through the same area, to the dismay of the guard. This was my first experience being racially profiled. I suppose I should be grateful that the guard didn't summon law enforcement to deal with me because I was "Driving while Black" and "perceived to be in the wrong place."

Drive-Thru Racism – Do You Want Bias with That?

One night in the late-1970s, at about 1:30 a.m., after leaving a teen dance at my Y in Fort Worth, Texas., I stopped for a burger and fries at a Jack-in-the-Box near my apartment. I was seated in the restaurant for some time, enjoying my meal. I think the White teenage worker at the drive-thru window didn't know, or remember, that I was there.

When a customer, who by his voice sounded to be "Black," placed an order over the drive-thru speaker, the young man who took the order laughed and said to his White co-workers, "That sounds like something a nigger would order!" Almost immediately, the young man and his co-workers looked toward me, realizing that I had heard his racist comment.

I sat quietly, finished my meal, and then—channeling John Wayne—I lumbered to the counter with my then-297-pound frame, beckoned the young man with my index finger, and said in my best Sidney Poitier voice from the movie *They Call Me Mr. Tibbs*—"The word is pronounced 'nēgrō.'" The young man, still wearing his wireless headset but without the bravado shown earlier, responded, "Yes, sir." I don't know what the young man might have said after I left the restaurant—or if the manager was made aware of the incident the next day—but at that moment, he gave respect to a Black man!

I believe that no one is born a racist. Could it be that this young man's racist language was learned behavior? Did he get this from his parents? His peers? Television or the movies? This was the first time that I witnessed someone treating another human being in such a vile, racist manner. While this was the first time that I witnessed a racial epithet, sadly, it wouldn't be the last.

Halloween Vitriol – Hatred Unmasked

On the morning after Halloween in 1981, I found a chalked Swastika on the driveway of our home in Olivette, Missouri, a suburb of St. Louis. Ours was a mostly White and Jewish neighborhood where I felt welcomed; however, someone apparently thought otherwise. We easily washed away the chalked symbol, but we could not erase the hatred in the people's hearts that perpetrated this atrocity.

I can't help but fast forward to the present when antisemitism is once again surging in America. This sad situation is evidenced by high-profile acts against Jews, such as the presence of neo-Nazis in Charlottesville, Virginia, in 2017, where White supremacists chanted, "Jews will not replace us," which resulted in the death of Heather Heyer, a 32-year-old woman; the mass shooting at the Tree of Life synagogue in Pittsburgh, Pennsylvania in 2018, where 11 people died, and seven were wounded; and the taking of four hostages at the Congregation Beth Israel synagogue in Colleyville, Texas in January 2022. No doubt, many other acts of racism, xenophobia, and antisemitism go unreported.

I was outraged by the senseless murder of nine Black congregants at Emanuel AME Church in Charleston, South Carolina, on June 17, 2015. Dylann Roof, a White supremacist, who, by his own admission, sought to start a "race war" between Blacks and Whites, opened fire on the church members and their pastor after participating in Bible study with the group. For the first time in my life, I felt afraid in my church, fearing that there would be copycats who might target other Black churches around the nation and in my community. I felt fidgety whenever unknown persons visited our Sunday services and meetings during the week. I had previously obtained a permit to carry a pistol. However, for the first time, I carried my weapon in church. This I did for nearly a year after the massacre at Mother Emanuel.

On Father's Day, June 21, just a few days after the murders at Mother Emanuel, my church, St. Peter's AME Church in Minneapolis, held a special remembrance during our morning service that was attended by members of our congregation, visitors, and Minnesota Governor Mark Dayton and several Minnesota state representatives. I also remember U.S. President Barak Obama attended a memorial service at Mother Emanuel AME Church in Charleston, where he consoled family members and friends of the victims of this act of hate. He also spoke to the nation about the need for love, unity, and healing and sang what seemed to be an impromptu rendition of the hymn, *Amazing Grace*.

However, the racial hatred continues. I watched in horror as CNN reported on Saturday, May 14, 2022, that a young White male—who espoused hatred towards Black people—had driven two and a half hours from his home in upstate New York to Buffalo, New York to target Blacks at a local grocery store. The assailant, a White supremacist who had surveyed the location previously, shot 13 people, killing ten. All of the dead were African Americans, ranging in age from 32 to 86. This senseless act of violence was fueled by racial hatred against Blacks. When will it end?

THE YMCA, RACISM, AND THE GOOD OLE BOY SYSTEM

Much to my surprise, the President/CEO of an Urban Group *YMCA* (a group of the 30 largest *YMCAs* in North America) allegedly asked when I was hired as the first African American President/CEO of the Omaha-Council Bluffs Metropolitan *YMCA* in Omaha, Nebraska, in 1989, "What's wrong with the folk in Omaha? Didn't they know they didn't have to hire a Black CEO?" Apparently, his assumption was that because the city of Omaha and the state of Nebraska had a small Black population, there was no need to hire a Black CEO. This was the first Y job where I had been hired to lead in a majority community. Although I became the first Black CEO in the Omaha-Council Bluffs Metropolitan *YMCA*'s 123-year history, I was keenly aware that even among *YMCA* leadership, systemic racism continued to stereotype me and others.

After achieving success as CEO of the Omaha-Council Bluffs Metropolitan *YMCA*, I was courted to apply for the position of National Field Executive for the Mid-America Field of the *YMCA* of the USA. The Mid-America Field was the largest of the Y's four fields, comprising more than 700 *YMCAs* in 18 states. I competed against Y executives from across the country; however, I won out and was appointed to the position in 1994. Still, there were naysayers who felt that I got the job because of my race, in spite of my education and experience, and had demonstrated success in other cities.

I went on to provide exemplary services through my team of National Field Consultants based in Minneapolis, Minnesota, Dallas, Texas, Indianapolis, Indiana, and Columbus, Ohio, and local Y consultants based in Management Resource Centers (MRCs) in Dallas, Texas, Denver, Colorado, and Chicago, Illinois.

On one occasion, my White boss didn't recognize me when I was in the breakroom of the *YMCA* of the USA's national office in Chicago. I was one of the most senior persons of color in the national Y structure; however, he interrupted my conversation with a colleague without saying "hello" or "excuse me." This happened on a Friday morning following a week of meetings in Chicago, and I was headed back to Minneapolis and stopped by the national office wearing business casual attire. It became apparent to me that he didn't recognize me, my attire did not match someone who should be important to him, or as a Black man, I was literally invisible to him. Shocked and embarrassed for him, I didn't call him out, a response I regret to this day. I wondered how he related to other people of color who held lower positions in the organization.

My new boss, in 1995, asked my National Field Executive colleagues and me for suggestions for persons to recommend to the *YMCA* of Phoenix for their CEO vacancy. I suggested the name of a Black person, who I deemed qualified, to which he responded, "Phoenix is not ready for a Black CEO." I immediately recognized that my boss, a White man who had served as CEO of an Urban Group *YMCA* previously, seemed unaware of his stereotypical attitude.

My boss' comment was emblematic of the "Good ole boy system." It was also the first time I had witnessed homosocial reproduction—where people in charge tend to hire, nurture and promote people who are socially similar to themselves. This prejudice made it problematic for people of color to land key *YMCA* executive jobs (CEOs, VPs, etc.) in predominantly White communities. Homosocial reproduction was on full display in the *YMCA* of the USA and in the Y movement nationwide. Some talented Black leaders may not have been hired or invited to interview for jobs in predominantly White communities as a result of systemic racism.

I benefited greatly from a cohort of African American *YMCA* leaders who met regularly to provide encouragement to one another. This proved to be a supportive network for learning and mentoring. The group, initially convened nearly 50 years ago by Jean Ann Durades, a former member of the National

YMCA staff, and over the years included current and retired, Black leaders including Jesse Alexander, Diane Baker-King, Kenneth Barnes, Janis Berry, Tanya Bluford, Jack Booker, Gayle A. Brock, Ralph Christian, Everette Christmas, George H. Coleman, Carolyn Creager, Chuck Dandridge, Jean Ann Durades, Douglas Evans, Franciene Gill, Jackie Gordon, John Green, Glenn Haley, Tom Hargrave, Sandra Harris, Yvonne Harris, Eston Hood, Maurice Horsey, Rick Hopkins, Jock Johnson, Julius Jones, Norm Joyner, Robin Lee, Lindiwe Lester, Eric K. Mann, Rodney Martin, William McAllister, Harold Mezile, Eric Nelson, Marcellette Orange, Lowell Overby, Willie Proctor, Rc Pruitt, Angie Reese-Hawkins, Dr. Jacob Rhodes, Ronald F. Sargent, George Shinhoster, L.T. Thompson, Norm Urquhart, Kevin Washington, Bob Wilson, Bill Wimberly, myself, and others.

WHY DID THEY HAVE TO HIRE A FUCKING NIGGER?

In late 2007, shortly after I was appointed Chief Operating Officer for the *YMCA* of Greater Cleveland, an obscene message was left on the voicemail of my office phone. The male caller, who sounded "White," asked, "Why did they have to hire a fucking nigger?" I found either word to be profane; however, together, they were diabolical. I was taken aback and appalled. (I have seen an uptick in overt racism and hatred in our country since the election of Donald Trump as U.S. President in 2016.) I shared the disturbing call with my boss. We had our IT director make a recording of the voicemail onto a CD, and I made a police report. The Black police sergeant who took the report phoned the number that appeared on my caller ID; however, no one answered. The officer promised to stop by the address associated with the number on his way home that night. I heard nothing further on this issue and can only hope that the officer's phone call and visit served as a deterrent for the maladjusted person who made the racist call.

Throughout my 35-year career, I was often stereotyped and perceived to be unready for jobs in Ys that served downtown business districts or suburban communities for fear that White residents would not relate to my leadership. This was the first racial epithet—that I was aware of—that was directed toward me.

Willie Dean

Lived Experiences of My Black Sons

In June 2020, after decades of deaths of Black men and women at the hands of law enforcement and vigilantes, I decided to ask my Black sons about their experiences with racism at the hands of police and others. Their responses were disheartening. I never gave them "the talk" when they were growing up; however, I wish I had. According to Wikipedia: "The talk is a colloquial expression for a conversation Black parents in the United States feel compelled to have with their children and teenagers about the dangers they face due to racism or unjust treatment from authority figures, law enforcement, or other parties and how to de-escalate them. The practice dates back generations and is often a rite of passage for Black children."

I should have sat down with my sons and told them the realities of being a Black male in America. I should have warned them about some (not all) law enforcement officers who would treat them harshly and differently than their White peers simply because of the color of their skin. I should have told them, "To always be respectful towards police, even if they are not always respectful towards you," because the goal is to come home safely. Here are their stories.

When our family lived in Omaha, Nebraska, Cedric and three Black male friends drove to a McDonald's and realized they were being followed by a Douglas County Sheriff's deputy. After he and his friends stopped properly at three stop signs, they were pulled over by the officer. Cedric had counted aloud to make sure he had made a complete stop at each stop sign. They were in a mostly White neighborhood where they all lived. After stopping them, the officer asked them lots of questions, including, "Where are you going?" "Where do you live?" He never, however, told them why he had stopped them. The father of one of the other boys called the sheriff's office to complain. This experience made Cedric feel devalued. He learned to watch his back around police. (He didn't tell me about this incident at the time but recalled his feelings after the murder of George Floyd by police in Minneapolis in 2020.)

In the fall of 1993, when Cedric was in the U.S. Navy, he, another sailor, and two marines, all Black males, were stopped by police officers near the marine airbase where they were stationed. Cedric and his friends were traveling to Santa Monica to get something to eat. One of the officers approached the driver's door with his hand on his gun, while another stood at the rear of the car with his gun drawn and pointed at the ground. The officer who had approached the driver's door alleged they had made an improper left turn and asked where they were going and what they were up to. Cedric's car had Tennessee plates and Department of Defense (DOD) stickers and could easily have been recognized as being owned by a service member; however, Cedric and his comrades felt they were stopped, questioned, and treated with disrespect because they were Black.

On another occasion, Cedric and some of his friends were going hunting in Minnesota and got pulled over by a Black cop. The officer asked for his driver's license and proof of insurance. Cedric was respectful and let the officer know that he was reaching for his wallet. Cedric has been stopped by police multiple times, and each time he said his goal was "to make it home that night."

On yet another occasion in Minnesota in 2016, a White female driver hit Cedric's SUV and left the scene without stopping. He chased her down and called the police. When the officer arrived, he questioned Cedric as to why his car was behind the lady's car if she struck him from behind. Adding insult to injury, the officer issued the White hit-and-run driver a "warning." The officer clearly wanted to comfort and excuse the driver because she was a White female and dismiss the importance of the incident. In addition to the damage to his bumper, Cedric's sustained back injuries that required more than a year of chiropractic care. This disparate treatment of White and Black citizens by law enforcement is eerily similar to a situation that occurred at a New Jersey mall in 2022. According to CNN:

> *A video showing police officers breaking up a fight between a Black teenager and a White teenager at a New Jersey mall has prompted outrage over the police response. New Jersey Gov. Phil Murphy said Wednesday that the "appearance of what is racially disparate treatment is deeply, deeply disturbing."*
>
> *One video of the incident reviewed by CNN shows the boys arguing before the White teenager points his finger at the Black teenager's face, and the Black teenager pushes the White teenager's hand back. The White teenager pushes the Black teenager, who begins to throw punches at the other boy. The White teenager punches back.*
>
> *The Black teenager ends up on the ground. Two Bridgewater Township police officers arrive and separate the two boys.*
>
> *The Black teenager begins to get up and is pinned to the ground by one officer and rolled onto his stomach, with his hands behind his back. The other officer pushes the White teenager onto a nearby couch and then assists in handcuffing the Black teenager. Eventually, officers stand the handcuffed Black teenager up.*
>
> *It is unclear from the video how the incident escalated between the boys or what happened after the Black teenager was handcuffed.*

> The Bridgewater Township Police Department said in a Facebook post that they know the video of the incident has upset members of the community. They have asked the Somerset County Prosecutor's Office to investigate the incident.
>
> "We recognize that this video has made members of our community upset and are calling for an internal affairs investigation," the department wrote.

This recent incident at a mall in New Jersey with a White teenager, a Black teenager, and police and the situation faced by Cedric in 2016, with a White female hit-and-run driver and police, speaks volumes about the disparate treatment received by Black and White Americans when encountering law enforcement. Police sometimes seem to forget part of their oft-used slogan, "to protect and serve," that should apply to all citizens equally. Too often, these types of incidents have occurred without the benefit of cell phone cameras or police bodycam footage. This frequently means that police officers' reports or White assailants' accounts of what occurred become the "truth."

Jarrod, too, has been pulled over numerous times by police. When he was attending Florida International University in Miami, he and several male friends (Black, Cuban and White) were followed and stopped by police at a gas station with what Jarrod describes as "cherries and berries"—flashing red and blue emergency lights. One of the men in the car was from Portugal, but for all intents and purposes, he looked "White." The police "asked" the driver for permission to search the car. Embarrassed by the situation, Jarrod and his friends had to sit on the curb during the search. The police asked, "Where are you going?" The officers never explained why they were stopped. Over the years, Jarrod has learned he always needs to ask permission before doing anything—getting his wallet, getting out of the car, etc.—when stopped by the police. On this stop, Jarrod had to calm his friend down, who was understandably angry about what happened and how they were treated. (We have seen in situation-after-situation with law enforcement stops involving Blacks that "standing up for yourself" against police for their disparate treatment seldom ends well for Black Americans.)

When we lived in the Twin Cities, Jarrod was pulled over by police for allegedly making a rolling stop on "420" (April 20, National Marijuana Day). Jarrod says his mom and I taught him how to relate to police—he learned to calm himself—especially when being racially profiled. He says being pulled over is always an uncomfortable feeling. Jarrod doesn't want to say anything to invite trouble; however, he doesn't trust the police. Whenever he feels that a police officer is following him, he lets them pass him by because he is not comfortable with them following behind him. (Unfortunately, this practice in and of itself may invite further scrutiny from suspicious police who may be looking for a reason to stop Black drivers.)

Jarrod has experienced racial discrimination in employment and has often felt that he was treated differently than his White peers. When Jarrod worked as an intern at FleishmanHillard, a global public relations firm located in St. Louis, Missouri, his White colleagues felt he was hired to satisfy a quota. He frequently felt a certain level of bias. White interns were given assignments; however, Jarrod had to ask for them. At the end of the summer, Jarrod talked to several of the White interns and realized that all of them had been given interviews that resulted in them being hired for junior positions at the firm. However, Jarrod wasn't offered interviews or employment. He inquired about employment opportunities like the ones his White peers had received. His supervisor denied that others had been given interviews and downplayed the situation. A White female, who worked in the office, observed what was happening. She apologized to Jarrod and remains a friend of his to this day. Jarrod says he learned that "You can't fight city hall!" Systemic racism permeates American society and makes getting ahead in the workplace problematic for people of color.

When Jarrod worked as a personal trainer at *Lifetime Fitness* in Bloomington, Minnesota, the head trainer told him that they had never had a Black trainer and that a Black man of his size might make some of the mostly White, female clients uncomfortable. (I find it ironic that Jarrod's 5'10," 170-pound muscular frame would have been a problem for a personal trainer who needs to model a healthy body type and lifestyle for clients.) Jarrod says he was called out in meetings by a supervisor who said that he looked like Michael B. Jordan, a Black movie actor. This made Jarrod feel stereotyped. As a light-skinned Black male, he has experienced "colorism" throughout his life. Frequently, Whites have asked him what race he is because some feel he doesn't fit the stereotype of how they expect a Black man should look.

Jarrod says it's hard to work and socialize in a White environment. He finds that Minnesotans are often passive-aggressive with their racism. He says you can sense it a mile away. They know they need diversity, but they don't want you to be the angry Black man. "I have encountered a lot of racism, particularly in my corporate work, and even now, I have to deal with it in therapy," says Jarrod. Dating in a White environment is a whole different dynamic for Jarrod. He felt he didn't discover himself until he lived in Miami, a multicultural community that has numerous Cubans, Africans, African Americans, and other people of color.

Jarrod took off from work on June 1, 2020, because he needed a break from all the things happening around the country following the murder of George Floyd. Floyd, a Black man, had been arrested by Minneapolis police for allegedly passing a counterfeit 20-dollar bill at a local convenience store. The four officers involved in the arrest were fired from the department later. Derek Chauvin, the officer who had pressed his knee on Floyd's neck for more than nine minutes, was arrested and charged with third-degree murder (Chauvin was later tried and convicted of murder). The remaining three officers, who failed to intervene in the inhumane treatment of Floyd, were charged with aiding and abetting third-degree murder. In the wake of all that was happening, Jarrod felt he needed a mental health day. Fortunately, his supervisor recognized the stress that Jarrod might have been under and asked him if he needed the day off. Jarrod says it pained him not to be able to be in Minneapolis to ensure nothing happened to his little brother, Matt.

My youngest son, Matt, has been stopped by police numerous times. Once when he was 17 years old, he was stopped near our home in Bloomington, Minnesota, while he was driving my 2000 *Saleen XP8 Explorer*, a high-end, limited-edition SUV. He was racially profiled and followed by a cop for two miles in our mostly-White suburban neighborhood. After being pulled over, the officer asked Matt, "What are you doing?" "Where are you going?" The officer never explained why he pulled him over, but Matt assumed he thought the vehicle was not his or that he did not have permission to drive it.

Another time Matt was driving with his wife, Kristine, who is White, to take her girlfriend to a wedding in Maple Grove, Minnesota. Matt was driving a friend's car. They had a blowout and stopped at a gas station to wait for a tow truck. Two police officers came up to them. Matt explained that they were waiting for a tow truck because they had a flat. Matt handed the officer his driver's license and explained the vehicle's papers were in the glove box. He also handed the officer his permit to carry a pistol, although he was not required to do so. All of a sudden, eight other officers showed up, and now there were ten officers surrounding their car with their guns drawn. Matt said he had done nothing to provoke them. He said he was not necessarily scared, but each time he is stopped by police, he feels, "This could be it, and this won't end well for anyone."

Once in Downtown Minneapolis, while celebrating with friends, a White male friend in Matt's group got drunk and slapped a police horse on its rump.

The mounted police officer assumed Matt had done this and shouted at him, "Don't fucking touch my horse!" Two mounted officers then pushed their horses' heads toward him, striking him. Matt feels police always assume that you are up to no good and you must be guilty. He says everyone believes that Minneapolis police are corrupt and racist when it comes to Black people.

Matt has experienced racism on several fronts and feels you can tell how people feel about you by the way they look at you. He has difficulty with anger management and gets enraged when he is profiled and treated unjustly by police. Matt says, "I guess most state troopers may be nice, but I make the assumption that most [police] are profiling me because the majority of them treat you like crap."

Matt has been treated unfairly in employment too. When he worked in construction, White workers frequently used swear words, made racial jokes, and laughed at references to Black Lives Matter. They saw the jobs in construction as union jobs that should be for Whites. Matt said, "On one project, they assigned me the task of carrying the heavy bricks. I told them I was going to the gym to work out after work to let them know they couldn't get the best of me." The two foremen who supervised the crew were racists. They never corrected the employees, which is why his White co-workers felt safe making racist statements in Matt's presence. Once when going to DQ for lunch, Matt offered to drive as his co-workers had trailers on their trucks. Instead of being appreciative, they said, "We're not going to get pulled over with cocaine in the car, are we?" Matt said he felt crummy, but he sucked it up and went on about his day.

Matt also relayed to me a time when he had a job interview with a White hiring manager. The manager took him around the plant and showed him the tasks that, if hired, he would be handling. Matt said their conversation was cordial and professional. However, the feedback the manager gave to the temp agency was that there was no "feng shui." In other words, he didn't feel Matt would fit into the culture; code for people who are different from the majority (culture, race, ethnicity, sex, gender preference, etc.) need not apply. White employers often look for "harmony" or "homogeneity" in their workforce, the epitome of homosocial reproduction. Whether intentional or unintentional, this tendency disadvantages Blacks.

A few years ago, I asked Matt to take me to my speed shop, located in Rogers, Minnesota (a predominantly White suburb of Minneapolis), to pick up my car. Matt was driving his friend's *Chevy Avalanche*. I didn't pay much attention to the car's tinted windows and "whiskey plates"—license plates in

Minnesota that start with the letter "W" to signify that the vehicle's owner has had certain driving while intoxicated (DWI) convictions. These plates alert law enforcement officers to the propensity for reckless driving; however, they don't give officers authority to pull over vehicles with these plates without cause. Kristine, Matt's wife, who is White, he and I were enjoying the drive when suddenly a Rogers, Minnesota police car pulled us over. Matt signaled and brought the car to a stop.

The White officer approached the driver-side window of the car, and Matt handed him his driver's license and permit to carry a handgun. The officer quickly looked into our vehicle and saw Matt and Kristine in the front seat and me in the back. He returned to his car. Soon there were two other cruisers on the scene. I asked Matt to remain calm, and I sat nervously, not knowing what was going to happen next.

The officer returned to the driver's side window, handed Matt back his driver's license and permit, and told him that they had to respond to another call. As he was departing, he told Matt that the vehicle's window tint was too dark and to get them fixed. Then, as quickly as they had appeared, the police were gone.

I asked myself, "Did the officer pull us over because the window tint was too dark?" "Because a young Black man was driving?" "Because a Black man was driving with a White woman?" Or, "Did the officers stop us to check the sobriety of the driver of a vehicle with a "whiskey plate?" I believe that had I not been in that vehicle—an older man—things might have gone differently.

Looking back, the stop involving Matt, Kristine, and me could have gone terribly wrong if we or the police had acted rashly, as this stop was eerily like the one involving Philando Castile in Falcon Heights, Minnesota—a suburb of Saint Paul, Minnesota—on July 6, 2016. Castile, a 32-year-old Black man, was stopped by a St. Anthony, Minnesota police officer. After being asked by the officer for his license and registration, Castile informed the officer that he had a firearm (Castile had a permit to carry). The officer told him, "Don't reach for it." Castile's girlfriend—who was in the vehicle along with her four-year-old daughter and who filmed the incident on her cell phone—told the officer that he wasn't pulling out the weapon. In the confusion, the officer fired seven close-range shots, five of which hit Castile, who died later that night at a local hospital.

Not until I asked my sons about their experiences with racism following the George Floyd killing in June 2020 did I begin to understand the significant number of racial incidents, pain, and humiliation that they had experienced as Black males in the predominantly White cultures that they had been exposed to growing up in the suburbs of St. Louis, Omaha, and Minneapolis. In my attempt to give them the best homes, educational opportunities, and life experiences, I inadvertently placed them in hyper-racial situations in the communities where we lived. They had to contend with racism from police officers, school teachers, and school administrators, as well as from co-workers and supervisors on their jobs. I had an epiphany about rearing Black families in America.

Had I to do it over again, I would look harder at the situations wherein I placed my family. Mostly White suburbs are not nirvana for Black children and teens, for there they often face disparate treatment in the schools they attend, in the communities where they live, and in the criminal justice system that is supposed to dispense "blind" justice. As a Black comedian once put it, the American justice system is often a place where you find "just us." I also recognize that in the real world, where Black Americans will raise their families, they can expect to often face unequal justice unless people of good conscious step forward and demand change.

BARRIERS TO UPWARD MOBILITY – RACISM AND THE YMCA

After graduating college and starting my career with the *YMCA* in Memphis in 1974, I became increasingly aware that I was only being considered for Y positions in inner cities working with communities of color. When I applied for jobs outside the urban core, I was told I didn't have experience managing a large membership branch. The irony was that all of the large membership branches were located in largely-White suburbs or in downtown business districts. Neither of these types of *YMCAs* was ready to have a Black executive at their helm for fear of losing White members and their financial support.

Even though I had a Bachelor's degree with a major in Recreation, 15 years of branch executive experience, and several years of experience as Vice President of Urban Services with one of the largest Ys in the country, I was unsuccessful in landing a CEO position in the *YMCA*. Then, in 1989, I was hired as President/CEO of the Omaha-Council Bluffs Metropolitan *YMCA*, becoming the first person of color to hold this position in the organization's 123 history. I also became one of the first Black CEOs of a major *YMCA* nationwide. Even then, there were doubters who questioned why I had been hired in a majority-White community.

Willie Dean

While in Omaha, I was blessed to be able to increase membership and program participation, raise more than $5 million in capital funds to enhance branch facilities and build a new Y in the inner city, and strengthen volunteer and staff leadership. I also obtained an Executive MBA from the University of Nebraska at Omaha to continue my education and professional development.

After a successful stint in Omaha, I was hired as the National Field Executive for the Mid-America Field of the *YMCA* of the USA in 1994. This position put me among the most senior staff nationwide in the Y movement. I successfully led the Mid-America Field Office, the largest of four field offices in the United States. My goal, however, was to become CEO of an Urban Group *YMCA* (a group of the 30 largest *YMCAs* in North America). Even though by this time, I had 20 years of *YMCA* executive experience and an Executive MBA, I was still unable to move up the ladder to become CEO of an Urban Group *YMCA*, as I saw many of my White peers do with less experience, education, and credentials.

Following my wife's tragic surgery and lapse into a chronic vegetative state in 1998, I went back to school to work on a doctorate, in part to continue my education, strengthen my resume, and occupy my mind during a very trying period in my life. I also wanted to identify and study the barriers to upward mobility that I had struggled to overcome in my career with the *YMCA*.

I enrolled in the Ph.D. program in the College of Education and Human Development at the University of Minnesota and chose my dissertation topic: "Barriers to Upward Mobility: A Case Study of the *YMCA*." The then-President of the *YMCA* of the USA, Dr. Kenneth L. Gladish, gave me permission to survey local Y staff nationwide as part of my research. I selected a random sample of *YMCA* program directors, branch executives, vice presidents, and CEOs. The sample included 50 Black and 200 White employees.

A literature review revealed that barriers to upward mobility exist in organizations preventing some members from achieving their full potential. The evidence suggested that dominant group members recruit, select, nurture, and promote individuals who are like themselves for trusted, senior positions. Barriers believed to be the product of homosocial reproduction (a theory developed by Rosabeth M. Kanter, which posits that managers seek to hire and nurture others who are socially similar to themselves), treatment discrimination, and differential investments in human capital and social capital, result in disproportionate representation of African Americans and other "people of difference" (other minorities, women, and men not represented in the "in-group") in lower-prestige positions.

I learned from my research that prejudice and discrimination, which form the basis for many barriers, are sometimes unseen and, perhaps more accurately, are unreported in American society. Organizational responses to discrimination and diversity are often symbolic rather than substantive and send mixed messages to management and staff that reinforce inequitable and inappropriate behavior. These responses tend to maintain the status quo and serve to magnify differences.

Managing diversity means looking beyond race and gender; however, until recently, little emphasis was placed on how to manage people with diverse backgrounds in the workplace. On the one hand, affirmative action seems to have been successful. More women and minorities are found in companies; however, many are disproportionately bunched in entry-level positions. This situation creates a "glass ceiling," which acts as a barrier to upward mobility for minorities and women in even well-intentioned organizations.

Numerous organizations, including universities, companies, and nonprofits like the *YMCA*, have embraced the concept of diversity. However, many still operate under a paradigm where some group members enjoy privileges and perks not available to others. Merely increasing the number of women and minorities is not enough to ensure that everyone is valued equally. In the desire to ensure diversity, it is important that leaders not overlook how prejudice and discrimination affect racial and ethnic minorities, women, and others, and likewise, how organizational policies, practices, and structures can sometimes create barriers to upward mobility.

The Young Men's Christian Association (*YMCA*), founded in London, England, in 1844, began in response to the growing ills of city life brought on by the Industrial Revolution. Men and boys of the era were moving in large numbers from the countryside to industrialized London in search of jobs and better opportunities. Many fell victim to houses of ill repute, gambling, and drinking, or they lived in otherwise unsafe surroundings.

George Williams, the *YMCA*'s founder, a young Christian man who worked in a drapery (forerunner of the modern-day department store), was concerned about the situation. Williams and 12 of his friends met in an upper room over the drapery and founded the *YMCA*. An evangelical Protestant movement, the organization's goal was to provide wholesome alternatives to the men and boys who were moving to the city. Initially, the organization focused on Christian Bible study and leadership development. Later it expanded to include an emphasis on "spirit, mind, and body" through Bible study, adult basic education, and instruction in physical fitness.

Willie Dean

According to Nina Mjagkij in her 1994 book, *Light in the Darkness: African Americans and the YMCA, 1852-1946*, "Like the nation, the *YMCA* was torn by the debate over slavery during the 1850s. Initially, the *YMCA* leaders tried to avoid a discussion of slavery in order to maintain a unified organization." The *YMCA*, although a Christian organization, failed to accept all men and women as brothers and sisters. Rather, the organization provided "separate but equal" services for African Americans, which gave birth to systemic racism in the organization.

Early African American leaders, like Dr. Jesse E. Moorland, Director of the Colored Men's Department of the International Division of the *YMCA* in the early 1900s, and others, recognized the inequality of this practice. However, they seized the opportunity to reach out to young Black men in the South and in other parts of the country as they worked to develop *YMCAs* to serve the needs of Black communities. Andrea Hinding, in her 2001 book, *YMCA in America: 1851-2001*, notes, "One of the first *YMCAs* was also one of the earliest African American organizations in the United States. Formerly enslaved, Anthony Bowen founded a Black *YMCA* in Washington, D.C., in 1853. "Colored *YMCAs*" held the hopes and aspirations of many young Blacks.

Precluded from participation in many forms of American life, the *YMCA* offered Blacks opportunities for education and leadership development. However, the *YMCA* was not willing to take on the Jim Crow laws—government-sanctioned segregation of the era—which prevented Blacks from living the American dream. Instead, the *YMCA* relegated the formation and administration of Black *YMCAs* to its International Division. According to Susan K. Chandler, in her 1994 article, "'Almost a partnership': African Americans, Segregation, and the Young Men's Christian Association," this tactic "enabled the Y.M.C.A. to avoid integrating African American work into the established local and state apparatus and thus sidestep the divisive subject of Black and White unity."

I presented a report to the *YMCA* of the USA based on research done for my dissertation that investigated whether African Americans and women had been marginalized into less prestigious positions in the *YMCA*. The results from my study suggested that homosocial reproduction (the tendency of leaders to select and nurture others who are socially like themselves) played a role in the hiring and promotion of Blacks, women, and other diverse people in some *YMCAs*. It was believed that there was a relationship between homosocial reproduction—which led to "treatment discrimination"—and, therefore, barriers to occupational mobility. Likewise, differential investments in human capital (education, training, skills, mentoring, and experience) and social capital (demographic similarity, psychosocial support, etc.) were believed to lead to differences in promotion rate and social support afforded Black and White *YMCA* managers.

There may be many reasons for the under-representation of minorities and women in senior management positions in some *YMCAs*, including discrimination, misperceptions, stereotypes, negative attitudes, and limited or disparate investment in human and social capital. I sought to discover if and why such differences exist. While homosocial reproduction and treatment discrimination were found to be present, it was unclear as to their sequence. It appeared to be a "chicken and egg" situation: "Which came first, homosocial reproduction or treatment discrimination?" It is clear, however, that the two were inextricably linked.

My study found, consistent with the literature that African Americans, women, and others may be discriminated against in the *YMCA* based on the preconceived notions of the individuals and groups responsible for hiring and promotions. I found that certain individuals within the organization both "knowingly and unknowingly" erected barriers that served to limit opportunities for some employees. The themes that emerged from the data suggested barriers faced by Blacks and others in the *YMCA* included: treatment discrimination (homosocial reproduction, etc.), lack of human capital (Blacks' inability to obtain diverse experience), lack of social capital (lack of racial and gender similarity with others in employees' advice and social support networks), the attitudes and behaviors of minorities and women, and organizational structural barriers. These instances were, in some cases, subtle and, at other times, overt.

Findings from my study revealed that treatment discrimination, which can occur at the individual, group, and organizational levels, was present in the *YMCA*. Individual-level discrimination, characterized by themes that emerged from the data, suggested that stereotyping, racial bias, age bias, gender bias, sexual orientation bias, a salary differential between men and women, pigeonholing, and the fact that minorities were viewed as a monolithic group, operated to form barriers that prevented African Americans, women and others in the *YMCA* from achieving career advancement on par with their White (often male) peers.

My study found that Blacks and women were often "pigeonholed" into certain positions; the former into branches that served inner-city communities and the latter into programs like childcare and youth sports. Like in collegiate and professional athletics, Blacks were often relegated to noncentral positions in the organizational hierarchy, where they appeared to be frozen at lower levels where salary and other remunerations were limited. I also found that biases held by some branch and corporate volunteers adversely affected decisions about candidates for employment and that age bias may have worked against both younger and older employees. These practices served to disadvantage employees in the YMCA's workforce. I did not, however, find significant differences between the self-perceived promotion rates of Black and White managers. This may be accounted for because Blacks were being promoted on par with Whites; however, they were not being hired to fill suburban jobs that lead to senior jobs on corporate staffs.

YMCAs, which are locally organized and operate with a high degree of local autonomy, are required by the organization's national constitution "to pay annual dues, refrain from discrimination and support the YMCA mission." On the one hand, local autonomy allows local Y leaders to make important decisions about programs, staffing, and the like; however, it inhibits the national organization's effectiveness in facilitating change in mandated areas like non-discrimination in hiring, placement, and promotion.

I found that the tendency of YMCAs to reflect the attitudes and demographic characteristics of the communities that they served acted to relegate minority managers, for the most part, to "minority communities." The organization maintained that reflecting on the communities that it serves was in the best interest of those communities, as the leaders were more sensitive to and able to work with community leaders to address community issues. This rationale, however, was flawed as no attempt seemed to have been made to ensure that YMCA senior leadership also reflected the gender make-up of YMCA service areas. The practice of matching the race or ethnicity of candidates to communities had a stifling effect on the upward mobility of minorities.

My study found instances of racial bias that ranged from one YMCA's desire to build a YMCA for "White people only" to another that didn't want to have photos of Black children on its brochures for fear of alienating White residents.

Respondents overwhelmingly reported that YMCA senior managers were almost always White, consistent with findings in the literature that suggested stacking and limited leadership opportunities for Blacks were occurring in collegiate and professional athletics. Some respondents went further to suggest that YMCA senior managers often were disproportionately male.

Bias served as a barrier for women and minorities in obtaining recognition, compensation, and advancement. According to one respondent, even when a Black male was hired into a senior position, he often still faced barriers, as he was "not fully in the club because he was a non-White man." This situation suggests that even though Blacks and women may make it to senior positions unless there is a change in both the attitudes and behaviors of those in charge of the system, structural barriers will persist, and nothing will really change.

Upward mobility often has been limited for staff at branches that serve minority communities. Staff in those units sometimes have been treated inequitably, as they don't have access to training, facilities, equipment, and funding on par with their suburban, often White, counterparts. In addition, the communities they served often had higher unemployment and higher levels of poverty, which made the ability to be self-sustaining a near impossibility for minority branches. However, the organization placed greater value on a branch and, consequently, its leadership when it had the ability to run large membership and health and fitness programs.

Black and other minority staff found it nearly impossible to gain experience managing a large membership facility with comprehensive health and fitness programs because they were not given opportunities to do so. As such, they didn't generally acquire the skills and experiences that were sought by those hiring senior positions in the organization. In order to become a vice president of operations or a CEO, one generally had to have had successful experience running large health and wellness and membership operations. However, Blacks, other minorities, and women generally weren't given opportunities to gain those experiences.

Black respondents in my study invariably saw reality from both the majority perspective, from conversations and accounts in the media, and from their own "lived experiences." This fact was evidenced by the accounts—given by Blacks, some women and a handful of White men—of barriers faced by Blacks in the organization.

Fear of losing membership and program revenues was a barrier that prevented Blacks from being hired as program directors and executive directors in suburban, often predominantly White communities. Middle and senior managers in some associations appeared to harbor these concerns. The assumption was that Blacks would not be welcomed by White constituents or they were not capable of managing comprehensive health and wellness programs.

While Whites sometimes saw the presence of people of color at *YMCA* meetings and conferences as an indication of how diverse the organization was, Blacks, on the other hand, saw it differently. Blacks said that they saw few Blacks in senior positions or in positions other than in "minority communities."

Blacks rarely got invited to apply or interview for jobs in non-minority communities. Blacks may have been "filtered" out of the candidate selection process long before their résumés were received by those responsible for hiring. Local senior staff and volunteers, as well as national staff, may have acted in ways that prevented minorities from even being considered for jobs that were deemed more suited for the majority. Because staff and volunteers had such tremendous influence, hiring committees often deferred to their recommendations on who got invited to apply or to interview for certain jobs. Likewise, their recommendations on who was ready to assume senior leadership roles weighed heavily on hiring decisions. These practices were evidence of homosocial reproduction, social closure, and treatment discrimination in the organization.

If reflecting "the ethnic composition of communities that are served" was important, then wouldn't "gender representation" be equally important? If one follows this logic, having female branch managers would be as important as having staff that reflected the community's ethnic composition. The *YMCA*, however, did not appear to place such value on having women in senior positions. Findings from my study suggested that males had more career options than females, as males more often served as branch executive directors, vice presidents of operations, and CEOs. Females, on the other hand, were frequently found in child care, youth sports, human resources management, finance, and marketing and were not given opportunities that would position them to assume senior executive leadership roles.

The *YMCA*'s culture was such that in order to become a CEO, one invariably had to have had line experience as an operator of a major branch or have served as an operations director, positions wherein women, as minorities, appeared to be underrepresented. The organization said Y's "serve their particular communities, and staff members tend to represent the ethnic composition of the communities served." On the one hand, this tendency may seem laudable. However, there seemed to be a disconnect between ethnic and gender representation among *YMCA* leaders. Blacks were invariably relegated to providing leadership in branches that served "Black" communities, and although women constituted more than half of the population in many communities served by the organization, women were not represented proportionately in senior-level positions. Blacks and women invariably were excluded from roles that would align them for upward mobility.

The "traditional" parental role of females as caregivers for children and families may have served as a barrier to their upward mobility. For these reasons, females as a group were seen by their male counterparts as less likely to relocate in order to pursue their careers. While this may have been true for some, it was not for all. However, some in the organization made that assumption and, therefore, failed to invite females to consider positions that involved relocation. Some saw "females" and "careers" as an oppositional binary. They saw careers as synonymous with males, and since males are not synonymous with females, they believed females, therefore, were not synonymous with careers. This kind of logic serves to limit females in the organization, for many who might be willing to relocate may never be invited to apply or never be considered in that regard.

Like residents of White communities, residents of Black communities sometimes may want to have someone of "their own kind" leading the YMCA in their community. While this might seem admirable or appropriate on the surface, it serves to undermine the principles of diversity and inclusion. If organization leaders allow these kinds of sentiments to dictate hiring and promotion practices, it will undo much of what has been accomplished in our culture since the landmark 1954 U.S. Supreme Court "Brown v. Board of Education" ruling, which struck down the "separate but equal" practices that were common in public education. Allowing communities, or individuals, to influence and ensure that only people of like color are given positions of leadership in YMCAs in their communities also goes against what the organization professes in its mission. As one respondent put it, "it's a slippery slope" from reflecting community attitudes and demographics in hiring and promotion practices to maintaining a separate system of YMCAs that, in effect, serves one racial group or the other. Diversity and inclusion are good for business; however, more importantly, it's the right thing to do. Youth and families benefit from seeing leaders from diverse backgrounds.

As the YMCA was initially a male organization, attitudes and behaviors may be hard to change. Some in the organization, just as some in society, find it difficult to accept females as equals. They find it hard to believe that women can do anything that men can do, and consequently, their biases prevent them from seeing women as full partners in the organization, capable of serving as branch executives, vice presidents of operations, and CEOs. Some of these fears are rooted in the culture in which YMCAs operate. Off-color jokes or comments at meetings that were reported by some female respondents suggested that some in society, and some within the organization, still questioned women's roles in the *YMCA*. While only a relatively small number of people may have voiced these sentiments overtly, the covert acts of hiring committees and senior executives seemed to bear them out. Several respondents in my study documented this sentiment.

Gender bias makes it hard for females to occupy "nontraditional roles," to be successful, and achieve career advancement. Women often had to work harder than their male counterparts in order to receive recognition in an organization that was dominated by males in senior leadership roles. This situation caused tremendous frustration among some females and may have led to their departure from the organization, if not in body but in spirit, for it is increasingly difficult to pour one's heart into an organization that appears to not fully value and appreciate your contributions. Barriers to upward mobility are doubly difficult for Black and other women of color.

The social closure practices of some *YMCA*s prevented minorities and females from becoming "fully part of the club." Respondents in my study, both male and female, recounted how females sometimes were not invited to participate in work-related social events like golf outings. A White female respondent suggested that the relationships one builds on a round of golf could be integral to one's career success. However, if females, like minorities, are routinely excluded from such events, they may face a disadvantage in comparison to their colleagues, who are often White males. Likewise, the opinions and ideas of females, sometimes even senior executives, were not given the same credence as those of their male colleagues. Women may be at a disadvantage socially if men talk only about sports and use sports analogies in their conversations and speeches. Males generally didn't see gender bias as an issue. Some males, however, did see gender bias in the organization.

A number of respondents suggested that the organization was not very accepting of people with different sexual orientations. This situation created both tensions and barriers for people whose sexual orientation was different from the majority.

A salary differential between men and women may have prevented women from seeking career advancement that required relocation. Several respondents felt that, on average, women were not paid on par with men; therefore, their worth to the organization was undervalued.

Because of certain stereotypes, minorities and females have been seen only in certain roles. This circumscription limits the positions that they can hold, the contributions they can make, and the recognition and rewards they can reap.

Minorities are sometimes seen as a monolithic group, and individuals are asked to speak on behalf of the group or to represent the sentiments and ideas of those in the group. This situation, according to several respondents, is both unfair and stressful for Blacks. The organization would be better served to invite multiple voices to discuss and debate issues important to the minority and majority communities.

The themes that emerged from my study suggested that group-level discrimination was present in the *YMCA*. Group-level discrimination includes lack of a clear career path and opportunity for upward mobility, lack of salary competitiveness, the majority group's comfort level with minorities working in inner-city jobs, fear of losing power, and wanting to maintain the "status quo."

It is easy for Whites to see a clear career path and envision how they will traverse through positions of increasing responsibility for the course of their careers in the *YMCA*; however, the situation is often starkly different for people of difference. Blacks, other minorities, and women, because of organizational policies and practices, may be unable to see many opportunities for upward mobility and often become frustrated and disenchanted with a system that seems to undervalue them and their contributions.

While some Whites in my study said that low pay may have been a barrier to attracting and retaining minority employees, none of the Black respondents reported that to be the case. Rather, most of the Black respondents suggested that the lack of opportunity to work in roles that would provide the skills and experiences needed to move up in the organization, and a system characterized by homosocial reproduction in its hiring and promotion practices, were tremendously frustrating to them.

Another barrier was the fact that some individuals in the organization believed that because Blacks were very good at working in the inner city, an assumption was made that they were content working there, failing to recognize that some Blacks may desire to use their skills in other roles as well. Some in the majority may not recognize the risks that minorities would face by openly voicing discontent with a system that is unfair. Blacks may feel they would be ostracized by those who already perpetuate a system that is unfair by being told that they are "being sensitive" or that by playing the "race card," they are trying to gain an advantage in an organization that is already offering opportunities "equally to all."

Some barriers appeared to be the result of some minorities' lack of preparation, i.e., human capital (education, training, experience) and social capital (networking and development of a system of social support). While the attainment of these resources may be hindered by organizational practices that limit their availability to minorities, some respondents in the study suggested that minorities can and should do more to determine their own destinies.

Those in charge may fear a loss of power should the status quo change. If that is the case, some may resist having more minorities and women in senior positions because it may necessarily mean less power, influence, and prestige for them.

Organizational-level discrimination was evidenced by policies and practices that the institution employed—whether consciously or unconsciously, implicitly or explicitly—the consequences were the same, they served to disadvantage minorities and women. Data suggested that homosocial reproduction, found to be a subset of organizational-level discrimination, operated to ensure those hired, nurtured, and promoted resembled those in charge, invariably White men. The themes that pointed to organizational-level discrimination included: homosocial reproduction (including a need to assimilate and the "good old boy system"), fear of losing membership and program revenues, lack of intentionality in promoting diversity (inadequate human resource development, lack of board diversity, lack of staff diversity, lack of mission focus, a tendency to reflect community attitudes, a tendency to reflect community demographics, and a tendency to undervalue the contributions of subsidized branches).

Many respondents spoke about the impact of homosocial reproduction, suggesting that organizational leaders tend to hire and promote people like themselves because it is an expedient way to ensure that those selected were compatible with existing norms and expectations. When candidates were being considered for senior, trusted positions, those in charge tended to look for others who were similar, which invariably meant someone who was both White and male. Homosocial reproduction was likely one of the primary barriers to upward mobility for African Americans in the *YMCA*. Often those responsible for homosocial practices were blind to the impact it had and failed to see themselves as perpetuating a discriminatory system.

Even when Blacks and other minorities were given opportunities to fill senior roles in the organization, they often were expected to assimilate and not "make waves." Black managers may find themselves in a quandary. On the one hand, in order to be successful, they must be innovative and decisive, yet by doing so, they may be perceived as being militant or rebellious. As one respondent said, "it's a 'no win' situation." Minorities and women also may feel the need to overcompensate when dealing with same-race or same-gender subordinates in an effort to avoid the appearance of favoritism, thereby creating stress for all involved.

The "good old boy system," a representation of homosocial reproduction, helped to ensure that key jobs were given to individuals who were like those in charge, often White males. The "good old boy system" is facilitated through biased recommendations and unfair hiring and promotion practices that generally worked to disadvantage minorities and women. A number of respondents suggested that "who you know" still played too large a role in staff selection and inhibited minorities and women from advancing to all levels of the organization. The "good old boy system" was enmeshed in the senior leadership in the *YMCA*, making the establishment of mentor relationships difficult unless you were part of the "the club." This, again, usually worked to the detriment of minorities and women.

My study recommended the following strategies to assist *YMCA* leaders in eliminating these barriers to upward mobility (Other organizations and companies may also find these strategies helpful in dealing with barriers.):

- Review policies and practices to ensure they are not discriminatory in design or in effect.
- Establish diversity committees within each corporate and branch *YMCA*.
- Ensure that programs and facilities are made available to all.
- Develop strategies to engage and reward managers for success in diversity efforts.
- Engage outside consultants to aid in goal attainment.
- Address personal biases and community attitudes.
- Diversify the composition and thinking of volunteer boards.
- Establish dialogue with minority organizations to aid in recruiting diversity to boards.
- Achieve board commitment to diversity.
- Reconcile fears about loss of revenue if minorities are hired in majority communities.
- Become intentional in promoting diversity.
- Become proactive in finding and inviting minorities and women to apply for jobs.
- Provide training and development for all staff equally.
- End the practice of candidate profiling.

- Address human capital barriers (education, training, skills, and experience).
- Address social capital barriers (demographic similarity, career-related support, and psychosocial support).
- Develop a national mentoring program.
- Dismantle the "good old boy system."
- Educate minorities and women on the impact of their attitudes and behaviors.
- Address structural limitations.
- Establish meaningful dialogue.

Organizational leaders must be committed to achieving a diverse workforce, have a well-thought-out plan, and seek ways to sustain the effort for the long term. Leaders must recognize that responsibility for achieving a diverse workforce rests with everyone and not just people of color and women. Ways must be found to change the behaviors of majority and minority, and male and female decision-makers, supervisors, subordinates, and coworkers, if meaningful changes that support diversity are to be made and sustained. Barriers to upward mobility and disparate treatment are real in the *YMCA*. It is incumbent upon *YMCA* leaders to recognize, study and work to eliminate their existence. Only through concerted efforts, which include reflection and intentional policies and practices, can the situation be changed.

Since my dissertation was completed in 2003, the *YMCA* of the USA and some local Y's have made significant strides toward improving their commitment to diversity, equity, and inclusion. Kevin Washington, the first African American to be hired as President/CEO of the *YMCA* of the USA, led the organization from 2015 to 2021. Following Kevin, the organization hired Suzanne McCormick, the first woman to serve in this role. In addition, a number of people of color and women have been hired as CEOs of local *YMCA*s. However, as of 2020, only 42 (5.3 percent) of the 795 Y CEOs nationwide are African American. On the other hand, 714 (90.1 percent) are White. To its credit, the *YMCA* of the USA has developed a Multicultural Leadership Development Strategy that "aims to identify, engage, inspire, develop, promote, and retain Y leaders of color in order to create a stronger pipeline of diverse Y leaders and volunteers at all levels and to increase racial representation at all levels within the organization."

The findings in my research should be a clarion call for change in the *YMCA* and other organizations. While significant strides have been made toward diversity, equity, and inclusion at senior levels of the *YMCA*, nationally and locally, much more still needs to be done to dismantle systemic racism in the organization and in our society.

I venture to say that the findings in my study of the *YMCA* may be similar for other nonprofits, for-profit businesses, and corporations. I invite readers to challenge their thinking and examine the ways your own organization creates a welcoming and rewarding place for all. I pray that God will continue to guide me as I attempt to work toward achieving diversity, equity, and inclusion throughout my community and in American life.

First Pitch – A Lesson on Humility

"Humble yourselves, therefore, under God's mighty hand, that he may lift you up in due time. Cast all your anxiety on him because he cares for you." 1 Peter 5:6-7 (New International Version)

AMID ALL THE SUCCESS and accomplishments that we may have achieved, God always has a way to humble us. He reminds us that He is in charge and that we can do nothing without Him. This is true for all of us, no matter how successful we are. Unfortunately, I have had to learn this lesson more than once. I sometimes think that my accomplishments are simply the results of my hard work and determination, failing to recognize the importance of God's unmerited favor in my life. Sometimes I don't think to pray to God before I go through a storm, thinking, "I've got this." But in reality, I should pray to God constantly and recognize that He and He alone is in charge.

One day in the fall of 2009, I received an e-mail from Rob Porras in the Community Affairs Department of Reliant Energy inviting me to view the August 18th *Texas Rangers* vs. *Minnesota Twins* game with other guests in their corporate suite. The *YMCA* of Arlington was one of *Reliant Energy*'s community partners and had benefited from their generosity. I gladly accepted the invitation and looked forward to enjoying food, fun, and fellowship with some fine people. As President/CEO of the *YMCA* of Arlington, I felt honored to receive this invitation.

On the day before the game, I got another e-mail from Rob asking if I'd like to "throw out the first pitch." After nearly falling off my chair, I tried to rationalize why I should or shouldn't accept this awesome invitation. I thought,

Willie Dean

"What if I flub the pitch and look silly?" "What if I get winded climbing the steps or pull something because I was just four months from having had two major surgeries?" I started no less than four times to phone my wife to ask her advice; however, my "pride" got the best of me. I phoned Rob, thanked him, and declined his invitation because of my "recent surgeries."

That night when I talked with my wife and shared my anxieties, she consoled me by telling me at least I followed my intuition. I lamented, however, that I was sorry I had turned down what was likely a "once-in-a-lifetime" opportunity. Finally, I did what I should have done in the first place; I prayed about it and asked the Lord for guidance.

The next day, less than 12 hours before game time, I sent an e-mail to Rob which said, "If the opportunity to throw out the first pitch is still available, I'd like to do it tonight. If not, please keep me in mind for this honor should it occur in the future." I knew it was likely that someone else had been asked since I had turned down the invitation the day before. However, Rob responded almost immediately, confirming that I would be able to do it, "Let's play ball.......you will have the honor to throw out the first pitch tonight." I was reminded that following the Lord's guidance always leads us in the right direction!

I sent out a joyous e-mail to about 150 of my supporters (board members, staff, family, and friends) around the country that said, "I will do something tonight that I never dreamed of doing...throw out the first pitch at a Major League Baseball game!" I went on to say, "This is an awesome opportunity, one that few people ever get. It turns out that Major League pitcher Dizzy Dean and I have something in common. We were both born in the South to sharecroppers and went on to achieve much in our lives. I thank God for every opportunity He provides me!" I closed by saying, "The game is tonight, August 18, at 7:05 p.m. I'll be the one wearing a red 'YMCA Activate America' t-shirt. Tune in and pray that all goes well...it could be the start of something BIG! I've got to go now and practice my pitching (smile)!"

In response to my e-mail, many colleagues and friends wished me well, and a few suggested that I not "bounce it off the ground!" Here are some of the comments I received:

- Go, Willie, go! So glad you included me in your good news. – Gay
- Congratulations! It's great having a major leaguer in the family!! – Ken
- Brother Dean, I am convinced that life, the sum total of our experiences, can, at times, be more precious than gold. Continue to be blessed by all that it offers you!!!!!! – Brother Rodney

- Congratulations, Willie! Your messages are always so inspiring, and I really enjoy getting them! – Susan
- Willie, I am jealous. What a well-deserved opportunity! Congratulations – Richard
- My brother always does great things! – Christine
- Congratulations, God's plans are always greater than ours! I will be watching for the 1st pitch! Blessings. – Lonzetta
- That's fantastic. Congratulations. I'm sure it will be a strike right down the middle. – Al
- Willie, practice makes perfect. I hope you do not leave it all out there on the first pitch. The Rangers may need you in the bullpen. – Jim
- Congratulations and well-deserved honor. – Jimmy
- Wow, Willie – That is fantastic! The Texas Rangers are doing so well too! Here's my tip – fire it in there – better to overthrow than underthrow! Good Luck – I'll be watching on MLB.com! – Charlie
- Willie – throwing the first pitch is the coolest thing I can imagine. Your life is blessed in many ways, and you are a blessing to others. I appreciate our Rotary ties and our business ties. Don't hurt your back; I am not sure if your insurance covers major league pitching. – Brian
- Outstanding Coach. You'll do well. Just throw a fastball right down the center. We'll see you on TV tonight, hopefully! – Louie
- Congratulations! As you said, not many people get this opportunity, and so many dream of being able to have this moment! Make us proud! – Brittany
- Just throw it at the guy with the glove. He will make you look good! Awesome! – Tom
- Good luck, Willie, on your first pitch! I think you're going to be drafted to join the Major League. We'll be cheering for you tonight. – Sophy
- Fabulous news! They chose the best person for the first pitch! Congratulations! – Glynda
- Congratulations, Willie! That's awesome! It's well deserved! I know you're going to throw a strike! – Hadley
- I even got an e-mail from Mark McLemore, former Texas Rangers great and Fox Sports Southwest sportscaster, who said, "I'll b covering the game tonight, so I'll c u there. By the way, a word of advice, when u throw out the first pitch, whatever u do, just don't bounce it!!! I'll b watching."

A number of other friends had similar admonitions:

- Congrats. I know it's a thrill. Oh yeah, just remember, don't bounce the ball. Ha, ha, ha. – Lee
- Wow, Willie. This is awesome. Wish I was in town; it would be worth the price of admission. Don't throw like a girl... – Terry
- Congratulations, Willie. I will be looking for you on TV, make sure you make a good pitch! – Eric

That's all I needed was to be reminded not to embarrass myself, or the *YMCA*, in front of 30,000 baseball fans. The nervousness was on...again!

Then to my relief, Mark Bradrick, *YMCA* Sports Director, sent me an e-mail, "Come on over, and I will have Jason work with you. He has done a lot of pitching in high school and college. You don't want to bounce it to the plate!! This is so awesome!! Make sure you take a lot of pictures. Congratulations."

I phoned Jason Simmons, one of our Sports Coordinators, who played baseball in high school and was a pitcher at his alma mater, the University of Texas at Dallas. Jason agreed to catch with me that afternoon. He was very supportive and offered tips after I had thrown several pitches from the 45-foot and 60-foot rubber he had laid out. I found that my control when throwing hard wasn't what I remembered as a teen some 40 years earlier. Imagine my amazement! So, I decided to throw at a moderate speed, aim for accuracy and avoid "bouncing it!"

I learned that another gentleman would also throw a pitch that night. The Rangers staff had him go first. He threw a blistering pitch that sounded off in the catcher's mitt, and the crowd responded in approval. Rather than try to compete with this gentleman who appeared at least 25 years my junior, I stuck to my plan. I positioned myself about three feet short of the rubber, wound up, and threw a moderate-speed pitch directly into the catcher's mitt.

My pitching experience was a blast! I had managed not to "bounce it," and I received a "thunderous roar" from the crowd! There isn't a video on YouTube; however, I placed photos on my Facebook page to prove to myself and my grandkids that the evening really did happen! In addition, former Texas Rangers pitcher, Tim Crabtree, stopped by the Reliant Energy suite where we watched the game and autographed his alumni card for the other guests and me!

Comments from family and friends following the game gratified me and helped me remember how important praise is for kids of all ages:

- CONGRATULATIONS, my friend! – Ann

- Congratulations, I'm glad to hear it went well. It looks like you threw from the mound, too—very impressive! - Jason
- I enjoyed the photos. Did the Rangers offer you a contract? - Ramona
- What a great day for the *YMCA* and you (glad no bounce) - Bill
- I hope you didn't have to ice your pitching arm…seriously I hope you had a great time at the Rangers game. - Sue
- Congratulations…What an awesome opportunity? I hope that you retained footage of the event. I know that you had fun! - Pastor E.

Normally I'm "cool, calm, and collected" on almost everything I do; however, I was nervous beyond belief with throwing out the first pitch. Just think, six months earlier, I was diagnosed with bilateral renal carcinoma. Three months earlier, I underwent two major surgeries to remove malignant tumors from my kidneys, and there I was throwing out the first pitch at a Major League Baseball game! Because of what I had gone through, these encouraging comments meant all the more, which is why I saved them.

I thanked my friends at *Reliant Energy* for the opportunity to throw out the first pitch. Family and friends commented on how cool my experience was. Being selected for the first pitch was a lesson on humility, for which I thank God. What a testament to His awesome power!

Caring for Aging Parents

"Honor your father and your mother, as the Lord your God has commanded you, so that you may live long and that it may go well with you in the land the Lord your God is giving you." Deuteronomy 5:16 (New International Version)

I CAME OF AGE during a period known as the "Sandwich Generation," when many adults found themselves rearing their children while simultaneously caring for their aging parents. It was my responsibility to raise my children and provide for my family; however, it was my honor to make the lives of my mother and father comfortable during their debilitating illnesses and, ultimately, their demise and transition to glory.

My mother was diagnosed in her mid-50s with multiple myeloma, a cancer of plasma cells that is a type of white blood cell in the bone marrow. She suffered from this malady until her death, in 1997, at age 65. I rarely saw Mom complain about her affliction or the pain that she endured. She continued her daily routine, cooking meals, washing clothes, and keeping our house going until her body could no longer withstand the pain and anguish. As the disease progressed, she spent more and more time on the couch and in bed. Dad, who had been laid off from his job when the trucking company where he worked went bankrupt, was able to spend time with her between daily trips to his farm to care for the farm animals and to tend the crops in his garden. Years later, it became apparent that it was providence that Dad's job had ended, providing him the flexibility to care for my mother. Also, the work on the farm was, in many ways, cathartic for my dad. It gave him the chance to get away daily from the stresses at home and to work with his hands tilling the soil, something he valued deeply.

Willie Dean

I got a call from Dad in early March 1997, informing me that my mother's health had taken a turn for the worse and that I should come to Memphis as soon as possible. I was living with my family in Bloomington, Minnesota, at the time. As soon as I could make flight arrangements and ensure my family was in good stead, I traveled "home." When I arrived in Memphis, my mother had already been admitted to the hospital. When I saw her, she was lucid and recognized me. I greeted her, held her hand, kissed her on her forehead, and asked her how she was doing.

My son, Cedric, who had relocated back to Memphis after his discharge from the U.S. Navy, came by the hospital to visit with his beloved grandmother. Cedric and I greeted each other with a huge hug, for we had not seen each other in months, and he sensed the seriousness of the situation and my need to be comforted.

Cedric suffers from asthma that he developed while stationed at a naval base near Lemoore, California, that was located adjacent to agricultural fields that were frequently dusted with aerial pesticides. During his visit to the hospital, Cedric had an asthma attack, perhaps brought on by the stress of seeing his grandmother's health waning before his eyes. A nurse asked him if he had an inhaler. He indicated that he did, and she retrieved it from his pocket and helped him administer the medication. After a bit, he was stable. Thank God for trained and observant medical professionals.

My mother's sister, Mayetta Walker, had traveled from Potts Camp, Mississippi, and was with us on the night of my mother's death. Aunt Mayetta wanted to visit another relative who had been admitted to the same hospital. I accompanied her to our relative's room for a brief visit.

When we got back to my mother's room, we learned that Mom had passed. I felt bad that I had not been at her bedside when she made her transition. I took her hand and kissed her forehead as I had done earlier. I opened the Bible that was on the nightstand in her room and read aloud the 23rd Psalm. This passage has always provided comfort and solace to me.

I was heartbroken when my father exclaimed, "What am I going to do?" Dad and Mom were just five months from celebrating their 50th wedding anniversary. I had never seen my father cry or express pain. I had experienced the death of both my maternal and paternal grandparents, but the death of my mother was the closest relative to me to die. (My mother's death foreshadowed the death of my wife, Pam, four years later. The strength that I draw from the Lord helped to comfort and sustain me during these difficult periods in my life.)

Overcoming

My mother passed away on March 18, 1997, following a heroic ten-year battle with multiple myeloma. We thought Mom was a hypochondriac because she seemed to come down with every malady that others had. However, I don't remember her ever complaining about her cancer and the pain she endured going through radiation and chemotherapy. I know now that we underestimated her strength and resilience. I regret we had sometimes made light of her medical concerns.

Planning my mother's homegoing was both gratifying and heart-wrenching. It was good having my father, brothers, and sister together under one roof again; however, the pain of the empty chair at our dinner table was difficult. My father, as usual, was our rock. Looking back, I realize I probably took on much of my persona from my dad, who showed little emotion although he must have been writhing inside with pain and grief.

After losing his life partner, my father went on with life. He continued being his nurturing self with his children and grandchildren. And, because all of us except for Bug did not live in the Memphis area, he grew increasingly close to his nieces and nephews in Mississippi and with children of all ages at his church.

I enjoyed talking with my father and siblings as we pieced together my mom's obituary and searched for a photo for her funeral program. We had a wonderful homegoing service at Baptist Hill Missionary Baptist Church (the family church where Joe and I confessed our faith nearly four decades earlier) in Potts Camp, Mississippi, and laid Mom to rest at Forest Hill Midtown Cemetery in Memphis.

Dad, a few years older than Mom, lived until age 92. He was active and even continued to drive his car until a few years before his death. As his health began to fail, I recognized the need to support him in any way that I could. I made it a point to visit him in Memphis whenever I could. I traveled by car, bus, or airplane to spend time with my dad.

I retired from my job with *YouthCARE* in December 2017, in part to be able to travel to Memphis to spend time with and care for Dad. And as fate would have it, I developed a relationship with Dr. Carol Johnson, who also had been widowed and had ties with the Memphis area. Carol and I wed in June 2018. She was loved by my dad and did everything possible to care for him. She prepared his favorite meals, which included turnip greens, deviled eggs, and meatloaf. She also made sure he always had his special request, a Kroger brand lemon pound cake, to satiate his sweet tooth.

Willie Dean

I believe the Lord made it possible for me to meet, fall in love with and marry Carol, and move back to Memphis, in part to be closer to my dad at a time he needed me most. Carol and I rented a *U-Haul* truck, loaded my belongings, and drove the more than 800 miles from Minnesota to Tennessee in June 2019. The move allowed Carol and me to live together under one roof and for me to be near my aging father and younger brother, Bug, who still lived in the house where I grew up in South Memphis.

I visited Dad and Bug frequently, making the 60-mile roundtrip almost daily. I fixed breakfast for them and took Dad to doctors' appointments. Initially, Dad was ambulatory, requiring only a cane to steady himself when he walked. As he got older and as his physical condition deteriorated, he would use two canes, a walker, or a wheelchair to get around. I noticed, too, that Dad's memory was failing as he frequently repeated himself during conversations. He could recount things that happened earlier in his life, but where he put his glasses or his memory of recent events was more challenging. He was exhibiting early signs of dementia, which would later be diagnosed by his medical team.

Dad was healthy during much of his life; however, as he aged, he was confronted with a number of health challenges. He suffered two strokes, following which he had only minor complications. He also suffered from breast cancer, which required a mastectomy, hypertension, and renal cell cancer, from which he succumbed. Through it all, my dad was a lover of life and relied on his faith, his family, and his friends.

Dad recognized the need to sell his farm as his health was declining, and there was a need to fund a special needs trust to help support Bug after his demise. Selling the farm was not an easy decision for dad or me. Many Black people don't own land, a primary source for building generational wealth. But, in the end, Dad made the decision that was best for his family. We found a Mississippi-licensed realtor, as his property was located in Olive Branch, Mississippi, and listed his farm for sale.

Dad bought the farm in 1986 from another Black farmer. He built a small farmhouse, barn, and storage sheds—all constructed with discarded wood, tin, and other materials that he often found alongside the road—that allowed him to care for a small herd of beef cattle. He also built a small garden that he took pride in tilling each spring. Working in the garden was cathartic as it allowed him to get back to his roots and work the soil with his hands.

Dad went by ambulance to Methodist University Hospital in January 2020. He was bleeding from his rectum, a condition that plagued him for the past few years, requiring numerous trips to the ER and several hospitalizations. He spent more than 24 hours in the ER waiting for an exam room due to the surge of patients caused by the early stages of the COVID-19 pandemic. I went home overnight, and when I returned to the emergency room the next day, I learned that dad had been told by the ER doctor that he had only six months to live. I was disheartened that my dad was alone when he got this news. It was difficult to accept that Dad had osteosarcoma and only six months to live.

It was difficult for me to hear the diagnosis, but the prognosis was even harder to accept. It couldn't be that I was soon going to lose the most important man in my life. The man that I loved, learned from and emulated my whole life. Dad, on the other hand, seemed ready to accept his fate. His treating physician suggested we consider hospice. I asked Dad if he wanted me to set up a family conference call to share the information we had received and to discuss the prospect of hospice. Dad said that he and I would make the decision. He was resolute in not wanting to prolong his life with extraordinary measures. This was something he and my mother had decided for themselves years earlier. More importantly, he was assured of his destiny, knowing his soul was in the hands of the Lord.

Finally, a room became available, and Dad was admitted to the hospital. The nurses and technicians provided him excellent care, and the doctors tried to explain to us in layman's terms what was happening to his body. They were afraid he might fall; he later was restricted to using a bedpan and urinal. It was difficult seeing this proud man, who all of his life was independent and strong, becoming bedbound.

As a devout Christian, Dad faced death with dignity, knowing that he was glory bound. He and I decided we would arrange for home hospice so he could die at his residence, the place he had called home for 62 years.

I noticed that Dad was increasingly becoming dependent on Bug and me to assist him in going to the bathroom rather than asking the nursing staff for assistance. This was even more apparent when he was being discharged. Bug and I assisted him to the bathroom, which in hindsight, I realize, masked his inability to move about. We would learn later that his mobility was becoming increasingly limited.

On one occasion, we attempted to take Dad for an appointment; however, his legs buckled when we got to his living room, and despite Bug's and my best efforts, we weren't able to keep him from sliding from our arms to the floor. After repeatedly trying to lift him, we realized that his less than 175-pound frame was like dead weight. It was nearly impossible for us to lift him safely. We wisely called 911. Within minutes a Memphis Fire Department engine company arrived. Two brawny firefighters assessed the situation and gently lifted Dad back into his wheelchair and moved him safely to the hospital bed that hospice had arranged in his bedroom. Sadly, this was the last time that Dad was out of his bed alive. We tried on several occasions, with the assistance of his hospice nurse; however, it was clear that his legs could no longer support his body weight.

The wonderful people from Methodist Home Hospice—nurses, aides, and chaplain—treated my dad with dignity and respect on the phone and whenever they entered his home. The nurses taught us how to administer medicine and change his foley catheter. We even learned how to change Dad's bed linens with him in the bed, as he was, by this time, bedridden.

I never thought I would have to help my dad onto a bedpan, wipe his bottom or hold his penis while a nurse inserted a foley catheter. I was doing many of the things for my dad at the end of his life that he likely did for me at the beginning of mine. I felt both humbled and honored to perform these duties.

Dad endured almost constant pain. Since the hospice program's goal was to keep him comfortable and pain-free, we administered a regimen of pain medications, including morphine. I was concerned about Dad becoming addicted; however, his pain management was more important as he was nearing the end of his life. I told him that everything was going to be alright. I was surprised when he told me, "Willie, you don't know that." I felt hurt; however, in reality, I couldn't truly understand what he was feeling. Here he was, in almost constant pain and bedridden at age 92. How could I tell him that I understood how he was feeling or that it was going to be alright?

Dad frequently lamented that he was in pain and wanted to die. He was tired. Most of his contemporaries (his wife, several siblings, many friends, and co-workers) were deceased. He was non-ambulatory and had suffered breast, pelvic, renal cell, and prostate cancer, as well as hypertension and two strokes. He also exhibited more pronounced symptoms of dementia, and he was slowly becoming less and less lucid.

As Dad's condition deteriorated, he complained more and more of pain. The hospice nurse reiterated that their goal was to keep him comfortable and pain-free. I continued to be concerned about the possibility of my dad becoming addicted to the painkillers. However, it became clear to me as his pain mounted that this concern had to be balanced against his comfort in his final days.

Late one night, Bug called me and said that Dad was hemorrhaging profusely from his rectum. I drove immediately to their home. When I arrived, I assessed the situation and phoned the on-call hospice nurse, who was nearly 45 minutes away. When the nurse arrived, she triaged Dad, took his vitals, and worked with me to change his nightgown and bedding. She told me that his bleeding was likely the result of his cancer. For the first time, I became very worried and realized the end might be near.

Dad became increasingly irritable and began to refuse to eat or drink an adequate amount of water. As he was not eating, we didn't put his dentures in his mouth daily. Soon I realized that his mouth had become constricted, and he couldn't open his mouth enough for me to insert his dental plates. We tried to give him sustenance like applesauce and other soft food with a spoon and water through a straw.

Dad's faith in God remained strong. He especially liked praying with the hospice chaplain. He also enjoyed visits from his pastor, the Reverend Dwight L. Saulsberry, who comforted both Dad and me during this very difficult time in our lives. He was a man of deep faith. Dad relished having these men of God to pray with him.

Bug and I worked hard to make Dad comfortable. When I came over, I usually prepared breakfast for us. My specialties included scrambled eggs with cheese, sausages (pork and turkey), wheat toast and jelly, orange juice, and tea. Neither Dad nor Bug liked the skim milk that I drank. Although it was breakfast time, Dad always liked to finish each meal with a slice of lemon pound cake. He had a "sweet tooth" to the very end.

A number of friends called and visited Dad during his last days, a testament to the kind of man that he was and the bonds he had made with others during his lifetime.

My siblings and I provided the best of care for our ailing father. Knowing the end was near, Joe and Chris hastened to Memphis to spend time with Dad. They each spent a week cooking meals, changing his bedclothes, and sharing memories. Either Bug or I was with Dad continuously for the final months of his life.

We celebrated Dad's 92nd birthday early on the Martin Luther King holiday weekend, January 18, 2020. (His actual birthdate was January 30.) The holiday allowed Joe and Chris to take advantage of the three-day weekend to travel from Princeton, New Jersey, and Baltimore, Maryland, respectively. It also allowed more friends and family to attend.

Carol and I had planned to host the party at our home; however, by mid-January, Dad had become bedridden, and moving him was not practical. We decided instead to hold the party at his home. On the day of the party, more than 30 family members and friends crowded into Dad's small, three-bedroom home to wish him a happy birthday and enjoy plenty of homecooked food characteristic of a southern family gathering. Although Dad couldn't get out of his bed, he seemed to enjoy talking with small groups of family and friends who visited with him in his bedroom. He also enjoyed the bountiful food, especially the deviled eggs and lemon pound cake, his favorites. This was the last time most of our family and friends got to see Dad alive. I was pleased that we had planned this birthday celebration for Dad and our family and friends.

Over the next few weeks, Dad suffered multiple internal bleeding episodes, believed to be the result of his renal cell cancer. He became increasingly agitated and refused to eat, drink fluids or take his medications. The hospice nurses warned that the end was near.

Dad passed away peacefully in his sleep at his home on March 3, 2020. As fate would have it—while Carol was out of town on business—I was staying over a few days to care for Dad and to give Bug a break. After Dad went to sleep that night, I watched TV for a while in his room and then retired to the guest room to phone Carol to say goodnight. Later that night, when Bug returned home, we discovered that Dad seemed not to be breathing. I checked for his pulse and found none. I felt blessed that I had chosen to spend the night with him.

I phoned the on-call hospice nurse, who arrived within the hour, checked my dad, and pronounced him deceased. She meticulously and respectfully cleaned up my dad and changed his bed linens, which were used later by the funeral home attendants to lift Dad's lifeless body from his hospital bed onto their stretcher. I read the 23rd Psalm and kissed Dad on his forehead, just as I had done with my mother when she passed away 22 years earlier.

I phoned my brother, Joe, and sister, Chris. Bug and I phoned other family members and friends with the somber news. I also phoned my wife, Carol, in Boston. She made arrangements to fly back to Memphis the next day. I appreciated her presence and support during a very difficult time in my life.

Joe and Chris flew to Memphis within just a few days, and we worked together to write Dad's obituary and create his funeral program, just as we had done for our mom two decades earlier. We enjoyed sharing fond memories with Bug, Skip (Chris' husband), Tana (Joe's partner), and Carol.

While growing up, I hugged my father at the dinner table after he got home from work. I felt his stubby beard against my face, and while uncomfortable, this connection with my father assured me that everything was alright. Now that he is deceased, I long to feel his stubby beard. I took pride in shaving him when he was in hospice and unable to shave himself. This was a humbling experience for him and a source of pride for me.

Dad's funeral was held at New Fellowship Christian Church. We were fortunate that his passing occurred at the beginning of the COVID-19 pandemic; otherwise, we wouldn't have been able to gather for his funeral service. Several dozen mourners, family members, friends, and church members attended. Pastor Saulsberry, who had become a dear family friend, gave the eulogy. I will forever remember the words to a moving song, written by Walter Hawkins, *Goin' up Yonder*, that was sung at the end of his homegoing service as his body and casket were being rolled out of the church sanctuary. I knew that my father was "going up yonder to be with his Lord!"

Dad was buried beside his beloved wife, Mattie, who passed away 22 years earlier, just months short of their 50th wedding anniversary. Mom and Dad—devout Christians—were together again.

I now had the responsibility of managing my dad's affairs. In administering his estate, I undertook the daunting task of hiring an attorney to assist with probate in the state of Tennessee and the state of Mississippi, as his home was located in Memphis, Shelby County, Tennessee, and his farm was located in Olive Branch, DeSoto County, Mississippi. Our family home needed many improvements. We determined that repairing and maintaining the property was not going to be practical and reluctantly decided to put the house and the farm on the market for sale.

Once the house and the farm were sold, we had to find housing for Bug, who had lived in our family's home for all of his 62 years. Carol and I scoured newspaper and online listings for affordable housing in and around the Memphis area. We toured over a dozen apartments, houses, and duplexes; however, we found nothing to our liking that fit Bug's income.

We moved Bug into an *Extended Stay Hotel* for several months and then signed a one-year lease on an apartment near where we live. Several days after signing the apartment lease and moving his belongings into the apartment, we got notice that an income-based apartment near the neighborhood where he grew up was available. The problem was we had just signed a 12-month lease and couldn't get out of it, short of the apartment management being able to lease the apartment to another tenant.

We abandoned the market-rate apartment, continued paying the monthly lease payments, and prayed that the apartment would be re-leased soon. Thanks to God, the apartment was re-leased after two and a half months, relieving Bug of the lease burden. My father would be pleased that my siblings and I worked together to settle his estate and to support Bug in the transition (ensure that he has affordable, stable housing) and that his future was now secure.

For the most part, Bug had always been at home with my parents, and I was sensitive to the fact that in one year, he had lost Dad—someone with whom he had laughed, traveled to the farm, watched TV shows, and attended church services. The same year, their dog, Tiger, also died. I reminded myself to be supportive of Bug as his life, like mine, changed forever with Dad's passing.

Bug loves his new apartment and decorates it constantly with *Dallas Cowboys* memorabilia to make it a place that is his own. He maintains daily communications with Carol and me, as well as with Pastor Saulsberry and the First Lady from his church. "God is good!"

Achieving Balance in My Life

"Come to Me, all you who labor and are heavy laden, and I will give you rest. Take My yoke upon you and learn from Me, for I am gentle and lowly in heart, and you will find rest for your souls." Matthew 11:28-29 (New King James Version)

I TOOK UP A number of interests to help me achieve balance in my life, maintain my health and wellness, and cope with the stresses of work, studying for my Ph.D., and my family's numerous medical and other challenges. I also engaged my sons and me in individual and family therapy to help us grapple with the loss of their mother and my wife. I found Tae Kwon Do, biking, photography, learning to play the guitar, sports cars, and even the demands of a doctoral program to be cathartic during trying times in my life. I stayed busy and also used compartmentalization to deal with adversity. This technique has been effective as a coping tool; however, it has fallen short in letting others—family, friends, colleagues, employers, and employees—know how I feel and where I stand on important issues. I have to constantly remind myself to be more emotive.

Tae Kwon Do – Self Defense and Self Discipline

I have been a lover of martial arts for more than 50 years since when I saw movie stars like Bruce Lee and Jean-Claude Van Damme perform unbelievable feats on the big screen. I participated briefly in an intramural Judo club while an undergraduate student at Memphis State University. I learned how to throw opponents and use their body weight against them. However, my serious training in martial arts began in 1992 at the South/Southwest *YMCA* in Omaha, Nebraska, when I began training in Tae Kwon Do, a Korean martial arts form characterized by the use of open hands and feet that was developed in the 1940s and 1950s. The five tenets of Tae Kwon Do—courtesy, integrity, perseverance, self-control, and indomitable spirit—fit wonderfully with my personal values.

In June 2003, more than ten years after I started training, I earned a first-degree black belt in Tae Kwon Do, at True Tae Kwon Do, in Bloomington, Minnesota. My school, headed by Master Ralph Truesdell, was conveniently located just a few miles from my home. At age 52, I was one of the oldest students in my classes; however, Master Ralph and my fellow students were always respectful of classmates of any age or ability. I was also the only African American that trained at my school. I felt welcomed and never felt out of place.

I earned a black belt and a Ph.D. in the same year. I guess you could say I was a glutton for punishment. However, these accomplishments were both important and therapeutic for me as I dealt with the stresses of caring for my wife, Pam, who continued in a chronic vegetative state, and the challenges I encountered, as a single parent, raising two teenage boys.

Biking for Fun and Fitness

My family gave me a mountain bike for Father's Day in 1997. I immediately set a goal to ride 500 miles before winter set in that year. I rode five to ten miles daily throughout my community. I especially liked biking to a nearby nature preserve. On Thanksgiving Day, while exiting the preserve, I had a flat tire. It had begun to rain, a precursor to sleet and snow during a Minnesota winter. I was within a mile of my home and of my goal.

As I walked my bike along the cold, wet streets headed home, a White woman in an SUV pulled alongside me, rolled down her window, and asked, "Are you, Willie Dean?" I said yes. She then asked if I needed a ride. I thought momentarily and replied, "Thank you, but no. I set a goal to ride 500 miles this season, and I'm within a mile of achieving it." The fact that the lady was White is relevant only to illustrate that not all Whites and Blacks are suspicious of one another.

I hoped my neighbor, who likely remembered me from neighborhood cookouts, would understand that I was not ungrateful but that achieving my goal was important to me. I trudged along in the cold rain, pushing my bike the last mile home. Goal attainment had become built into every facet of my life.

This was the same drive that had been instilled in me from a young age by my father and by Mr. Terrell, my junior high basketball coach.

One summer, after the death of my wife, Pam, a dear friend, Harold Mezile, invited me to accompany him on a bicycle trip around Prince Edward Island, Canada. We were the only African Americans on the biking tour. It was a scenic and grueling journey where we saw small towns, forests, and seashores. We even saw the fictional home from Ann of the *Green Gables*, a popular book for young girls. While I had been an avid biker most of my life, riding up and down the hills and dells of Prince Edward Island proved to be very challenging; however, one of our guides made it a point to ensure that he was always nearby. The trip combined two of my loves, biking and the outdoors.

I used my interest in biking to help raise funds for the Sioux *YMCA*, the only *YMCA* in the U.S. that served Native American youth and families. I recruited several Y staff and volunteers to bike a 50- or 100-mile trip that ended at the Sioux *YMCA* on the Cheyenne Reservation in Dupree, South Dakota. I secured a number of pledges and selected the 50-mile trip as my goal. Riding beside me was Don Kerr, then-Executive Director of the Missouri Valley Family *YMCA* in Bismarck, North Dakota. Having Don by my side provided me with constant encouragement.

The ride was much more difficult than I had anticipated. The rolling hills of South Dakota are a lot more challenging when riding a bike than when riding in a car! A number of times, I thought I was going to have to "throw in the towel" and signal for our chase car to carry me to the finish line. But somehow, I dug deep, prayed for strength, and continued on, knowing the importance of finishing what I started.

The pain of the last few miles was surpassed only by the exhilaration of turning the last corner and seeing the finish line in sight. The throng of Y volunteers (from across the Midwest) and youth and families from the reservation were gratifying. Together, we raised more than $50,000 to help support the Sioux *YMCA*'s programs. The pain and exhaustion I felt were worth it. The Sioux *YMCA* volunteers gave me an ornamental, handmade blanket in appreciation for my support of their Y.

Photography – Window to My World

From an early age, and my first *Instamatic* camera, I have been a camera bug. I remember sending my negatives off to the drugstore for development, only to learn upon retrieving my photographs that my fingers had often obscured my camera's lens. I took some great photos, if you didn't mind the presence of my fingers in the frame. I welcomed the advent of through-the-lens metering, which allowed me to see my subjects, and any obstructions, through the camera's lens.

My brother, Joe, bought a *Minolta SRT 101* 35mm camera when he was in college. He took it with him to Europe during a summer abroad and took probably 1,500 slides. When I saw his beautiful pictures, I was hooked. Years later, when I was in college, I bought a *Minolta SRT 201* 35mm camera; once again, I was walking in the footsteps of my big brother; however, by this time, I was physically larger than he.

Over the years, I have refined my photography skills and now shoot with a *Nikon D3*, a professional digital camera. I have probably taken more than 25,000 digital photographs, many of which were to support the ministries of churches that I have attended, the *YMCAs* where I have worked, *KFAI Radio*, and *YouthCARE*. I also have many shots that I have taken just for fun and to express my creativity. I even operated a small photography business for a brief period. I plan to revamp and reopen the business again in my retirement. I enjoy immensely creating images in this art form.

Guitar – Music to My Ears

I started taking guitar lessons at my home in Bloomington, Minnesota, in 1992. I always loved music; however, I had never taken music lessons of any kind. Learning to play has been challenging. (Not knowing how to read music and the fact that I have large fingers both seemed to be problematic. However, I have seen other guitarists with equally large hands who have mastered the instrument.)

I continued lessons at a community center when I moved back to Texas and at a music studio upon my relocation to Minnesota. COVID-19 interrupted my in-studio lessons when I relocated to Memphis; however, I dabble with learning to play a number of songs by watching instructional videos on YouTube. I love listening to music and playing music on my guitar. It soothes my soul. I played for my late wife, Pam, when she was in a chronic vegetative state at the Masonic Home near our home in Bloomington, Minnesota. I play my guitar from time to time for family members. Carol encourages me and has invited me to play for family birthdays and for our Sunday School class.

I also played my guitar during student recitals when I took lessons in Minneapolis. I nervously performed as I didn't want to embarrass myself. Only one other student performing in the recitals was over age 50; the rest ranged from about age six to 16. I was out of my comfort zone, but I persevered, never giving up until the job was finished. I recently played *Amazing Grace* during a brunch for my Sunday School class. It was a gratifying experience

Fast Cars – You Can Never Have Too Much Horsepower

A *YMCA* colleague once called me a "renaissance man" because of my varied interests. One of my interests, a love of fast cars, is one that I now share with my sons, Cedric and Matt. We each own a *Mustang*, an iconic American-made muscle car. The first car that I bought, however, was a royal blue 1972 *Dodge Demon*. It had a 340 cubic inch, 240-horsepower engine, a 4-barrel carburetor, and a 4-speed manual transmission. It also had a white stripe along the sides. A real head turner with a throaty growl when you opened it up, this car was fast. I put yellow traction bars, a rear lift kit, chrome mag wheels, and 9.5-inch-wide, L60-14 tires on the back. This car looked fast even when it was standing still. However, it didn't have air conditioning, which was problematic when I moved to Texas. I regret to this day that I added an aftermarket A/C unit, which often overheated in the Texas heat and robbed the engine of power.

My second car, a gray 1978 *Dodge Challenger*, had a 2.6-liter *Mitsubishi* engine and a 5-speed manual transmission. It was not a muscle car by any means. It was fuel-efficient, which was important during the national oil crisis that started in 1973 when the Organization of Oil Producing Exporting Countries (OPEC) declared an oil embargo designed to pressure countries thought to be pro-Israel. The net effect of the embargo reduced supply and increased demand (and prices) for petroleum nationwide. I remember federally mandated energy-saving practices like a 55-m.p.h. national speed limit. Everyone was encouraged to turn off lights in unused rooms and to set thermostats to moderate levels. There were increased thefts of gasoline from vehicles and long lines at gas stations as gasoline allotments were limited. Gasoline prices nearly tripled from the beginning of the crisis until its end in 1974, leading consumers and manufacturers to look for more fuel-efficient automobiles and trucks. Regrettably, I failed to change the oil properly in my *Challenger* and damaged its engine on one of my drives from Fort Worth to Memphis. I had the engine rebuilt; however, it never ran the same. I learned a valuable and expensive lesson about taking proper care of my cars.

Willie Dean

The next car I owned was a black 1985 *Toyota Supra*. It had a 161-horsepower engine, a 5-speed manual transmission, and a sunroof. This car was powerful yet sophisticated and reflected my laid-back, strong persona. I hand-washed my car just about every week and hand-waxed it twice each year. I reluctantly traded this beauty—after driving it for more than 160,000 miles—when I determined it was not practical for my family of five to drive in the snow and ice during Omaha winters.

I bought a black 1997 *Ford Mustang Cobra* in early 1998. This car, which came standard with a 305-horsepower engine, and 5-speed manual transmission, had only 75 miles on its odometer when I bought it as it was a limited-edition vehicle, and dealers knew prospective owners didn't want a lot of miles on them. I had to buy the vehicle without test driving it; however, I knew what I wanted. Looking back, it was my son, Cedric, who had recently bought a black 1996 *Mustang GT*, who encouraged me to get a Cobra. Our mutual love of cars was becoming apparent. Not only did we both have black Mustangs, but we also loved going to car shows and to MN Cars and Coffee, a gathering of car enthusiasts. At MN Cars and Coffee, owners showcased everything from souped-up domestic vehicles like *Chevy Corvettes* and *Ford GTs* to exotic foreign makes like *Lamborghinis*, *Ferraris* and *Porsches*, and other supercars! Many of the owners also allowed visitors to see their elaborately decorated garages, complete with their exotic cars, automotive memorabilia from past years, sleeping quarters, and even bars and snack areas.

A year or so after buying my Cobra, I decided that 305 horsepower was not enough. I took my car to a motorsports company in Minneapolis and had a supercharger installed along with a new six-speed transmission. While I loved the 460 rear-wheel horsepower that resulted from this modification, there were problems with the workmanship; I ended up with a cracked cylinder head. Cedric told me about Casey, a friend he had met, who recommended I take my car to Danny Wolfson at DB Performance in Rogers, Minnesota.

I called Danny and arranged to take my car to him. Danny, a Ford-trained automotive technician, was doing vehicle modifications on the side in a garage he built on his parents' farm in Rogers. I found Danny to be personable and, most important, reputable.

Danny diagnosed the problems with the set-up on my Cobra and asked if I had considered a total rebuild. That began a business and personal relationship that has become very important to us both. Danny rebuilt my engine and added a custom exhaust system with headers and high-flow mufflers, and a supercharger. He worked for weeks in his shop after his day job repairing cars at a local Ford dealership. Danny's mother told me she often would assist him when he was working on my car by holding the brake pedal down or turning the steering wheel when Danny needed an extra pair of hands. I visited Danny's shop often to take pictures of the project as it was unfolding. When my vehicle was put back together, Danny trailered it from Minnesota to California to have it tuned by a master technician who was highly regarded for tuning high-performance cars. When Danny returned to Minnesota, he and I took my Cobra for a test drive. I was more than pleased with the power and throttle response of my supercharged Cobra.

A few years later, Danny asked me if I had ever thought about converting my supercharged Cobra to a twin-turbocharged beast. I told him I thought turbos were only for foreign car applications. I soon learned that was not the case and that turbos were being used successfully in foreign and domestic cars. I was totally hooked.

Danny developed a conversion plan that I approved, and when the modifications were done, I had a 731 rear-wheel horsepower, twin-turbocharged monster. Danny estimated that my Cobra had a top speed of 180 m.p.h., up from the 161-m.p.h. top speed from the factory. We were off to the races, figuratively and literally. (I took my Cobra to a track in Wisconsin where Cedric's friend, Casey, was getting married. I served as the wedding photographer. Along with other wedding guests—including the bride and groom—I raced my car on the quarter-mile track.)

I ordered new Cobra insignia chrome mag wheels and leather racing seats with Cobra script from England. (These may have been the first seats of this type imported to America.) I also installed a custom 1000-watt AM/FM stereo radio with a dedicated amplifier, eight speakers, and a trunk-mounted subwoofer.

In addition to trailering my Cobra to California for tuning, Danny also trailered it to me when I moved to Cleveland and Memphis. A couple of times when I had mechanical problems, Danny consulted with a Cleveland-area *Ford* technician to order parts and make repairs on my highly modified car. Danny watched and listened to a video clip that I texted him from Memphis and determined that my fuel pump had failed and needed replacement. He ordered the part and had it drop shipped to me for installation at a Memphis-area repair shop.

When I moved from the Twin Cities to Cleveland in 2005, Danny told me it felt like he was losing a brother. I, too, felt a void because we had grown in our friendship. We talked about our families, business plans, and life's challenges, in addition to our interest in powerful cars. I value Danny's automotive expertise and, more importantly, his friendship.

The next car I bought was a black 2000 *Ford Explorer Saleen XP8*. The day I bought my high-end SUV, I was actually taking my son, Jarrod, to look for a used SUV to replace the *Geo Tracker* of mine that he had been driving. After we made a deal to buy a late-model *Ford Eddie Bauer Edition* SUV for Jarrod, I asked our salesman about the *Saleen XP8* on the sales floor. I had seen the vehicle there for almost a year and surmised that no one wanted to pay the hefty sum they were asking for a *Ford*. One could buy a *BMW* or another foreign vehicle for what they were asking. I was dressed in worn jeans, and I don't think the salesman thought I had the financial wherewithal to buy one vehicle, let alone two. But that's what I did. I guess my ego and impulse got the best of me.

My *Saleen XP8*, numbered "15," was one of only about 200 manufactured that year, making it a rare vehicle. It had Recaro leather bucket seats, power steering, power brakes, power windows, a power moonroof, race suspension, chrome 18-inch mag wheels, and all-wheel drive. I later added a supercharger, which increased my Saleen's horsepower from 160 to 225. I also added a 1,200-watt custom AM/FM radio, CD/DVD player, television receiver, and three video screens to my roadster. My sons and I enjoyed this vehicle as we drove locally or on long trips to Missouri and Tennessee. I only sold it in 2020 when my son, Matt, needed more reliable transportation for a courier job he was doing. Even with 213,000 miles on it, the Saleen still looked good.

The next vehicle I bought was a special ordered, black 2018 *Jeep Grand Cherokee Trackhawk*. This limited-edition vehicle—that has a 6.2-liter Hemi, 707 horsepower, supercharged Hellcat V-8 engine, and all-wheel-drive—can accelerate from zero to 60 m.p.h. in 3.5 seconds and has a top speed of 180 m.p.h. When it was manufactured, it was advertised as the most powerful and quickest production SUV in the world. I haven't taken it to the track yet, but that's coming. Once again, I am hooked on speed. You can never have too much horsepower!

A penchant for fast cars is one of my few obsessions. I take pride in owning, driving, and maintaining unique vehicles.

As I said earlier, my hobbies and interests have helped me cope with adversities and to enjoy my life. While I have enjoyed these activities and the items I have acquired, they don't compare to the satisfaction I get from spending time with my family and helping others. To God be the glory!

Overcoming

Throwing out the first pitch at a Major League Baseball game was both exhilarating and nerve-wracking. What an honor, but what if I "bounce it" to the plate?

Caring for our ailing father was a taxing but rewarding experience. We were blessed with the opportunity to help him die with dignity in his home, surrounded by the people who loved him.

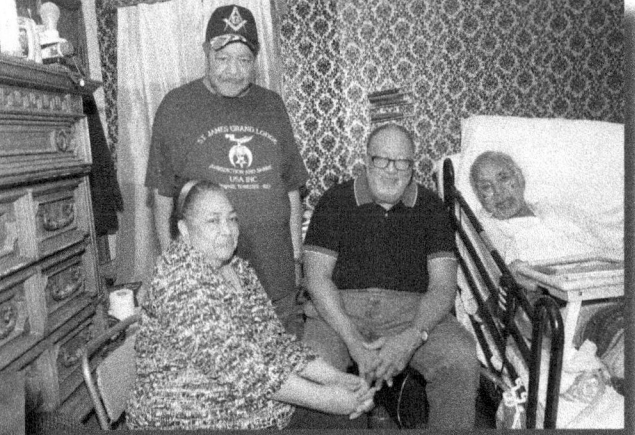

I earned a first-degree black belt in Tae Kwon Do and my Ph.D. in the same year. I guess you could say I'm a "glutton for punishment!"

Willie Dean

I've taken over 10,000 digital photos, many of which were snapped as a volunteer for churches I have attended.

I'm learning to play the acoustic guitar and find playing it relaxing and enjoyable for myself and others.

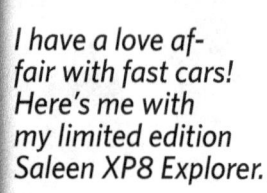

I have a love affair with fast cars! Here's me with my limited edition Saleen XP8 Explorer.

PART FOUR:

THE GOLDEN YEARS – FRUITS OF MY LABOR

Finding My Soulmate

"Therefore, a man shall leave his father and mother and be joined to his wife, and they shall become one flesh." Genesis 2:22 (New King James Version)

SUNDAY, APRIL 9, 2017, is a date that will be emblazoned in my memory forever, for this is the day I found my soulmate. This is the day I talked with Dr. Carol Rawls Johnson at St. Peter's AME Church in Minneapolis, Minnesota. Carol was in town, from Memphis, for her brother-in-law Bob Goff's memorial service in Saint Paul, Minnesota. I was familiar with Carol, former superintendent of schools in Minneapolis, from when we both lived and worked in the Twin Cities. In fact, Carol and her late husband, Matthew, had attended St. Peter's AME Church, as had my late wife, Pam, and I had two decades earlier. Carol had also served as superintendent of schools in Memphis and Boston and was well-known in our church.

I had been single for a number of years and had prayed to God to bring me an attractive, well-educated, Christian lady. I even shared my prayer request with members of my church during a leadership retreat the previous fall. It was difficult, being an introvert, meeting women. I dated off and on; however, I never found the right lady that I sought. Divorced twice and widowed, I was about to give up on my quest to find my soulmate.

Then, on April 9th, my prayers were answered. I had previously heard that Carol's husband, Matthew, had passed. I didn't know what to expect when I approached her during the period reserved for greeting members and visitors following the sermon. I don't even know why I approached her. Perhaps it was God answering my prayer but telling me I had to walk across the sanctuary and say hello. I had butterflies in my stomach, just like when I was nervous at the prospect of walking across the gym to ask a girl to dance in junior high. This time, however, I followed through and greeted Carol.

As fate would have it, this was the day that I had been assigned to give a testimonial to the congregation during morning service. Speaking from a podium off to the right of the pulpit, I shared how God had comforted my family and me in the wake of my late-wife Pam's tragic medical emergency that resulted in her lapsing into a chronic vegetative state. I shared that our neighbors, some of whom were Christians and many of whom we didn't know very well, had cleaned our home and brought us meals for almost a year. I also shared that my faith comforted me during this trying time and that our church choir had visited and sang to Pam at the Masonic Home, where she spent her final days. I shared my personal story of how my faith and God's grace had sustained me.

When I went up to Carol after she greeted the congregation during the welcome period, I told her that I, too, was from Memphis and that my dad and brother still lived there. She gave two other members and me her business card and suggested we might connect sometime when I visited family in Memphis. That night I sent Carol an email saying that I enjoyed speaking with her earlier in the day. I also said I looked forward to getting together with her the next time I was in Memphis. (Carol told me later that she was impressed that I had followed up with an email the same night after we had spoken in church. Although she made it clear she was not looking for someone, and it had only been four years since Matthew's passing, I had made an impression on her.)

In early June of the same year, my dad had a stroke and was hospitalized. This was the second stroke he had suffered in four years, and I knew I needed to check on his health. After my arrival in Memphis and determining that Dad was recovering successfully, I phoned Carol to see if she was free for lunch or dinner. When I talked with her, she expressed her concern for my dad's health. She said she was scheduled to spend much of the week in Minneapolis, attending a Links, Inc. meeting. There we were, Carol, to be in Minneapolis while I was in Memphis. Was fate trying to play a dirty trick on me? However, we arranged to meet for dinner the evening before she left town.

Carol picked me up at Dad's hospital, and we drove a short distance to Capital Grille, one of my favorite restaurants. Our conversation was cordial and free-flowing. We talked about our families and friends that we had in common and the importance of our faith. It was clear to me that the synergy I felt was real. Carol offered me the use of her car while I was in town to avoid my having to rent a vehicle. I graciously turned down her offer as I didn't want to assume such liability. It was a kind offer, especially from someone who didn't know me well at that point in time.

Carol sent my dad a bouquet of flowers and a card wishing him a speedy recovery. She even stopped by the hospital to visit with him and me before she left for Minneapolis. Dad was elated that the former superintendent of Memphis City Schools had taken notice of his condition and demonstrated such concern. I would learn later that love and compassion for others is emblematic of Carol.

After Dad recovered from his stroke, and when I was visiting Memphis again, he invited Carol and me to attend service at his church. We arrived at New Fellowship Christian Church in Olive Branch, Mississippi, for the 9:30 a.m. service. We were greeted by the ushers and by my brother, Bug, who serves on the church's security team. We sat behind Dad and his friend and fellow deacon, Mr. Osbie Lyons.

I had known the pastor, the Reverend Dwight L. Saulsberry, for a number of years. He and members of the congregation had prayed for me following my cancer surgeries nearly a decade earlier. After Pastor Saulsberry finished his sermon and opened the doors of the church to anyone seeking membership, he turned to greet Carol and me. Dad had asked Pastor Saulsberry if we could offer words of encouragement to the youth in the congregation. I spoke about my experiences working with youth through the *YMCA* and YouthCARE and the importance of youth development through the church. Carol talked about her experiences working with youth as a teacher, principal, and superintendent of schools. We shared our belief in the importance of youth development and education in the maturation of youth. Dad was proud to have Carol and me attend his church with him.

After service, we toured Dad's farm, which was only about a ten-minute drive from his church. Carol strode among the weeds in the pasture and tried to get near the cows that meandered about. Wearing high heels and a yellow suit, she seemed out-of-place yet at home among the yellow dandelions. Having grown up in Brownsville, a small town in West Tennessee, Carol was no stranger to rural life. We saw the barn and farmhouse that my dad had assembled himself from discarded wood and tin that he picked up over the years. Carol was impressed that my dad seemed to have a personal conversation with his cows; they responded to his voice and watched for Dad's directions. We drove around the pasture and saw the man-made pond and barbed-wire fencing that kept the cows within. After touring the farm, we went to lunch together at an *Outback* restaurant, one of my dad's favorite eateries.

Willie Dean

Carol spent Labor Day that year in Minneapolis. She stayed with her sister, Phyllis, in Saint Paul but spent as much time as possible with me. We attended Cars and Coffee, the gathering of sports and luxury car enthusiasts, with my son, Cedric, and my granddaughter, Madison (Maddie). Carol met the other members of Cedric's family, his wife, Melissa, son, Cedric Jr. (CJ), and daughter, Samantha (Sammie). She also met my son, Matthew (Matt), and his wife, Kristine. Carol and I talked daily by phone, sometimes multiple times, after she returned to Memphis.

I visited Memphis that Thanksgiving and looked forward to spending time with my dad, Bug, and Carol. She invited me to attend Thanksgiving dinner at her home along with scores of her family and friends. An annual tradition for her family, Carol prepared dinner for some 75 guests. I felt remarkably at home and only a little anxious as I met many of her relatives for the first time.

Carol and I went on our "first date" to the movies and to *Baskin-Robbins* for ice cream afterward. We saw someone who recognized her as the former superintendent of schools, something that happened almost wherever we went. Carol and I continued our courtship. I had concerns, however, about maintaining a long-distance relationship.

I met Carol in New York City when she attended a business meeting there. We had a romantic weekend where we went sightseeing on a double-decker bus, took a ferry boat ride around Ellis Island, and saw *The Lion King* on Broadway. This was my first visit to the Big Apple. I turned down a previous invitation years earlier by my brother, Joe, and his wife, for I was a bit overwhelmed by the prospect of being in the nation's largest city; however, this time was different. I was with Carol, and everything seemed okay. I soon learned that this would be a constant theme. When I am with Carol, everything seems okay. She has a remarkable way of caring for others.

The more I got to know Carol; I realized how compatible we really were and that we were both committed to our faith, family, and friends. Like me, she had been in church almost all of her life. She attended First Baptist Church as a youth growing up in Brownsville, Tennessee, a small town about 45 miles west of Memphis. And she had been active in churches in the cities where she had lived. And like me, Carol had excelled in her chosen field, education. She had been a teacher and the first Black female superintendent of schools in St. Louis Park, Minnesota, and the first female superintendent of schools in the 50,000-student Minneapolis Public Schools. Carol also had been superintendent of schools of the 120,000-student Memphis City Schools and the 50,000-student Boston Public Schools. Carol is one of the most respected educators of our time. She was named Interim President of LeMoyne-Owen College, the only HBCU (Historically Black Colleges and Universities) in Memphis. Under her leadership, the college received a $40-million endowment to ensure continued educational opportunities for students of color in the Memphis area and throughout the nation. I also found that Carol values the friendship of her former classmates at Fisk University.

Carol is very community-minded, as evidenced by her membership in numerous civic and social clubs, including The Girl Friends, Inc., Links, Inc., the Assisi Foundation Board of Directors, Facing History Board of Directors, University of Minnesota Alumni Board, Memphis Symphony Orchestra Board, and Delta Sigma Theta Sorority, Inc.

In a relatively short time period, our affection for one another grew. Carol told me that she loved me. I was not quite sure how I felt, so I resisted responding right away. I wanted to be sure. I asked the Lord for a sign and soon realized that Carol and I were right for each other. I told Carol that I loved her and that I wanted to be her husband. We discussed our relationship and determined that we were in love, we both loved our families, we both had been blessed with careers supporting youth development and education, and most of all, we both loved God. We decided to get married and spend the rest of our lives together in holy matrimony. We bought wedding rings, and I decided that I would ask her for her hand in marriage on Valentine's Day 2018 when I would be in Memphis again. We decided to get married that June.

Carol's sister, Phyllis Goff, agreed to help us plan what was to be a small, intimate ceremony with family and friends. The only questions were: "Would we get married in Memphis or Minneapolis?" And, "Where would we live?"

We planned a small wedding ceremony that was to be held at my church, St. Peter's AME Church, in Minneapolis. Before it was done, however, the guest list had swollen to more than 200 family and friends from Tennessee, Minnesota, Michigan, Massachusetts, and several other states. And, because the wedding ceremony was going to be in Minneapolis, we felt it necessary to have a wedding reception later in July in Memphis for family members and friends who were unable to travel to Minneapolis. The reception, held on the top floor of the Crescent Club in Memphis, attracted more than 150 guests. Because we were both settled in life, we asked our relatives and friends to consider our charities, St. Peter's AME Church in Minneapolis, Minnesota, and Fisk University, in Nashville, Tennessee, in lieu of wedding gifts. We were thrilled to start our lives together and looked for a way to help others.

Willie Dean

On June 9, 2018, I married Dr. Carol Rawls Johnson at St. Peter's AME Church in Minneapolis. Our "small" wedding, with nearly 200 family members and friends, was the highlight of our courtship. Our marriage ceremony was the first wedding officiated by my pastor, the Reverend Carla M. Mitchell. (We became and remain good friends with Rev. Carla!)

Carol and I divided our honeymoon into two different trips. Initially, we drove to Chicago, Illinois, and St. Louis, Missouri. We went sightseeing in Chicago and had dinner at a blues club, where a native Memphis blues singer was performing. While in St. Louis, we toured the Monsanto *YMCA*, the location of my second Y executive position. I was humbled when the current executive director said that I was revered by a number of his volunteers. I wanted Carol to see where I had served during the early days of my career. We flew to Myrtle Beach, South Carolina, in October 2018, for the second half of our honeymoon. In Myrtle Beach, we went on a helicopter ride, had dinner at a blues-themed restaurant, and attended a show at a comedy club. Since it was the off-season, we didn't have to contend with throngs of people on the beach or in the hotel pool.

Carol and I had two equally commanding options for where we should live. We both had children and grandchildren who lived in the Minneapolis area. Carol also had a sister who lived in Saint Paul. My father, and brother, Bug, lived in Memphis, and Carol had sisters who lived in the Memphis area. She also had a daughter and sister who lived in the Nashville, Tennessee, area. My son, Matt, lobbied for us to live during the spring and summer in Minneapolis and during the fall and winter in Memphis. After much discussion and prayer, we decided that I would relocate to Memphis. We would live together in Carol's Cordova, Tennessee home, and I would sell my Bloomington, Minnesota, townhouse. The fact that my aging father's health was failing and I could spend more time with him during his time of need helped us make our decision.

I relocated to Memphis in June 2019. We gave some of my furniture to my son, Matt, and to Carol's son, Paul. We then rented a *U-Haul* truck, and Carol and I drove it and my furnishings from Minnesota to Tennessee. It was a two-day trip that was filled with sunshine and rain (literally and figuratively), which was to be symbolic of the next few years. I was able to spend quality time with my father during the last year and a half of his life. God is good!

Carol and I enjoy our time together in our home, walks in the park, going to movies and eating theater popcorn, and keeping in touch with our family. We look forward to when the COVID-19 pandemic is under control, and it is safe to have our family visit us for Thanksgiving and to attend family reunions and other gatherings. We also look forward to traveling together around the world. I pray to God daily and count my blessings for having Carol in my life.

The Lord is My Shepherd – He Guides Me the Right Way

"The Lord is my shepherd, I lack nothing. He makes me lie down in green pastures, He leads me beside quiet waters, He refreshes my soul. He guides me along the right paths for his name's sake." Psalm 23:1-3 (New International Version)

My life has been enriched through my relationship with God. His love and grace have sustained me through many years and many tears. He has led me through dangerous situations on the streets of the cities where I have lived and on the highways that connected them. He has been my guide throughout my life, encouraging me when I have been obedient and chastising me when I have gone astray. Like any good father, He holds me to account when I am rebellious, or I think only about myself.

My sons have a hard time buying gifts for me. Finding Christmas or birthday gifts for me can be daunting because I lack almost nothing. That is to say, I have much in terms of material possessions, and I don't want to continue to accumulate "things." What is most important for me at this stage of my life is the love of my wife and family, good health, and most of all, the love and saving grace of my Lord and Savior, Jesus Christ.

God has allowed my seed to fall upon fertile ground, and I have grown personally and professionally. With His guidance, I have learned to be a loving husband and father, obtained a Ph.D. in Education, earned a Black Belt in Tae Kwon Do, and ascended to the highest ranks in the *YMCA*. Through it all, I have maintained strong connections to my faith, my family, and my friends. God continues to lead and guide me and give me opportunities for growth and development, times for quiet reflection, and challenges to refresh my spirit, mind, and body.

I started life in Mississippi, lived briefly in Arkansas, and spent my elementary, high school, and undergraduate years in Tennessee. With nearly a fourth of my life spent in the Mid-South, one could say that I'm a southerner. However, with the remaining three-fourths of my life spent in Texas, Missouri, Nebraska, Minnesota, and Ohio, one could say I am a mid-westerner. The various locales where I have lived and the diverse people and situations that I have encountered give me a unique perspective on life in the United States. The challenges that I have overcome have helped to make me the man that I am today. More importantly, how I dealt with these challenges gets to the crux of my lived experiences as a Black man in America. I am the sum total of all the experiences I have had and the people I have known. I am proud to say that I have benefited immensely from both.

The year 2019 marked 50 years since I graduated from Hamilton High School in Memphis, Tennessee. My 50th anniversary high school class reunion that was held June 21, 2019, at the *Holiday Inn-University* in Memphis was the first reunion I have ever attended. I lived out of town during past reunions, learned about them at the last minute, and could not adjust my schedule to attend. But this time was different. I had gotten married the prior year and moved back to Memphis in June 2019. It seemed my life had come full circle. I had spent the bulk of my formative years in Memphis, and now I was celebrating this momentous event just days after relocating to Memphis after having lived in multiple cities around the United States. I had gone out and made my mark in the world. I had retired from a successful 35-year career with the YMCA, earned a terminal degree, earned a black belt, and provided leadership to churches throughout the country.

I had dreamed of attending my high school class reunion after earning a doctorate and ushering my beautiful wife on my arm. Vanity aside, my dream finally came true. I attended several reunion planning meetings and got reacquainted with a number of classmates, including Pamela Bailey-Morris, Ronnie Booze, Trent Cobb, Early Drane, Gwen Cowans-Flowers, Regina Gates Haley, Evonne Shipp Henderson, Gladys Freeman-Houston, Sharon Lewis-Henderson, Cheri Jackson-Harrell, Ruby Jackson Payne, Janis Paxton, James E. Powers, Dr. Lilly Roberts, Rev. Elmer Shelton, Jr., Brenda Partee Taylor, Diane Tennial-Haley, Juanita Fifer Watkins, Isaac White, Jr., Rhonda Jones White, Laverne Williams-Banks, and others.

I have had the opportunity to travel the world, well, three continents anyway, and I plan to visit at least three more of the remaining ones. I'm not so sure about Antarctica.

I am blessed to have been able to live in multiple cities and to have known diverse friends and colleagues along my journey to discover who I am and God's purpose for my life. God continues to be my shepherd and my guide.

Love and Unity – What the World Needs Now

"Make every effort to keep the unity of the Spirit through the bond of peace. There is one body and one Spirit, just as you were called to one hope when you were called; one Lord, one faith, one baptism; one God and Father of all, who is over all and through all and in all." Ephesians 4:3-6 (New International Version)

THE APOSTLE PAUL, IN his letter to the church at Ephesus, admonished Christians to live in a way that expresses God's unity. I believe our lives and our interactions with one another should be characterized by humility, gentleness, patience, love, unity, and peacefulness. I believe that we should seek unity through nonviolent, yet determined, means.

Unity, while important in human discourse, does not mean unanimity, which implies full agreement with others. Likewise, unity does not mean uniformity, which suggests sameness, without recognition of individual differences. We can, however, operate in unity with a shared set of values to achieve common goals for the good of all—not just for some. We can achieve unity by embodying the unconditional love that is exhibited by Jesus in each of our human interactions.

When I was in grade school, America was touted as a giant "melting pot," with people from many nations coming together as one. Some say that the words of Emma Lazarus's famous 1883 sonnet, *The New Colossus*, inscribed on the Statue of Liberty says in part—"Give me your tired, your poor, Your huddled masses yearning to breathe free, The wretched refuse of your teeming shore,"—symbolizes America's thirst for diversity and inclusion. While millions of immigrants have been processed through Ellis Island, I doubt that few, if any, of my African ancestors were. Many African Americans find it difficult, if not impossible, to trace their heritage beyond a few generations because of the horrors of "slavery," our nation's original sin. It's difficult to imagine that fellow humans could divide families, treat others inhumanely, and lynch and kill thousands without remorse. Today, proponents of diversity and unity view America as a "mosaic," with racial and ethnic groups coexisting and everyone enjoying the richness of their cultures and the nation benefiting from their diverse contributions to society.

As Americans, we are one people, and we must work together to ensure that all people, without regard to race, ethnicity, religion, country of origin, sexual orientation, gender, socioeconomic status, etc., have equal opportunities for life, liberty, and the pursuit of happiness.

Race relations have been an issue in this country since the first Europeans "discovered" America. From the beginning of this great nation, slavery was at the center of commerce and controversy. Hypocrisy aside, for a variety of reasons, enslaved people were described as three-fifths human. This provision gave southern states more power in the Union; however, it prevented enslaved people from enjoying the "inalienable" rights that were guaranteed to Americans.

Some Whites attempted to justify slavery by asserting that enslaved people were present throughout the Bible. They also alleged that "Negroes" had no soul or that they were less than human. This, they thought, gave them the moral authority to use and abuse enslaved people. Others placed commerce and economic gains above the concern for their fellow human beings. Enslaved people provided the cheap labor that fueled the vast cotton and tobacco plantations of the South and the shipbuilding industry of the Northeast. Sadly, many plantation owners took female slaves as mistresses, raping them and fathering mulatto children, many of whom became outcasts among both the White and Black races. (Not surprisingly, my son Cedric's research of our genealogy revealed White progenitors in our family's lineage.)

Even after the Civil War, a war that supposedly freed the Black man, many in America resisted change. A system of Jim Crow laws, a separate but equal doctrine for public accommodations (schools and other public buildings and institutions), and even coercion by groups like the Ku Klux Klan forced Blacks to live in poverty, fear, illiteracy, and desperation. Poll taxes and literacy tests were just a few of the techniques employed by Whites to prevent Blacks from voting. Likewise, discriminatory hiring practices, redlining, and underfunded schools in segregated communities continued to disenfranchise Blacks from achieving the American dream.

Dr. Martin Luther King, Jr. has been referred to by some as one of the greatest leaders of the 20th century. This man, who came from humble beginnings, was thrust upon the international stage when he and others dared to confront the injustices of segregation in our country. Dr. King was a Baptist preacher who believed in the precepts of brotherhood and unity. Inspired by Mahatma Gandhi, he also embraced nonviolent protest and civil disobedience as techniques to combat social injustices and Jim Crow laws (a system of legal segregation common during the era).

Dr. King's dream, rooted in the American dream, was predicated on the fact that all men are created equal; that we each have certain unalienable rights to life, liberty, and the pursuit of happiness. Dr. King's dream embodied the precepts of equality, justice, brotherhood, faith, and unity. But, how can these precepts be achieved when the memories of distant, and not so distant, racial atrocities (murders, beatings, and disenfranchisement of Black people) are beckoned to our minds almost daily on the evening news or 24/7 on incessant cable news broadcasts.

Some maintain that we should not teach students about our nation's history of slavery and racial discrimination for fear that it might traumatize young minds. Should I forget that as a young boy traveling with my family from Memphis to visit relatives in Oklahoma City in 1961, I witnessed a White driver speed up to prevent my dad from passing, nearly causing us to crash head-on into oncoming traffic? Should I have felt despair when I saw the same kind of vitriol and hate displayed by White supremacy groups that marched in 2017 in Charlottesville, Virginia, shouting, "Jews will not replace us?" Should I have been afraid for our democracy and for my life when I saw insurrectionists storm the U.S. Capitol on January 6, 2021, and parade around the rotunda with a Confederate flag? Unless we learn from our history—all of our history—we are destined to repeat it.

I remember growing up in Memphis and hearing on the radio and seeing on television the unfolding of the Civil Rights Movement. It was surreal learning about events that were occurring just a few miles from where I lived. I remember hearing about protests and marches and seeing Blacks, and sympathetic Whites, who were being subjected to brutal beatings, attack dogs, and tear gas at the hands of law enforcement officers—the very people who were sworn to "protect and serve." The mass shootings and murder of eight African American members and their pastor at the Emanuel AME Church in

Charleston, South Carolina, in 2015, and the murder of 11 members of the Tree of Life Congregation synagogue in Pittsburgh, Pennsylvania, in 2018, bring back unpleasant memories of the burning of churches and the murders of innocent children and adults during the 1960s. Many continue to ask, "What will it take for us to learn to love and value one another?"

ONLY LOVE CAN CONQUER HATE

Enslaved people prayed for relief from oppression and bondage but also for the forgiveness of the sins of their oppressors. Even while in chains and unimaginable pain and degradation, many enslaved people managed to give thanks and recognition to God.

Christianity demands that regardless of where we live—whether in the inner-city or the suburbs, the poor house or the White House—we must demonstrate love for our fellowman, without regard to race or creed. Each of us has an obligation to address racism in our community and in our nation and to work with others to ensure everyone is treated fairly and with dignity and respect. We must remember Dr. King's words, "Only love can conquer hate."

I remember going to stores in Memphis where signs over water fountains and restrooms read, "Whites" and "Coloreds." I remember riding the bus downtown to the Malco movie theatre and entering through a side door to get to the balcony, the only place where Black people were permitted to sit, in a previous period of American history. While we might not have overt segregation any longer in this country, we still have "two Americas." One for the rich and powerful and one for the poor and disenfranchised. The latter, more often than not, are people of color.

I remember vividly April 4, 1968, the day Dr. King was assassinated on the balcony of the Lorraine Motel in downtown Memphis. School officials and city leaders feared the city would erupt in violence. I didn't understand the gravity of the situation. Within hours there were police in riot gear and National Guard troops patrolling our city. I was in the 11th grade at Hamilton High School in Memphis, and as a young person, I didn't recognize the significance of these events until years later.

Conspiracy theories abound, and while unproven, I believe that James Earl Ray did not act alone in the assassination of Dr. King. I believe this atrocious act was fueled by the vitriol against Black people in this country and the hatred of those who wanted to maintain the status quo. Dr. King, and other leaders like him who espoused change, both Black and White, posed a threat to White supremacists and those in power. I believe that racial hatred has led to attacks against and assassinations of sympathetic White leaders as well.

We, as a nation, we as a people, must learn to love one another and work together for the good of all.

Dad asked Carol and me to attend his church shortly after we began dating. Our relationship got started in church; we pray together daily and keep Christ at the center of our lives.

Carol and I got engaged on February 14, 2018, Valentine's Day!

My son, Cedric, also a photographer, took our engagement photo.

Carol and I married on June 9, 2018, at St. Peter's AME Church in Minneapolis. My son, Cedric, was my best man, and Rev. Carla, our pastor and friend, officiated.

Dr. Carol Johnson Dean and Dr. Willie Dean, newlyweds.

Carol and I honeymooned in Myrtle Beach, South Carolina, and enjoyed walking together along the seashore.

Carol and I enjoyed time together on one of our many road trips.

EPILOGUE

"There is not a liberal America and a conservative America – there is the United States of America. There is not a Black America and a White America and Latino America and Asian America – there's the United States of America." Barak Obama, Former U.S. Senator

As I continue my journey to discover God's purpose for my life, I feel it incumbent to work to help build understanding to bring our country together as "one nation under God, with liberty and justice for all." Former U.S. President (then U.S. Senator) Barak Obama said it best, "there is only one America." We must work together to defeat a resurgence of Jim Crow-type laws, aid the Black church and the family, expand evangelism and social action and close the equity gap in education. We must also expand economic development and wealth creation for communities of color, increase political participation for Blacks and other people of color, develop healthy family roles and relationships, enhance family communications, nurture respect and responsibility, and focus on the importance of church involvement for youth, adults, and families. And most important, we must work to understand what God expects of us.

Continuing My Faith Journey

I will continue my quest to discover what God's plan is for my life by using scripture to guide my path forward. I will also continue to use the lens of faith, family, and friends to elucidate my journey. And I will reach out to others to share my story and invite participation in my quest to help build a more just society.

Let us not forget the importance of regular church attendance as we work to love others and unify our nation. Many of the values that we live by are taught and internalized in the context of worship, Bible study, and Sunday School. Keep your family involved in your church.

Churches and the family have been two of the strongest forces within American society since the founding of this nation. Despite the "separation of church and state" principles that are embedded in our nation's founding, the church has been integral to our nation's success. The church has provided hope, ideals, and an invitation to salvation, as well as a conscience for the formidable and a voice for the weak. Likewise, the family has provided the glue that holds our society together. For it is at home that we learn the basic skills, values, and behaviors which determine whether we are predisposed to go to the state university or the state prison.

I am who I am today because of the tremendous influence of the Black Church and my family. I fondly recall attending Sunday School and church services as a young child, where I learned about the Bible and the teachings of Christ. I went from being a Sunday School student at a young age to becoming a Sunday School Teacher at age 13 and Assistant Superintendent of my Sunday School at age 16, at Cane Creek Baptist Church in Memphis, Tennessee, to President of the Congregation at age 24, at the Community of Hope Lutheran Church in Fort Worth, Texas, to becoming Steward Board Pro Tem, at the age of 61, at the St. Peter's AME Church in Minneapolis, Minnesota. The Black church affirmed me as a person, enhanced my leadership skills, and helped me to understand the link between my faith and my responsibility to my community.

I formed much of my value system from my experiences in Sunday School and at church. I learned to love God and value myself and how God expects me to treat others. I learned how to be a good leader, and as importantly, I learned how to be a good follower. Without the strong, positive influence of the Black Church and the family, the world might never have known the brilliance of the Rev. Dr. Martin Luther King, Jr., the Rev. Fred Shuttlesworth, the Rev. Ralph David Abernathy, Sr., and many others.

Since the days of slavery, the Black Church has been instrumental in providing solace and hope for African Americans. For more than 400 years, the Black Church and the family have been the primary means of survival for a people who were summarily uprooted from their homeland, heritage, and culture and forced into servitude.

My African forefathers, like Native Americans, were proud, free men who cared for their families and their tribal communities. Work, which was required of everyone, consisted of hunting, fishing, gathering nuts and berries, and providing clothing and shelter. They respected nature and themselves.

Thanks to the efforts of missionaries and progressive Whites, many Africans and African Americans were "converted" to Christianity. Many enslaved people prayed not only for relief from oppression and bondage but also for the forgiveness of the sins of their oppressors. Even while in chains and in unimaginable pain and degradation, many of our forefathers managed to love and give thanks and recognition to our Lord and Savior, Jesus Christ.

Advances in Civil Rights would not have been possible without the support, foresight, and protection of the Black Church. The Black Church has also been in the vanguard in the fight for equity in housing, education, public transportation, medical care, and voting rights.

Now is the time for churches, synagogues, mosques, and other houses of worship to come together to address systemic racism, antisemitism, sexism, xenophobia, religious bias, and other prejudices wherever found in our country. Now is the time for individuals and groups, houses of worship, governments (local, state, and federal), and political parties to work together to help cure our nation's ills and to ensure a free and democratic society for all.

Churches should be active in voter education and registration. They should provide forums for a greater understanding of the political process, the issues, and the candidates. Of equal importance, churches should work to register and validate the necessity for every American to vote. Churches should also provide non-partisan forums for debates, workshops, and other events that serve to educate and inform the electorate. All this should be done while adhering to the separation of church and state provisions of state and federal laws against lobbying, etc.

EVANGELISM AND SOCIAL ACTION – TWO SIDES OF THE SAME COIN

Evangelism and social action are not mutually exclusive. As suggested by Lucille Whipper in her article, *Focusing on Issues: Social Action*, involvement in community life or social action is not new for the Black Church. Whipper reminds us, "Since the days of bondage, the African American's religion has produced leaders and movements that contributed to his freedom and throughout the years continue to contribute to the struggle for justice and equality…"

Whipper's article, found in the Study Guide for the National Baptist Congress of Christian Education, asserts that Christian social action is religion in practice. Christians are expected to be "doers of the word, and not hearers, only" (James 1:22a). In other words, we must not only hear and understand God's word, but we must also apply it in everyday life.

This daily application of our faith, whether you call it witness or social action, should guide us in our relationships with our brothers and sisters. The complex issues of today's world require that the Church respond in a comprehensive fashion, using the talents and resources of all its members. In addition to telling the good news about Jesus and his salvation, we must also work to improve life for our brothers and sisters. In the words of the Apostle John, "Whoever claims to love God yet hates a brother or sister is a liar. For whoever does not love their brother and sister, whom they have seen, cannot love God, whom they have not seen. And he has given us this command: Anyone who loves God must also love their brother and sister" (1 John 4:20-21, New International Version). In short, God expects us to love everyone.

The Black Church was a driving force in the Civil Rights Movement of the 1950s and 1960s. Black pastors, owing to their love of God and their people, provided forums and facilities for Blacks and sympathetic Whites to meet, pray and develop plans and strategies to address segregation, racial violence, and other inequities in American society. Leaders like Rev. Dr. Martin Luther King, Jr., Rev. Adam Clayton Powell, and others promoted non-violent social change. Women of the movement, like Coretta Scott King, Ida B. Wells, Maxine Smith, and others, also worked tirelessly to help bring about social change.

Many private historically Black colleges and universities are affiliated with Black churches. These connections helped to develop the minds and values of generations of Black leaders. Likewise, Black fraternities and sororities—most of which had their nexuses around the turn of the 20th century, mostly on HBCU campuses—laid the foundation for an educated Black citizenry.

It is incumbent upon each of us, and especially those who profess to be Christians, to give nourishment, care, and assistance to even the least among us. Sometimes it's easy to be a Christian when all we do is listen to the Word in church on Sunday morning, live in suburbia, and work downtown. But for many of our brothers and sisters, living in the inner-city, with a minimum wage job or surviving on public assistance, is a way of life. When people are struggling with basic survival issues like safety, health care, food, and shelter, it is difficult for them to hear the good news about Christ, especially when it's delivered by seemingly aloof brothers and sisters from outside of their community.

Christians—regardless of where we live and work, be it the inner-city or suburbia, the poor house or the Whitehouse—must demonstrate to our fellow-man that we care. And we must manifest that caring through good stewardship of the resources that we collectively control. Individuals and churches can do a better job of managing their financial resources for the improvement of all. The old adage, "people don't care how much you know until they know how much you care," rings as true today as it has throughout time.

Church and community leaders, along with parents and elected officials, must examine the systems that are in place to aid children, adults, and families in our communities. Systems that are biased, antiquated, or no longer effective must be reformed or replaced. New or revamped systems should be developed to channel resources to meet present and emerging community needs.

BUILDING STRONG KIDS, FAMILIES, AND COMMUNITIES

Churches and community-based organizations should work together to improve the plight of children, families, and communities. The family, the basic unit of civilization since time primordial, is still the most critical cultural link in contemporary society. Churches can and should, as a part of their evangelism, provide assistance and comfort to needy families. This might be in the form of workshops and seminars, Sunday School lessons, sermons, missionary work, the provision of safe, affordable housing, and connections to jobs and educational opportunities.

Developing healthy family roles and relationships can be accomplished by nurturing respect and responsibility among family members. This process is dynamic and must be parent-to-child, child-to-parent, parent-to-parent, and sibling-to-sibling. Children model what they observe. The old adage is true, "What you do speaks so loud I can't hear what you say." We must ensure that our behavior matches our rhetoric.

Effective family communications are a combination of speaking and listening. Family members need to practice expressing themselves clearly and succinctly, and children need to see respectful communication between the adults in their lives, even when there are different opinions. Likewise, it is imperative that everyone learns to listen effectively to what others are saying, both verbally and non-verbally.

According to Fred Schott in his book *Families We've Never Been Here Before!*, "Generally speaking, one of the best things families can do to improve the quality of family life is to assess the habits that they have fallen into in their daily communication." Schott says, "Most families would do well to follow this principle—less talk about the negative and more talk about the positive. I think families need to get in the habit of sending each other compliments."

Schott illustrates how a lifetime of put-downs, warnings, and doom and gloom predictions about the consequences of negative behavior can unwittingly become kind of a "self-fulfilling prophecy." Conversely, children (or anyone for that matter) need and relish genuine praise and compliments for their actions and deeds. (A case in point is the difference in motivation I received from a "caring and supportive" junior high basketball coach and a "belligerent and sadistic" high school coach. I performed better under the former when I received genuine praise and constructive feedback.)

Everybody needs encouragement, recognition, and a positive self-image. This fact is expressed cogently by the intrepid five-year-old who says, "Mom, let's play ball. I'll try to hit the ball off the tee, and whether I hit it or not, your job is to say, 'Way to go!'" (Author unknown)

A technique that we in the YMCA used during values clarification exercises with individuals, families, and groups involves identifying and writing down "house rules." These rules include important points that can be useful in nurturing respect and responsibility among family and group members:

1. *Speak for yourself.* Speaking for yourself suggests that you and you alone are responsible for seeing that others understand you, your feelings, your opinion, or your position on a given topic. Don't let others speak for you or "put words into your mouth." Likewise, it is important that you learn how to assess your wants and needs and then practice verbalizing your thoughts and feelings to others.

2. *Listen to others.* Listening to others is important because you can learn from everyone. Take care to observe not just the words but the feelings that the words and expressions evoke. Ask yourself, "How would I feel if I were in a similar position?"

3. *Avoid put-downs.* Avoiding put-downs is pretty obvious. The more that we learn to appreciate others and their inherent differences, the better equipped we will be to understand diverse opinions and value systems that may be unlike our own. In other words, "If you can't say something good about someone, don't say anything at all."

4. *Be responsible for your own learning.* Being responsible for your own learning implies that you and you alone control your destiny. You can be anything that you aspire to be when you are in control of yourself. Family members should understand the importance of respecting the unique personalities of each child and teaching children to be

self-reliant. This, however, does not imply that anyone should be left to be totally independent or callous to the needs of others.
5. *You have the option to pass.* Having the option to pass says that you need not feel compelled to comment, ask questions, or otherwise do something if you choose not to. This axiom is particularly important when youth deal with peer pressures like bullying, pre-marital sex, illicit drug use, smoking, etc. This point can also be instrumental for use internally with siblings and even parents. Obviously, one needs to understand the consequences of an action that might be out of sync with parental rules and values.
6. *Respect others.* Respecting others provides a framework for dealing rationally with family members. Although you might disagree vehemently with someone's opinion, you can still respect the person. It is possible to disagree without being disrespectful.
7. *Expect unfinished business.* Expecting unfinished business suggests that there will always be times when everything will not fall completely into place. Some issues and problems will require more time and effort to resolve. Don't get discouraged if one family member seems to be out of step. Fred Schott suggests that family crises are inevitable and sometimes OK!

These rules, adapted from the *YMCA* and other sources, should be followed during conversations and discourse among and with family members and can be used in other situations as well.

Developing Healthy Family Roles and Relationships

In order to develop healthy roles and relationships in families, we must provide parents with proper preparation and training, help parents and children to understand their respective roles and responsibilities to each other, and ensure flexibility and a proper amount of humor. We must also respond to the changing needs of families by providing: counseling and support, quality, affordable child care, and parent-child programs with values and family development components. We have learned through our COVID-19 experiences that there can be unexpected challenges that add stress to everyday living.

With increasing problems of drugs, youth gangs, gun violence, crime, and poverty, even the best of families will face challenges. It is incumbent upon each of us to nurture and respect the family, in whatever configuration it might be.

Single parents can't be everything for their children and should rely on the absent parent (when possible), grandparents, extended family members, and friends for emotional support. I know this from my own experience, having been a single parent on two occasions in my life. As a single parent, I had to overcome feelings of guilt, inadequacy, and the fear of "Whether I'm doing a good job." Positive role models through the church, school, and community-based organizations, like *Big Brothers/Big Sisters, Boy Scouts, Girl Scouts, Four H, Junior Achievement*, the *YWCA*, and the *YMCA*, etc., can be rich resources for parents.

Families should encourage their children to develop bonds with other students at school and in their neighborhood. Parents should get to know their children's friends and their parents. Parents should maintain open, two-way communications, but they should not be afraid to say no when they see or feel their child's well-being might be compromised. They should be attentive and take advantage of "teachable moments," and recognize that disciplinary problems and low achievement may be symptomatic of other underlying concerns.

According to Dr. Ken Blanchard in his book, *The One Minute Manager*, "People who feel good about themselves produce good results." Help children reach their full potential, catch them "doing something right!" Nurture and encourage positive behavior, and soon you will see positive relationships which are fortified through respect for yourself and other family members.

Life is not always predictable, easy, or without problems, but we can develop healthy roles and relationships in families by being open, honest, and sincere with our children and ourselves when the unexpected happens.

Let's Close the Equity Gap in Education

One system that needs immediate fine-tuning is the educational system. We are fortunate to enjoy free public education in this country for every child as a constitutional right. Yet many schools in inner-city, rural, and poor areas don't have adequate resources to teach and support our children. A good-paying job was my father's ticket out of poverty, which led to a better life for our family; education was the ticket that placed my family solidly in the middle class.

Some of the persistent challenges that need to be corrected include 1) the inequality of resources between rich and poor school districts due to the reliance on property taxes to fund schools, and 2) the loss of Black male children in primary years from less access to quality pre-kindergarten learning experiences, resulting in low achievement, high dropout rates, and lack of caring and supportive adults present throughout a child's school experience.

A November 1989 issue of *Essence Magazine* featured a story on "How Schools are Destroying Black Boys." The article suggested, "Many educators believe that negative stereotypes of black men as – lazy, violent, troublemakers, drug dealers, irresponsible, low achievers are locked into the psyche of the educational system and that these images influence teachers when they teach black boys." The notion that Black boys are incorrigible and are predisposed to fail in school seems to be prevalent in far too many schools in our American education system. "Many of us don't realize that what happens to boys in school between the ages of 9 and 13 will determine whether they go to college or jail and how much income they will earn in years to come," according to Dr. Jawanza Kunjufu, author of *Countering the Conspiracy to Destroy Black Boys*.

A March 2016 *Education Week* online article discussed racial disparities in teacher expectations of students, based on a June 2016 study entitled, "Who believes in me? The effect of student-teacher demographic match on teacher expectations," published in the journal *Economics of Education Review*. The study reported significant disparities between Black teachers and White teachers with regards to their expectations of future school success of Black students. The study found that White teachers are more likely than Black teachers to expect Black students to not be successful in school:

> *Researchers found that, compared to black teachers, white teachers were about 30 percent less likely to predict the same student will attain a four-year college degree and 40 percent less likely to expect their black students will even graduate high school. By contrast, black female teachers were 20 percent less likely than white teachers to predict their students wouldn't graduate high school and 30 percent less likely to make that prediction than black male teachers.*

According to the National Center for Education Statistics (NCES), there have been improvements in the overall status dropout rate in the past two decades. The data indicate that the rate for White 16- to 24-year-olds (4.5 percent) is not measurably different from the rate for Black 16- to 24-year-olds (5.8 percent):

> *The status dropout rate has decreased since 2000. The status dropout rate is the percentage of the civilian noninstitutionalized 16- to 24-year-old*

population who are not enrolled in school and who had not completed a high school program, regardless of when they left school. (People who left school but went on to receive a GED credential are not treated as dropouts.) Between 2000 and 2018, the status dropout rate declined from 10.9 to 5.7 percent (table 219.70). During this period, the status dropout rate for Black 16- to 24-year-olds declined from 13.1 to 5.8 percent, and the rate for Hispanic 16- to 24-year-olds declined from 27.8 to 9.0 percent. In 2018, the status dropout rate for White 16- to 24-year-olds (4.5 percent) was lower than the rate for Hispanic 16- to 24-year-olds, but it was not measurably different from the rate for Black 16- to 24-year-olds.

According to NCES:

In 2019 and in all assessment years since 1990, the average mathematics scores for White students in grade 4 have been higher than those of their Black and Hispanic peers. Although the White-Black and White-Hispanic achievement gaps in grade 4 did not change measurably from 2017 to 2019, the White-Black achievement gap narrowed from 32 points in 1990 to 25 points in 2019. (Digest of Education Statistics: 2019)

Much of the student performance data in the Digest of Education Statistics are drawn from the National Assessment of Educational Progress (NAEP). The NAEP data illuminates the White-Black achievement gaps in reading, mathematics, and science:

- The White-Black achievement gap in reading for 12th-grade students was larger in 2015 (30 points) than in 1992 (24 points).
- In 2015, the mathematics score for White 12th-grade students was 30 points higher than the score for their Black peers.
- For 12th-grade students, science scores for White students remained higher than those for their Black and Hispanic peers in 2015.

According to data from NCES:

- In 2019, Black boys had a status dropout rate (percentage of high school dropouts among persons 16 to 24 years old) of 6.6 percent, compared to 5.3 percent for their White peers.
- In 2020, Black males 16 to 24 years old (24.4 percent) were 16.4 points less likely to have a bachelor's degree or higher than their White peers (41.0 percent).

Too many educators in this country seem to expect the worst from Black boys, and as a result, more often than not, it becomes a self-fulfilling prophecy. For the past decade, many researchers have documented that both White and Black teachers have low expectations of Black male students.

- Black boys continue to score lower than any other group on standardized tests.
- Black boys are disproportionately misclassified and placed in classes for the mentally retarded or tracked into slow learning classes more than any other group.
- Black boys are suspended, expelled, and corporally punished more often for lesser offenses than white youngsters.

Nearly a third (29.4 percent) of Black male students dropped out of high school in 1970, the year after I graduated, more than double the rate of their White peers (12.2 percent). Put bluntly, Black males of my generation had only a 70 percent chance of graduating high school. Thanks to the grace of God, and the support and encouragement of my family and friends, I was able to beat the odds. I not only graduated high school, but I also obtained bachelor's, master's, and doctoral degrees. For me, sixth grade was a pivotal year with encouragement from a caring teacher and incentives and support from my mother and father, who valued education.

The per capita lifetime cost to the U.S. economy for high school dropouts, $272,000, is a combination of lower tax contributions, higher reliance on Medicaid, higher reliance on welfare, and higher rates of criminal activity.

There are several factors that can be used to predict high school dropout risks, including students with poor grades in middle school, students who don't read well in third grade, and students in families with financial and housing insecurities. The low percentage of minority teachers may also be a contributing factor to the poor performance of students of color, which might be inferred from the lower expectation for school success of Black students by some White teachers than from some Black teachers. Research shows that for minority children having at least one teacher that looks like them is a key to their success (Clemson University). A Johns Hopkins University study found that low-income Black students with at least one Black teacher in elementary school are significantly more likely to graduate from high school and consider attending college.

During the 2018 school year, 79 percent of the teachers in public K-12 schools were White, and 47 percent of the students were White (U.S. Department of Education, 2018). On the other hand, only 21 percent of teachers and 53 percent of students were persons of color (NCES). For Black students, the disparity is even starker. Black teachers represented only seven percent of all teachers, while Black students comprised 15 percent of the total student population.

We need to make school resources available equitably, regardless of where students live. We need to ensure that teacher pay is competitive and that our best teachers are valued and retained. We need to strengthen early childhood education so that kids get a "head start" and do not start school already behind. And we need to ensure schools are led by professional educators and that policies are set by elected or appointed school board members who put students' needs first and have the best interest of all students and the total community in mind.

My education allowed me to live a good life, take care of my family, and give back to my community. I was able to overcome many obstacles because the Lord was with me. I pray for the same blessings for today's youth.

Let's Close the Wealth Gap and Achieve Economic Parity

We need to work to achieve economic parity in this country. Economic development—a broad concept that can include: encouraging small businesses, minority set-aside programs, enterprise zones, tax abatement, entrepreneur assistance, etc.—is one way to do this. The Church, and other organizations, should encourage and, in some cases, demand action and fair treatment for minorities from local, state, and federal agencies and officials. Elected officials who are unresponsive to community needs should be challenged. There are those who do not acknowledge these inequities and who resist attempts to level the playing field. We must work to close the wealth gap that exists between Whites and people of color and men and women. This might include set-asides on public projects that give preference to minority- and female-owned businesses. Achieving economic parity in our communities and in our nation is paramount in order to develop a more just society.

Houses of worship should be encouraged to engage in social responsibility initiatives in their communities, which is a manifestation of God's love. Churches have a responsibility to monitor and assure that all segments of their communities receive equitable shares of goods and services. Sometimes this might mean that in addition to offering food and clothing pantries, a church might serve as a small business incubator. In this capacity, the congregation might sponsor a new entrepreneur in her quest to provide goods or services to others and thereby provide a better living for herself, her family, and her community. As the Bible says, let's not just give people fish; let's "teach them to fish" so that they will hunger no more. A church might also offer space for financial literacy training to ensure community residents, young and old, learn how to manage their finances. (This is a lesson I wish I had learned early on in my life.)

Racism Part Deux – Let's Address It Now!

Having grown up in the South in the 1950s and 1960s, I remember the sights and sounds of racism, segregation, and Jim Crow laws vividly. However, my parents never taught my siblings and me to hate Whites or to feel sorry for ourselves. Rather, they taught us about the love of Jesus Christ and insisted that we attend church and Sunday School at a young age, get a good education, and work hard in spite of what others might do.

Today, in the early decades of the 21st Century, racism, segregation, and Jim Crow-type laws are seen in high definition daily on 24-hour news outlets. We have entered a period of renewed attempts to "legally" disenfranchise Black and other minority voters. This new era of racism—that some have labeled "Jim Crow 2.0"—is as insidious today as it was five decades ago when it first emerged on the American landscape. Regretfully, a number of states are developing legislation that serves to limit the participation of people of color, often Democrats, in free and fair elections. Gerrymandering of state and federal voter districts to benefit one political party over the other makes a farce of the voting process and serves to disenfranchise whole groups of citizens, not to mention undermine the democratic principles that are the foundation of this country's constitution. More often than not, gerrymandering serves to weaken the impact of minority voters. Without the assurance of free and fair elections, our democracy is at risk. Every citizen should work to ensure free and fair elections; our democracy depends on it.

Racism is not limited to the South. I will forever remember a racial incident that happened to me in Minnesota just a few years ago. It was early December 2003, just five months after I received my Ph.D. As I pulled into Dred Scott Automotive, a gas station in my suburban Minneapolis neighborhood, the announcer on the radio station that I was listening to bellowed in a deep radio announcer's voice, "It's 8:00 a.m. and one degree!" In addition to being bitterly cold, there was dirt and grime on everyone's car from a recent snowstorm.

As I proceeded to gas up my limited-edition *Saleen XP8 Explorer* and cleaned my headlights and windshield, a well-dressed White woman in an expensive vehicle pulled up to the pump in front of me, with her vehicle's front end nearly touching my car. She was on her cell phone and I couldn't help but hear her tell the person she was talking with that she was looking forward to getting away to Arizona to escape the bitter Minnesota winter.

As I continued cleaning my windshield, the woman addressed me and asked if I could clean her windshield. I said to her, "Ma'am, I don't work here." She proceeded to gas up her car and clean her windshield. As I continued filling my gas tank, I heard the lady say, "I'm doing a lousy job with this. Could you help me?" Being the Good Samaritan that I am, I said, "Okay," and went over to squeegee her windshield. She got back on her cell phone and retreated to the warmth of her vehicle.

Just as I finished cleaning her windshield, the lady let down her window and asked, "Can you check my oil?" Incredulous, I looked at her and said, "Ma'am, I told you I don't work here. You need to ask one of the employees." She said sanctimoniously, "Oh, I thought you worked here." It became apparent to me that this woman saw me as a Black man who was likely working at this gas station. The fact that I was well dressed, articulate, and driving an expensive vehicle, like her, made no difference…she only saw me as "the help."

The irony is that this encounter happened in my middle-class, mostly White suburban neighborhood, at a gas station located across the street from a city park, both named after Dred Scott, an enslaved Black man who took his case for freedom all the way to the U.S. Supreme Court. According to Britannica, the U.S. Supreme Court ruled that a slave who had resided in a free state and territory was not entitled to his freedom; that African Americans were not and could never be citizens of the United States:

> *Dred Scott decision, formally Dred Scott v. John F.A. Sandford, was a legal case in which the U.S. Supreme Court, on March 6, 1857, ruled (7–2) that a slave (Dred Scott) who had resided in a free state and territory (where slavery was prohibited) was not thereby entitled to his freedom; that African Americans were not and could never be citizens of the United States; and that the Missouri Compromise (1820), which had declared free all territories west of Missouri and north of latitude 36°30', was unconstitutional. The decision added fuel to the sectional controversy and pushed the country closer to civil war.*
>
> *Among constitutional scholars, Scott v. Sandford is widely considered the worst decision ever rendered by the Supreme Court. It has been cited in*

particular as the most egregious example in the court's history of wrongly imposing a judicial solution on a political problem. A later chief justice, Charles Evans Hughes, famously characterized the decision as the court's great "self-inflicted wound."

The Dred Scott case took years to be decided and was believed to have been a contributing factor to the commencement of the U.S. Civil War. Dred Scott did eventually get his freedom. According to *Britannica*:

Dred Scott did, in fact, get his freedom, but not through the courts. After he and his wife were later bought by the Blow family (who had sold Scott to Emerson in the first place), they were freed in 1857. Scott died of tuberculosis in St. Louis the following year. Harriet Scott lived until June 1876, long enough to see the Civil War and the Thirteenth Amendment (1865) abolish slavery in the United States.

It appeared that the White driver who asked me to clean her windshield and check her oil was unaware of the history of the name "Dred Scott." Nor did she see the irony of assuming that a Black man must be part of "the help."

My family's relocation from Mississippi to Memphis in the early 1950s was a game changer. With a good-paying job, my father was able to lift our family from poverty and set us on a path to a better future. I must ask myself, "What have I done to lift my brothers and sisters?" Many poor people are not looking for a "hand out"; rather, they are looking for a "hand up." We must put away the fallacy of "pulling oneself up by one's bootstraps" when many of our brothers and sisters don't even "have boots."

Many Blacks feel that they are living in an American society where numerous acts of racial discrimination occur—beatings, denial of constitutional rights, insults, limited opportunities, economic distress, food desserts, social problems, unequal justice, etc.—under laws that were created to protect all citizens. Many Blacks have been followed in department stores, pulled over by the police, or otherwise profiled and treated differently simply because they are Black. Many Black families have sons and daughters, grandsons and granddaughters, nephews and nieces, or other relatives and friends who have suffered such indignities.

In many respects, we are living in two Americas, a bifurcated country where the "haves" and the "have nots" have very different life chances and outcomes. We are living in an America where Blacks, and other people of color, find obtaining the "American Dream" to be elusive, if not impossible. The few Blacks who are able to experience the "American Dream" are used as examples by those who argue that racism no longer exists. Further, Blacks, whether educated or not, well off or not, still experience discrimination and racism

According to researchers from Harvard University, Blacks are more than three times more likely to die at the hands of police than are their White peers:

> Black Americans are 3.23 times more likely than white Americans to be killed by police, according to a new study by researchers from Harvard T.H. Chan School of Public Health. The researchers examined 5,494 police-related deaths in the U.S. between 2013 and 2017. Rates of deadly police encounters were higher in the West and South than in the Midwest and Northeast, according to the study. Racial disparities in killings by police varied widely across the country, with some metropolitan areas showing very high differences between treatment by race. Black Chicagoans, for example, were found to be over 650% more likely to be killed by police than white Chicagoans.

Some believe the 2008 election of Barak Obama, the first Black President of the United States, signaled that we now live in a post-racial America. However, the circumstances that led to the deaths of a number of Black people since the turn of the Century, many at the hands of police, or vigilantes, suggest otherwise. This disturbing trend is illustrated by the tragic deaths of numerous Black people:

- Trayvon Martin, a 17-year-old Black boy, was killed by George Zimmermann in Sanford, Florida, on February 26, 2012, after Zimmermann, a White vigilante, deemed him suspicious, and an altercation ensued. Zimmermann was later acquitted of the charges.
- Terrance Franklin, a 22-year-old Black man, was shot 10 times, including multiple times in the head, by Minneapolis police SWAT officers in the basement of a Minneapolis home in 2013. Franklin was wanted for questioning in a burglary. A grand jury declined to indict the officers involved in the shooting.
- Eric Garner, a 43-year-old Black man, was killed by a New York City Police Department (NYPD) officer on July 17, 2014, after the officer put him in a prohibited chokehold while arresting him. Garner, who was suspected of selling loose, untaxed cigarettes, died on a Staten Island sidewalk. Video footage of the incident generated widespread national attention and raised questions about the use of force by law enforcement.
- Michael Brown, Jr., an 18-year-old Black man, was fatally shot by a White Ferguson police officer during a traffic stop in Ferguson,

Missouri (a suburb of St. Louis) on August 9, 2014. A St. Louis County grand jury decided not to indict the officer.
- Tamir Rice, a 12-year-old African American boy, was killed in Cleveland, Ohio, by a 26-year-old White police officer on November 22, 2014. Rice was carrying a replica toy gun when the Cleveland officer shot him almost immediately after arriving on the scene.
- Freddie Gray, a 25-year-old African American man, was arrested by the Baltimore Police Department over possessing a knife on April 12, 2015. While being transported in a police van, Gray sustained injuries. Gray died on April 19, 2015; his death was ascribed to injuries to his spinal cord.
- Sandra Bland, a 28-year-old African American woman from the Chicago area, was taken into custody in southeast Texas following a confrontational traffic stop on July 10, 2015. She was found hanging in a jail cell three days later in what was officially ruled a suicide.
- Philando Castile, a 32-year-old Black man, was stopped by a St. Anthony, Minnesota police officer in Falcon Heights, Minnesota—a suburb of Saint Paul, Minnesota— on July 6, 2016. After being asked by the officer for his license and registration, Castile informed the officer that he had a firearm (Castile was licensed to carry). The officer told him, "Don't reach for it." Castile's girlfriend—who was in the vehicle along with her four-year-old daughter and who filmed the incident on her cell phone—told the officer that he wasn't pulling out the weapon. In the confusion, the officer fired seven close-range shots, five of which hit Castile, who died later that night at a local hospital.
- Ahmaud Arbery, a 25-year-old unarmed Black man, was murdered in Satilla Shores, a neighborhood near Brunswick in Glynn County, Georgia, on February 23, 2020. Three White Georgia men, who said they suspected Arbery of committing a series of break-ins in their neighborhood, were found guilty of murdering Arbery and were sentenced to life in prison. (A former Brunswick Judicial Circuit District Attorney was indicted on misconduct charges for failing "to treat Ahmaud Arbery and his family fairly and with dignity," stemming from her reluctance to file charges against the two suspects because of her past work with one of them. The Arbery case received little scrutiny by authorities until a videotape was released to the public.)
- Breonna Taylor, a 26-year-old African-American woman, was fatally shot in her Louisville, Kentucky, apartment on March 13, 2020, when

White officers of the Louisville Metro Police Department forced entry into the apartment on a no-knock warrant as part of an investigation into drug dealing operations.
- George Floyd, a 46-year-old Black man, was murdered by Derek Chauvin, a White Minneapolis police officer in Minneapolis, Minnesota, on May 25, 2020. Chauvin held his knee on Floyd's neck for nearly nine minutes following an altercation with police that ensued after a store clerk accused Floyd of passing a counterfeit 20-dollar bill. Chauvin was convicted of the murder of Floyd. The other three officers were found guilty on federal charges of wantonly denying Floyd medical assistance.
- Amir Locke, a 22-year-old Black man, was shot and killed by a Minneapolis police SWAT officer on February 2, 2022. The controversial shooting occurred seconds after police burst into an apartment to serve a no-knock warrant.

I pray to God for comfort to the mothers, fathers, and other relatives and friends of these and other Blacks and other people of color who have suffered, and in some cases died, at the hands of law enforcement, vigilantes, and others.

"Black Lives Matter" is more than a slogan or a hashtag. It is recognition that Blacks should be afforded the same rights and privileges granted under the Constitution as any other individuals and groups in this country. It is not a diminution of the worth of other groups (Whites, police, etc.). Rather, it is an attestation that we have a problem with systemic racism in this country; a problem that puts Blacks at risk of harm, and even death, in a culture that ignores their humanity, and assumes "guilt," versus the "presumption of innocence" until proven in a court of law.

Whites are sometimes quick to suggest that Blacks are "oversensitive." They attempt to minimize racism by saying that Blacks are pulling the "race card." This tends to shut down communications and indicates an unwillingness to understand the issues, a desire to maintain the status quo or both. Some Whites are simply in denial about their own attitudes and behaviors. Whether intentional or unintentional, the consequences to the Black community are the same.

Black males are often vilified and viewed as lazy, dangerous, or incorrigible. They're often profiled by a law enforcement system that sees them as criminals and stereotyped by an educational system that expects them to fail. They're often pulled over by police for no reason other than "driving while Black." They're suspended from school at disproportionate rates—even in kindergarten and elementary grades—because they're perceived as violent, incorrigible, and unwilling or incapable of learning.

I was disheartened when I heard my son, Cedric, say that he worried about the possibility of civil unrest in our country in the early days of the Trump administration in 2017. He felt a need to develop a contingency plan to move his family to Canada if the uptick of racial violence in our nation intensified further. I have heard similar sentiments expressed by other Black Americans. The events following the 2020 U.S. presidential election seemed to have borne out those fears.

Ironically, the armed insurrection and attack on the U.S. Capitol on January 6, 2021—an unprecedented act of civil disobedience and sedition—was likely encouraged and condoned by the then-President and those sympathetic to his "big lie" about the "stolen" 2016 U.S. presidential election. During the insurrection, rioters walked the halls of Congress, destroying artifacts and defecating on its hallowed walls. Shamelessly, the Confederate flag—a symbol of our nation's racist past—was flown in the U.S. Capitol, something that didn't happen even during the Civil War. I can only imagine how different the response would have been had those "protestors" been Black and they tried to carry out insurrection against this nation.

An opinion piece written by Michelle Goldberg in the January 6, 2022 edition of the *New York Times*, entitled, *Are We Really Facing a Second Civil War?* suggested that civil war in the United States is a real possibility:

> Barbara F. Walter, a political scientist at the University of California, San Diego, has interviewed many people who've lived through civil wars, and she told me they all say they didn't see it coming. "They're all surprised," she said. "Even when, to somebody who studies it, it's obvious years beforehand."
>
> This is worth keeping in mind if your impulse is to dismiss the idea that America could fall into civil war again. Even now, despite my constant horror at this country's punch-drunk disintegration, I find the idea of a total meltdown hard to wrap my mind around. But to some of those, like Walter, who studies civil war, an American crackup has come to seem, if not obvious, then far from unlikely, especially since Jan. 6.
>
> Two books out this month warned that this country is closer to civil war than most Americans understand. In "How Civil Wars Start: And How to Stop Them," Walter writes, "I've seen how civil wars start, and I know the signs that people miss. And I can see those signs emerging here at a surprisingly fast rate." The Canadian novelist and critic Stephen Marche is starker in his book,

The Next Civil War: Dispatches From the American Future. "The United States is coming to an end," Marche writes. "The question is how."

In Toronto's Globe and Mail, Thomas Homer-Dixon, a scholar who studies violent conflict, recently urged the Canadian government to prepare for an American implosion. "By 2025, American democracy could collapse, causing extreme domestic political instability, including widespread civil violence," he wrote. "By 2030, if not sooner, the country could be governed by a right-wing dictatorship." As John Harris writes in Politico, "Serious people now invoke 'Civil War' not as a metaphor but as literal precedent."

Attempts by Republicans in some states to rewrite election laws, falsify election results, or gerrymander Congressional districts in an apparent attempt to weaken Democratic (often Black) voter impact in elections are troubling, to say the least. Some have said the "big lie," promulgated by many on the right, is serving to put our democracy at risk, for if citizens can't believe in the integrity of the election system, we are doomed as a Republic. This, in part, is why a scholar who studies violent conflict "urged the Canadian government to prepare for an American implosion."

While doing research for my dissertation, I found that people of color and women are often treated as second-class citizens in the workplace and in our society. We must work to improve relations in this country and help people with different views—political, philosophical, or otherwise—accept and include men and women from all areas of American life. We must address and excise the malignancy known as systemic racism from our beloved country.

BLACK HISTORY IS AMERICAN HISTORY

"We hold these truths to be self-evident, that all men are created equal, that they are endowed by their Creator with certain unalienable Rights, that among these are Life, Liberty and the pursuit of Happiness..." These words, part of our nation's Declaration of Independence, rang hollow at their inception as they didn't fully apply to people of color (and women). A number of our "Founding Fathers" owned slaves or failed to recognize or stand up against racist policies. Persons of African heritage were relegated to being only three-fifths of a man. Through it all—the horrors and indignities of slavery—Black people believed in God and in themselves.

Black people and Black institutions—Black churches, Historically Black Colleges and Universities (HBCUs), the National Association for the

Advancement of Colored People (NAACP), Black fraternities and sororities, etc.—helped to make America great. Black history is American history!

Black Americans have achieved significant accomplishments in every facet of American life. For example:

- Crispus Attucks – first to die in the American Revolution
- Benjamin Banneker – mathematician and astronomer
- Richard Allen – founder of the AME Church
- Frederick Douglas – abolitionist, orator, statesman
- Harriet Tubman – abolitionist, humanitarian, armed scout, and spy for the U.S. Army during the U.S. Civil War
- Garrett Morgan – along with others, invented the three-light traffic signal
- Elijah McCoy – invented the process for keeping locomotives lubricated while running
- Booker T. Washington – founder of Tuskegee Institute
- Mary Church Terrell – Civil Rights leader
- George Washington Carver – scientist, humanitarian
- Madam C.J. Walker – entrepreneur, first self-made female millionaire in America
- William C. Handy – jazz composer
- Jesse Owens – winner of four gold medals at the 1936 Olympics in Berlin, who disproved Hitler's Arian superiority assertion
- Jack Johnson – first Black Heavyweight Champion of the World
- Jackie Robinson – first Black to play in Major League Baseball in the modern era
- Shirley Chisholm – first Black woman elected to the United States Congress
- Mary McCleod Bethune – educator, philanthropist and civil rights activist
- Hon. Thurgood Marshall – first Black justice of the United States Supreme Court
- Rev. Dr. Martin Luther King, Jr. – Civil Rights leader
- Capt. Charles L. White, member of the famed Tuskegee Airmen
- Col. Guy Bluford, Ph.D., astronaut and first African American in space
- Gen. Colin Powell – former Secretary of State and former Chairman of the Joint Chiefs of Staff
- Barak Obama – first Black President of the United States
- Kamala Harris – first Black female Vice President of the United States

- Ketanji Brown Jackson – first Black female Justice on the United States Supreme Court

Growing up in Memphis, Tennessee, during the 1960s, I was witness to Black history in the making. I remember hearing on the radio and seeing on television the struggles for civil rights. Names like James Meredith, the first Black student at the University of Mississippi, were household words. I was in the 11th grade on April 4, 1968, when Dr. Martin Luther King, Jr. was assassinated in my city. Schools had been let out early, and students were sent home as school officials feared for students' safety in a city where tensions were high. I walked my girlfriend home, and although I later saw National Guardsmen driving about with their weapons at the ready, I didn't understand the gravity of the situation. Many neighborhoods and cities across the country experienced riots and were in turmoil. Years later, I visited the National Civil Rights Museum, built adjacent to the Lorraine Hotel, the site where Dr. King died, and more fully understood the struggles that Blacks and sympathetic Whites had experienced.

As a child, I remember seeing signs that read "Whites" and "Colored" on water fountains and bathrooms. I didn't understand why we always had an empty soda bottle in the car when we traveled.

I didn't understand that going up to the balcony at the Malco movie theater in downtown Memphis was not a treat but a relic of the days of segregation when this was the only place where Blacks could sit.

I remember driving with my family to Oklahoma City late at night on a two-lane highway when my dad attempted to pass a vehicle. Just as we were passing, the White driver looked over and saw that we were Black and sped up, putting us in peril of colliding into oncoming traffic. I can still fill the driver's seatback press against my knees as my dad exclaimed, "He's speeding up!" as he punched the accelerator and our Buick's Dynaflow transmission kicked into passing gear, taking us to safety!

I remember feeling pride in seeing Guy Bluford (Ph.D., USAF Colonel, Astronaut) become the first African American in space in 1983.

I also have great memories of meeting a number of notable Black Americans, including:

- Captain Charles L. White – Former educator and a member of the famed Tuskegee Airmen, who was my realtor when I relocated to St. Louis, Missouri

- Usher (Usher Raymond, IV) – Pop music sensation and former part-owner of the Cleveland Cavaliers, who spoke to my *YMCA* youth group in Cleveland, Ohio
- Bob Gibson – Former St. Louis Cardinals Major League Baseball Pitcher, with whom I had the privilege to have lunch when I was President/CEO of the *YMCA* In Omaha, Nebraska

In spite of numerous indignities and against the odds, Black Americans have excelled in every facet of American life and have helped to make American opportunities more accessible to women, other people of color, and people with limited resources. Take a moment to think about the impact of a Black leader, teacher, pastor, coach, entertainer, or sports figure on your life, and you will realize that Black history is American history! The efforts to make America better for Blacks have always benefited all Americans.

WHAT GOD REQUIRES OF ME

As I carry on my quest to understand what God requires of me, I must continue to be resilient and espouse positive values, like those exhibited by the many role models that God placed in my life. I must demonstrate the importance of love and responsibility that I learned from my mother and father. I must be a role model for my Black sons and others who come behind me. I must show them the determination I learned through athletics, especially from my junior high basketball coach, Mr. Robert L. Terrell, who valued "stick-to-it-tive-ness"—finishing tasks that you set out to do. Equally important, I must demonstrate the values of caring, honesty, respect, and responsibility—values that I learned through my work with the *YMCA*—to everyone with whom I come in contact. I must share and model these values with others without preaching or proselytizing. I must demonstrate what is expected of a man to my sons and other men and boys, who might see me as a role model. And, from my church upbringing, I must do what God requires of me, to act justly and to love mercy and to walk humbly with Him (Micah 6:8).

Appreciation for social justice, love for humankind, humility, and reverence for God have become hallmarks of my life. I pray that as I reflect on my life, that God will continue to reveal my purpose and that I will be attentive and obedient to His will.

After three score and 10 years, I have come to understand more clearly that God wants me to seek justice in all human interactions and advocate for the poor and disenfranchised. I tried to help the poor and downtrodden through my professional work with communities of color as a *YMCA* leader in the cities where I worked. I sought to provide superior programs and facilities for all. Research for my doctoral dissertation shone a light on the disparities in opportunities offered to Black and female employees in the Y. My findings helped to underscore the importance of effective diversity, equity, and inclusion efforts in the *YMCA* and other organizations.

God also wants me to seek justice by taking care of our earthly home. This includes the animals, the birds of the air, and the fish of the sea, as we have been given dominion over them. Likewise, we must seek environmental justice as we have a responsibility to guard against the destruction of the environment—the earth and all of its natural resources, water, air, mountains, and forests. As an environmentalist once said, when it comes to the health of our planet, "there is no planet B."

I also believe that God wants me to love my neighbors as I love myself and to be kind to everyone, even those who persecute and despitefully use me. This love should be like the love of Jesus Christ. This love—agape love—should be unconditional. I must love others without regard for how they treat me. I must love others, even if they don't love me back. And, I must love others without regard to their race, ethnicity, gender, country of origin, socio-economic status, religion or lack thereof, sexual orientation, political viewpoint, legal status, etc.

God also expects me to be humble in all my endeavors. I must recognize that I can do nothing without Him. I know now that I must pray on all matters and leave my troubles in His hands. In the words of the old spiritual, I must "Take my troubles to the Lord and leave them there." Too often, I have prayed at the altar, and instead of leaving my problems there, I have taken them with me back to my pew. It takes a tremendous amount of faith for us to trust in the Lord when we're facing challenges like cancer, the death of loved ones, loss of employment, financial ruin, or the inability to feed our family. However, like the words I once saw on a church marquee, "If God is your co-pilot, change seats." We must let God lead and guide us.

Despite all the "doom and gloom" that we hear during 24-hour news cycles that we have become accustomed to today, I am optimistic about America's future. I believe that there are good people of conscience who will stand up for the values that have made this country great. I believe that there are good people who will support the rule of law and will do the right thing when it comes to election integrity. I believe that with the grace of God, we will address racism, poverty, unemployment, education inequities, the wealth gap, comprehensive healthcare, inadequate housing, and disparate treatment of individuals and groups in this country.

I am heartened as I look back over my life and see glimmers of hope. As I rewind the videotape of my life, I see my father, Eddie Dean, Sr., a man who taught me what it is to be a man. I see Mr. Robert L. Terrell, my junior high basketball coach, who taught me about resilience and fortitude. I see Dr. Charles S. Modlin, a urologist, and friend who saved my life by performing surgeries to excise malignant tumors from my kidneys. I see Winnie R. Scott, former-Childcare Director of the McDonald Family *YMCA* in Fort Worth, Texas, a woman of character who worked with me and who served hundreds of kids and families during her career. And, I see Al Porter, a former lifeguard at the Monsanto Family *YMCA* in St. Louis, Missouri, who told me I had helped save his life. He said he was an "angry young Black man" until he met me at the Y in 1981. Al, now a successful entrepreneur, credits his success to the kind of man he saw in me.

As I continue to examine the scenes of my life, I see a Black female Y desk clerk who threw her arms around my neck in a heartfelt hug as I was leaving my office for the last time as President/CEO of the *YMCA* in Omaha, Nebraska. I had just left a going away party sponsored by my board and staff to celebrate my hiring by the *YMCA* of the USA as one of only four National Field Executives. This unexpected, loving gesture by this young woman meant as much to me as the accolades I received from my board, my staff, the mayor, and the governor. We may never know how we impact others. To know that through my leadership, I have touched hundreds of thousands of lives, even in small ways, is fulfilling beyond measure.

There is but one body, one Spirit, one Lord, one faith, one God and Father of all; therefore, we are all brothers and sisters. Dr. King's dream was predicated on brotherhood and unity. As Christians, we have an obligation to care for one another because we truly are our brother's, and sister's, keeper. America, now is the time to ensure life, liberty and the pursuit of happiness for all! May God bless and keep you, and may God bless America!

Cedric is my eldest son, a high school graduate, U.S. Navy veteran, and a software engineer.

Jarrod, my middle son, college graduate, and writer, hamming it up on our drive to San Diego.

Celebrating Dad's 90th birthday. Dad and his children.

Dean family at my wedding.

Family gathering in Philadelphia.

Family gathering at my home following Dad's homegoing.

Four generations of Dean men at our wedding rehearsal dinner.

Swimming lessons at the Y.

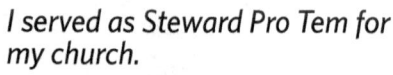

I served as Steward Pro Tem for my church.

Overcoming

A self-portrait

During my wedding ceremony, I reflected on my many blessings.

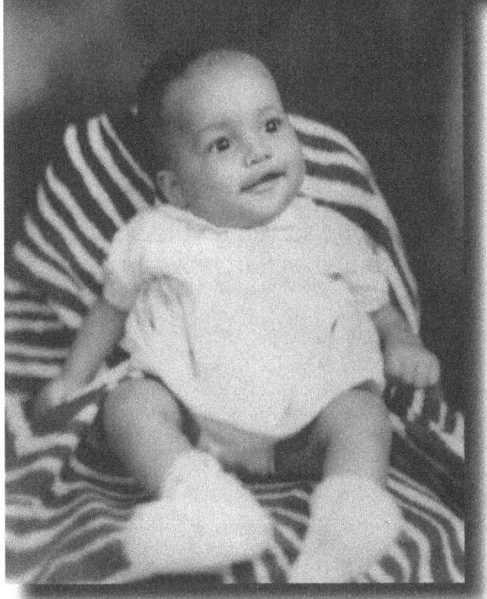

My mother said she hid behind the blanket in my baby photo to support my back. She had my back for the rest of her life.

Serving as President/CEO of the YMCA of Arlington, Texas, was a tremendous honor.

A member of Keystone Lodge 39, Dad—like his father, Anderson, and my brother, Eddie Jr.—was a proud Mason.

Dad, who served on the Deacon Board of his church, was a dapper dresser.

Four generations of Dean men at wedding rehearsal dinner.

Joe, Dad, and me on a road trip to Philadelphia.

Joe, Dad, and I attend service at Dad's church.

Kristine and Matt invited friends and family to their destination wedding in Jamaica.

Matt relaxing at my home in Memphis.

My family joins me at a pancake breakfast to support YouthCARE.

Overcoming

Family at our wedding rehearsal dinner.

Family outside my townhouse at our wedding rehearsal dinner.

Family celebrating Cedric's birthday.

ACKNOWLEDGEMENTS

First and foremost, I thank my Lord and Savior, Jesus Christ, for His saving grace and His unconditional love. I also thank my family, especially my parents, the late Eddie Dean, Sr. and the late Mattie Brown Dean, and my siblings (Joenathan, Christine, and Eddie Jr.), for their love and support. I also thank my wife, Carol, and our children (Cedric, Jarrod, Matthew, Rucker, Tina, and Paul), and our grandchildren (Madison, Cedric Jr., Samantha, Rucker Jr., Layla, Laniya, Imany, Paul Jr., and James), for their love and inspiration.

I would like to thank my wife, Carol, and my son, Jarrod, for their assistance in proofreading and editing the text for this book. I would also like to thank: Martha Perine Beard, the Reverend Dr. Michael A. Evans, Sr., Dr. Ellen Kennedy, Harold Mezile, the Reverend Carla M. Mitchell, Dr. Charles S. Modlin, Dr. Corliss Outley, and Gloria Spight for their friendship and for reviewing and offering their praise for this telling of my life story. And I would like to thank my pastor, the Reverend Dr. Byron C. Moore, for his pastoral leadership and for writing the foreword to this important work.

Finally, I would like to thank the many family members, friends, colleagues, Rotary Club members, Omega Psi Phi Fraternity brothers, and church members, past and present, who have in some way—sometimes without knowing it—inspired me to be the best version of myself. Space does not allow me to list everyone who has made a difference in my life; however, I would like to pay tribute to a few individuals who have enhanced my learning along my journey in many meaningful ways:

Dr. Joseph P. Atkins, junior high principal
Mrs. Regina Anglin, church member, and friend
Ms. Fairy P. Austin, sixth-grade teacher
Mr. Hank Bagelmann, colleague and friend
Ms. Beverly Baker, elementary school classmate
Mrs. Martha Perine Beard, board chair and friend

Willie Dean

Mr. James Beatty, board member and friend
Mr. Jose Casado, colleague and friend
Mrs. Leslie Chamberlin, colleague and friend
Mr. Charles Cleveland, colleague and friend
Mr. Warren Davis, church member, and friend
Mr. H. Eugene Dooley, colleague and friend
Mr. O.C. Duckett, custodian and first supervisor
Ms. Jean Ann Durades, colleague, mentor, and friend
Mr. George Elliott, board chair and friend
Rev. Dr. Michael A. Evans, Sr., pastor and friend
Mr. Terry Gaines, board chair and friend
Ms. Carmelita Gallo, colleague and friend
Mr. Walter F. Griese, colleague and friend
Mr. Glenn Haley, colleague and friend
Mrs. Lauri Hanson, colleague and friend
Ms. Alice Faye Harmon, colleague, mentor, and friend
Dr. Mel Humphreys, professor and mentor
Mr. Oliver J. Johnson, Jr., high school principal
Mr. Rodney H. Johnson, board member, fraternity brother, and friend
Dr. Ellen Kennedy, Rotary Club member and friend
Dr. Harold E. Massey, church member and friend
Mr. Harold Mezile, colleague, mentor, and friend
Rev. Carla M. Mitchell, pastor and friend
Dr. Charles S. Modlin, surgeon and friend
Rev. Dr. Byron C. Moore, pastor
Mr. N. Webster Moore, board member and friend
Rev. Frederick L. Norris, colleague and friend
Ms. Mary Beth Ormiston, colleague and friend
Lt. Col. Clyde H. Orr, board chair and friend
Dr. Corliss Outley, graduate advisor, professor, and friend
Mr. Jerry Pipes, colleague and friend
Mrs. Marsha Pope, colleague and friend
Mr. Willie Proctor, colleague and friend
Mr. Rufus Pulley, Neighbor, high school classmate, and friend
Ms. Madeline Rawlings, colleague, mentor and, friend
Rev. Gordon A. Roesch, pastor and friend
Mr. Ronald F. Sargent, colleague, mentor, and friend
Ms. Gloria Spight, junior high teacher and Sunday School teacher

Mr. Rodney Kase Tyrone, deacon and friend
Mr. Rich Schoffelman, colleague and friend
Mr. James D. Schuldt, colleague and friend
Mr. Robert L. Terrell, teacher, coach, and role model
Mrs. Van, third and fourth grade teacher
Mr. Louie Warren, colleague and friend
Mr. Bill Wells, church member and friend
Dr. Karen Wells, church member and friend
Mr. Isaac White, Jr., classmate, teammate, and friend
Mrs. Sue White, colleague and friend
Mr. Len Wilson, colleague and friend
Mr. Danny Wolfson, automotive technician and friend
Mrs. C.W. Young, second grade teacher

ABOUT THE AUTHOR

Dr. Willie Dean was born in mid-20th century Mississippi. While his mother and father had only a fifth-grade and an eighth-grade education, respectively, they wanted more for their offspring.

Dr. Dean earned a B.S. degree from Memphis State University, an Executive M.B.A. from the University of Nebraska at Omaha, and a Ph.D. from the University of Minnesota.

Dr. Dean started his *YMCA* career in 1974 as Program Director of the Glenview Branch of the *YMCA* in Memphis, Tennessee. In 1975, he was named Executive Director of the McDonald Branch of the *YMCA* in Fort Worth, Texas. Later in 1981, Dr. Dean was appointed Executive Director/District Director (and later Vice President-Urban Services) for the Monsanto *YMCA*, a branch of the *YMCA* of Greater St. Louis in Missouri. Under his leadership, the Monsanto *YMCA* was recognized by the *YMCA* of the USA as one of the "Ten Model *YMCA*s Serving Urban Communities in the United States."

In 1989, Dr. Dean was named President/CEO of the Omaha-Council Bluffs Metropolitan *YMCA*, becoming the first Black CEO in the organization's 123-year history. He also was one of only a handful of Black CEOs of large, multi-branch *YMCA*s in the nation.

In 1994, Dr. Dean was appointed National Field Executive for the Mid-America Field of the *YMCA* of the USA, making him one of the senior-most Black executives on the Y's national staff. In this role, he supervised offices in Minneapolis, Minnesota, Dallas, Texas, Columbus, Ohio, and Indianapolis, Indiana, and provided consulting services to 700 *YMCA*s in 18 states.

In 2005, Dr. Dean was appointed Chief Operating Officer (and later Senior Vice President/COO) of the *YMCA* of Greater Cleveland in Cleveland, Ohio, where he managed operations of a $17-million urban *YMCA*; provided programs through nine branches, four program sites and 19 child care sites; served 27,600 members and 10,800 program participants through 719,800 annual visits; supervised 500 full- and part-time employees; and developed the organization's strategic plan.

In 2007, Dr. Dean was named President/CEO of the *YMCA* of Arlington, Arlington, Texas, where he developed a strategic plan; managed a $7.7-million budget; supervised 365 employees; operated three branches, 20 program sites, and 21 childcare sites that served 17,500 children; served 56,300 members and 36,000 program participants, including 11,200 kids in sports.

Dr. Dean retired in 2012 from an illustrious 35-year career with the *YMCA*, having provided leadership to Ys that served hundreds of thousands of members and participants around the United States.

In 2013, Dr. Dean was appointed Executive Director of KFAI Radio, a Minneapolis, Minnesota, nonprofit community radio station that served 18,000 listeners through 89 on-air programs in 13 languages. And in 2015, Dr. Dean was named Executive Director of YouthCARE, a Minneapolis, Minnesota, nonprofit youth development agency that annually served 600 urban youth.

Dr. Dean is a member of the St. Andrew AME Church in Memphis, Tennessee, where he is an active member of the Digging Deeper Sunday School Class. Formerly, Dr. Dean was a member, board member, and Community Service Director of the Minneapolis University Rotary Club in Minneapolis, Minnesota; past member of the Arlington North Rotary Club in Arlington, Texas; and past member of the Omaha Downtown Rotary Club, in Omaha, Nebraska. Dr. Dean is also a former president of the Jennings-North St. Louis Kiwanis Club in St. Louis, Missouri. He is a graduate of Leadership Arlington (Texas) and Leadership Omaha (Nebraska).

Dr. Dean is a proud member of the Omega Psi Phi Fraternity, Inc., an Advisory Board Member of Uplift, Inc., and a past member of the 100 Black Men of St. Louis, Missouri, and the 100 Black Men of Cleveland, Ohio.

Dr. Dean is a *YMCA* Senior Director, a graduate of the Dale Carnegie Course, and holds a first-degree black belt in Tae Kwon Do. His interests include playing acoustic guitar, taking digital photography, reading, writing, and driving fast cars.

Dr. Dean is available for board membership, speaking engagements, graduations, board development workshops, leadership retreats, strategic planning, and nonprofit management consulting. He can be contacted at: willied744@gmail.com.

"Dr. Dean shares with the reader his heart and the struggles that men of faith encounter as they attempt to navigate the tragedies and triumphs of life. The reader of this work will discover that with God, all things are possible. Prepare to find in yourself the 'will' to press through life's most difficult trials and live to tell others about it.

You will realize that even though the "playing field" is filled with obstacles, pitfalls, and inequities, God has equipped you for the journey and the challenges ahead. This is a great book for your next book club and care group. Prepare to cherish this instant classic and the comforting real-life joy that is expressed in these well-thought-out pages."

—REV. DR. MICHAEL A. EVANS, SR., Senior Pastor, Bethlehem Baptist Church, Mansfield, Texas; Mayor of the City of Mansfield, Texas

"Dr. Willie Dean was born the son of a Black sharecropper in Jim Crow Mississippi, where racism was part of daily life. He defied all odds and had a remarkable career as a CEO, earned a Ph.D., and served as a leader in faith and civic organizations throughout the country.

Dr. Dean faced challenges with the support of his constant companions of faith, family, and friends. He is a survivor - and a THRIVER."

Dr. Dean writes, "You have to see a man to be a man." The man he saw was his beloved father. He is now the model for the next generation, urging us to dismantle the caste systems of color, religion, gender, and sexual orientation to become one America.

—DR. ELLEN KENNEDY, Executive Director, World Without Genocide, St. Paul, Minnesota

"*Overcoming* is a compelling memoir of one Black man's life, from rural Mississippi to an executive-level position within the National *YMCA*. This book will particularly benefit young Black males as Dr. Dean shares professional challenges, racism experiences as a child and as an adult in his personal life and the workplace, and the emotional impact of multiple medical challenges. But, as a man of God, he never ceases to praise God through the good and bad."

—MARTHA PERINE BEARD, Former Board Chair, Monsanto Family *YMCA*, St. Louis, Missouri

Willie Dean

"Dr. Willie Dean takes us on a powerful journey that few readers would expect. This is a raw story that reflects the richness and strength of who he has become by focusing on not only the hardships in his life but each of the triumphs as well.

Overcoming depicts Dr. Dean's experiences as a husband, father, and widower, from becoming one of the first Black Executive Directors in the *YMCA* despite extreme discrimination to finally finding love once again. Each passage provides a 'window to his world' that allows the reader to connect at a spiritual level through the sharing of his pain, vulnerability, laughter, purpose, love, and healing. Today, his legacy continues, and its influence is seen in the policies and practices enacted within various national and local organizations and his family's love and dedication.

Overcoming is a testament to the strength of Dr. Dean's love, courage, and ability to overcome any obstacles by not only opening up the hearts and minds of so many people but by placing faith in God above all else."

—DR. CORLISS OUTLEY, Professor and Director of REYSE Collaboratory, Clemson University; Former Graduate Advisor, University of Minnesota

www.ingramcontent.com/pod-product-compliance
Lightning Source LLC
Chambersburg PA
CBHW050127170426
43197CB00011B/1749